THE MOVIE
THAT CHANGED MY LIFE

THAT CHANGED MY LIFE

THAT CHANGE
D MY LIFE
THE M

THE MOVIE
THAT CHANGED MY LIFE

THE MOVIE
THAT CHANGED MY LIFE

CHANGED MY LIFE

THE MOVIE
THAT CHANGED MY LIFE

THE MOVIE
THAT CHANGED MY LIFE

THAT CHANGE
D MY LIFE
THE M
THAT AM O THA

THAT CHANGED MY
T CHANGED MY LIFE
HAT CHANGED MY LIFE

T CHANGED MY LIF
THAT CHANG

OVIE
THAT CHANGED MY

Also Edited by David Rosenberg

Congregation

Testimony

THE MOVIE
THAT CHANGED MY LIFE

Edited by David Rosenberg

VIKING

VIKING
Published by the Penguin Group
Viking Penguin, a division of Penguin Books USA Inc.,
375 Hudson Street, New York, New York 10014, U.S.A.
Penguin Books Ltd, 27 Wrights Lane, London W8 5TZ, England
Penguin Books Australia Ltd, Ringwood, Victoria, Australia
Penguin Books Canada Ltd, 10 Alcorn Avenue, Suite 300, Toronto, Ontario,
Canada M4V 3B2
Penguin Books (N.Z.) Ltd, 182–190 Wairau Road, Auckland 10, New Zealand
Penguin Books Ltd, Registered Offices: Harmondsworth, Middlesex, England

First published in 1991 by Viking Penguin, a division of Penguin Books USA Inc.

10 9 8 7 6 5 4 3 2 1

LIBRARY OF CONGRESS CATALOGING-IN-PUBLICATION DATA
The Movie that changed my life / edited by David Rosenberg.
p.   cm.
ISBN 0-670-84087-4
1. Motion pictures.   I. Rosenberg, David.
PN1995.M66   1991
791.43'75—dc20   91-50167

Printed in the United States of America
Set in Aldus
Designed by Cheryl L. Cipriani

ACKNOWLEDGMENTS

I am indebted for support to Grace Schulman, Marina Tamar Budhos, Madelyn Marcus, Jody Leopold, Janine Steel, and, for haven, to The Writers Room. My mother, Shifra Asarch, added extra allowance for popcorn during my formative years. Finally, the rare talents of Lew Grimes and Mindy Werner made this book possible.

David Rosenberg

CONTENTS

CONTENTS

INTRODUCTION
BRINGING THE SCREEN HOME
DAVID ROSENBERG

an a movie, or any work of art, change a person's life? In place of the word "movie," consider substituting "adult experience." When immature, an encounter with adult experience can mystify and change us; as adults, reliving the experience may disarm us. And whether we're immature or simply caught off guard, being immersed in moving pictures can yield dreamlike associations, looking larger than life.

Even when ordinary, movies have served as mirror to our culture, its myths, its manners and style, down to the tiniest details—so telling a looking glass, in fact, that we hardly think of American movies as art. But for insights that actually pierce contemporary culture, sometimes as hard to see as the air we breathe, we more often turn to our best writers. Now, in this book, these writers look inward to their experience of one movie—lodged in memory and confronted again on videotape.

Twenty-three prominent novelists, poets, and literary critics recalled a movie that influenced their younger years, contrasting it with a recent re-viewing. They were asked to speak as individuals, not film critics, and in that way they represent anyone who learned as a child to empathize with adults in movies. These authors grant us the personal and the unconventional: imaginative autobiographical writing. We get two narrators in most essays, and both are the author—one in youth, one in the present, and sometimes additional ones in between.

Just about everyone has experienced their own astonishments on seeing a particular movie at different stages of their life, and these essays read like tales of self-revelation. While I had doubts about the supernatural in my own youth, the mysteries of adult life were full of magnetic dread; my emotions were fully exhausted by the tug of war between wanting answers and wanting to avoid what I wasn't ready to understand. As an adult I'm drawn to the genre of writing that reproduces the conflict most poignantly. *The Movie That Changed My Life*, about memory and about archetypal encounters with art and film, invited truly personal essays that look for answers in the reflection of childhood, family—the original truths.

I chose writers of all ages who are acclaimed for their personal vision. If not all, then certainly some of these essays will provoke a response in every reader, striking a chord of personal history: a coming of age, a budding sexuality, a broken heart, an intellectual advance. Each contributor to *The Movie That Changed My Life* has a style and concern of her or his own.

A unique portrait of American culture thus emerges. The intimacy with cultural history we witness here can only grow more affecting in the future, as films are restored and the evolving technology puts them at everyone's hand. But even now, details we missed in childhood jump out at us, from the clothes we wore to the gestures we used, and buried memories return, prompted by the attention to detail that movies heightened. Movies are like dreams in the realistic, startling clarity of details: a forgotten style of shoe, a license-plate logo not glimpsed since childhood.

Wouldn't most of us acknowledge we were first up close in the dark with the myths of adult life—love, sex, death, evil—in movies? It wasn't like being home with our families and friends, because in the movies we weren't inhibited from identifying with the *mystery of adults*. We were bewildered by their experiences, from passionate kisses to death-defying struggles. The personal conflicts we witnessed resembled our dream life—uncensored in the way of school and library books written for children.

The Movie That Changed My Life can be a disturbing work about American culture. It's as if there were *two* significant films in each life—the one that played to a desire for escape and the one that played to a desire for facing ourselves, resolved to being made better somehow. Yet this book honors the act of discovery, however painful the self-criticism. The authors face their early encounters with popular culture and transform them into memoirs. In a pre-vious collection of original essays by writers, *Testimony: Contem-porary Writers Make the Holocaust Personal*, I wrote that the most challenging task for a writer, the most engaging for a reader, is the contrast between childhood and adult knowledge. The candor of a creative memoir, as it fights for maturity, can reflect a reader's own unfolding sense of the past. In *The Movie That Changed My Life*, the writers go beyond criticism of the obvious to discover as well some overlooked questions about art and experience.

Donald Hall was not even sure of the name of his film, other than it had a train and a fascist city in it, and was made before we entered World War II. When I found *Night Train to Munich* in a video catalogue and he viewed it, a sad phone call followed: that was not it at all. I finally tracked down *The Last Train from Madrid*, since no other movie could have the authenticity of this one in his memory. First, a librarian at the UCLA film archives located a former Paramount Pictures executive for me (when I called Paramount directly, I was told that they had dispersed their old films long ago), and then we traced a collector in New York.

Two months later, at 8:00 in the morning, Hall and I knocked on Professor William Everson's door. We were ushered into a living room that had been turned into a tiny movie theater, the walls lined with film cases. There were a dozen rows of authentic cinema seats, about eight across, and we settled into the second row (two seats in the first row were occupied by napping cats). Mrs. Everson turned down the lights; we placed our takeout-coffee cups on adjacent armrests and the film rolled. During the showing, we exchanged excited comments like, "I never imagined Dorothy Lamour could be so young, so voluptuous" and "Anthony Quinn looks like a boy, but he's already playing the cynical adult." Typical conversation, no doubt, for millions in front of their VCRs. . . .

These actors appeared as young today as they were fifty years ago. Not just their roles came back, as they would from a book, but the living actors themselves. And they had aged far less than "real people" in documentaries, because we relived the roles they were playing along with them. This tension between living and dead resembles the way early memories can remain more vivid than recent ones in our own minds—although what is remembered is often a distorted fantasy of the real thing. Hall was amazed to discover how mixed-up the plot was in his memory. In the same way, all of us—along with the authors in *The Movie That Changed My Life*—are witnesses: of the movies and of ourselves.

Compare how memory works to a movie: both are large and unwieldy, yet we rarely remember something, even from a dream, while a Beethoven quartet plays beneath it, as in a movie scene. The complexities of movie elements—from camera angle to music—make the best directors playful in all candor, whether it be

Hitchcock or Cocteau. And where most movies fail in their awkward grasp for art, the medium remains magical in its bewildering wealth of ingredients.

The position movies hold in culture is even more phenomenal today than it was in the past, as we gain personal control over the viewing of a century of films. In a startling article on the significance of movie literacy, the *New York Times*'s chief movie critic, Vincent Canby, wrote: "The development of the videocassette recorder has been the greatest boon to theatrical films since the refinement of sound. It has reclaimed audiences that had stopped going to movie theaters. It also provides virtually instant access to the entire heritage of movies." Further, Canby writes, "There once was a time when movies, having been seen in a theater, could be stored only as memories, often distorted ones. Today audiences can rerun movies indefinitely." The seed planted in this sentence is the awareness that culture involves memory and its retrieval. Much of this century's cultural history involved becoming accustomed to sitting in a darkened theater with a humming machine—and suspending consciousness of the machine, both the camera and the projector. The movie camera is the invisible narrator, omniscient yet dumb, granting the appearance of intimacy. In an essay that establishes a psychological connection between movie images and dream or fantasy images, one contributor to *The Movie That Changed My Life* focuses on children and the darkened room that movies required. He suggests that films forbidden in childhood are connected to repressed fantasies in adults; that, in fact, our subconscious fantasy life is visualized by us like a movie. In the process of writing, he indicates, the writer awakens hidden fantasies by probing taboos.

The formative films for most authors preceded the civil rights and sexual revolutions of the sixties and the feminist revolution following it. Yet many authors describe an intellectual growth and awareness of political and social issues. Louise Erdrich confronts the dictators in Greece; Valerie Sayers exposes urban blight in the

South; Bharati Mukherjee reflects the American dream in India; and David Bradley looks at the same dream in the distorting mirror of Ivy League pieties. Probing psychologically, Meg Wolitzer, Amy Hempel, and Leonard Michaels explore sexual issues, while Leslie Epstein uncovers the antisocial character of sex exploitation. Harold Bloom reveals how he found his way to the heart of Shakespeare's Macbeth; Jayne Anne Phillips feels her way toward buried knowledge.

Just about all of the authors allow for the influence of recent events; in the same way, I experienced a new twist of irony to the not-so-old customs of a "bachelor's party" I attended for one of this book's contributors. Instead of viewing stag films, eight literary males sat around a table in a Chinese restaurant talking almost exclusively of movies. Not more than three of us were likely to have read the same book recently, but all of us had seen Coppola's *Godfather III* and had an opinion about its relationship to his earlier films. We didn't expect greatness from these films, but rather a shared culture. For art, history sufficed, more often foreign than not: a heated debate opened up about the top three Japanese directors, with Mizoguchi winning out over Ozu, and Kurosawa, the only one still alive, not even in the running.

Rarely were actors more important than directors to us now, a turnaround from early youth, when the actors seemed everything. Yet the directors' personal struggles as "artists" were largely irrelevant to us; in the case of an Orson Welles, for instance, we devalued his accomplishment to the extent that he forced his life's details on us. We cared little, now or back in college, about Preston Sturges's or Stanley Kramer's bios—while simultaneously consuming what we could of the lives of writers—Kerouac, Plath, or Lowell. And the movies can remain as pure an object now— unadulterated by biography—as a poem by T. S. Eliot was in our adolescence, before we knew anything about him. A powerful film can still remind us of that time in our clever youth when we be-

lieved that art—or, more accurately, love—would change everything for us.

Several contributors to *The Movie That Changed My Life*,
both men and women, expose their early obsessions about love.
Yet there is a striking difference when it comes to issues of gender
and ethnicity. Several essays by women reveal a new consciousness
brought to bear upon movies that disturbingly support sexist stereotypes. Some of the essays by men show an awareness of sexism
but are more concerned about uncovering the shortcomings of
myths about the sexual revolution and family life. When it comes
to issues of prejudice, it's primarily the minority writers themselves
who expand our awareness of bias. An accurate reflection of contemporary culture in action, *The Movie That Changed My Life*
further unfolds a story of mainstream writers in America.

Beyond American experience, movies cross cultural boundaries: Doris Day alive in Bombay, and Cocteau's beast beguiling
New York, as in two of the book's essays, remind us that we may
find ourselves anywhere in the world and have a common culture
based in cinema. Even in films we dislike, we can find elements
that mesmerize our sensibility, from landscape to a curl of the
lip—small revelations of time, place, and character, a shameless
camera casting a spell on our unconscious.

◤

SUSPENSE / FANTASY

BAMBI
A BOY'S STORY
RUSSELL BANKS

ho can say that one and only one movie
changed his life? Who can name with confidence *the* movie that
accomplished so much? No, there have been many movies—or
"films," as I called them in my late teens and twenties—which
altered my thinking about the world and thus about myself and
which, therefore, could be said, to a greater or lesser degree, to
have changed my life. (Although I must say that there have not
been as many movies as books that have had this effect—but that's
in the nature of a more or less bookish adult life, isn't it?)

Even so, I am an American child of the twentieth century, so
that, before books began to change my life—books, and then travel,
sex, death, and divorce—which is to say, before I reached adolescence, there were surely movies to do the serious work, and in my
childhood, in the absence of books, in the absence of even a merely

4 provincial cinematic context against which I could place and measure the movie, and, going back still further, in the absence of *any* world larger than the one provided by my immediate family, in the absence, then, of church, school, community, in the absence of a conscious culture of any kind, yes, a single movie did have the capacity to alter and then shape my inner life with a power, clarity, and speed that would never be available to me again. Not in movies, anyhow, and certainly not in books.

I was little more than a baby at the time, but a person nonetheless; no tabula rasa, no amorphous unformed amoeba of a consciousness, but a true *person*; and I recently discovered that there was a single winter afternoon at the movies that did indeed change my life, and in such a thoroughgoing way that I am utterly unable to remember today the person I was before the moment I sat down in the Scenic Theater, the only movie house in the small mill town of Pittsfield, New Hampshire, with my younger brother Steve on one side, my cousin Neil, also younger, and Uncle Bud Eastman on the other, and the lights went out. One person—a child very much like the newborn fawn Bambi, of no particular gender, a creature whose destiny was shaped merely by his species—seems to have died that afternoon; and another—a child defined by his gender—got born.

The power and clarity and speed of ritual is what I'm referring to here. My secularized New England Protestant bar mitzvah. Though I had long remembered the event, the name of the movie, the circumstances surrounding my viewing, and a few vivid details, until I happened in recent months to see it again, I recalled little else of it. And exactly who I was before I first saw the movie is lost to me now, except as I'm able to observe him in another child that age or younger; and who I was afterward remains to a disturbing degree the person I am today. That's how powerful it is, or was—*Bambi*, the Disney movie version of the Felix Salten story, which I saw at the age of four.

How do I know this took place, this transformation? The truth **5** is, I was taught it by a child and, in part, by another Disney movie. I have a three-year-old granddaughter, Sarah, and last summer Sarah spent a week, without her parents, visiting my wife and me in our home in the Adirondack Mountains in upstate New York.

I am a relatively young grandfather, and my wife (not Sarah's grandmother) is even younger, but nevertheless we soon tired of carting this energetic, curious, but easily bored child to Santa's Workshop, Frontiertown, and the Great Escape Amusement Park. We began to look for diversions for her that were located closer to home and that we ourselves would find amusing, too.

There is very little television programming for children her age, especially way up in the north country, where the only channel we receive, and receive badly at that, is the NBC affiliate from Plattsburgh. We tuned in, but most of the children's shows seemed alternately hysterical and simple-minded. Sarah was neither, and we liked her that way, as did she.

But she seemed too young for movies—she was barely three, and too sidereal and digressive in her perceptions of time to care for plot, too curious about background to bother distinguishing it from foreground, and too far outside the economy to have her fantasy life targeted for colonization by sexual imagery. She was, we thought, media innocent. Possibly media immune.

We concluded all this when we rented the more popular children's movies and played them for her one after the other on the VCR. She watched them, *Mary Poppins, Cinderella, Peter Pan,* even *The Wizard of Oz*; but she watched them obediently, passively, sleepily, as if narcotized by a little too much cough medicine; and reluctantly (*we* were interested, after all), we rewound the movies halfway through, with no protest from her, and returned them to the video outlet in nearby Elizabethtown.

Then, one evening, for the first time, we ran a movie that instantly seized her attention, drew her forward in her seat and

6

engaged her emotionally in a way that none of the others had so far. She had locked onto it like a heat-seeking missile. It was Disney's *The Little Mermaid*. Relieved, my wife and I brought in a bowl of popcorn and sat down to watch it with her, but after a few moments, to our dismay and slight embarrassment, we realized that *The Little Mermaid* was essentially a dramatized tract designed to promote the virtues and rewards of female submissiveness and silence. Not the sort of thing we wanted our granddaughter to watch while in our care. She was *not* too young, it now seemed, to have her fantasy life structured and rearranged by sexual imagery, not too young to be colonized by the masters of the medium.

She wept when we rewound the film and removed it from the VCR. We replaced it with *Bambi*, the last of the children's films in Elizabethtown that was not science fiction or horror. My wife, born in 1950, had not seen *Bambi* since her own early childhood and remembered it no more clearly than I, although she at least knew that Bambi was a boy, which I did not. All I'd remembered of it, as I said, was that I had seen it at the Scenic in Pittsfield when I was four, with my brother and cousin and uncle. In my memory, it was a *girl's* story about a fawn—Bambi is a girl's name, right?—and there was a forest fire, and Bambi's mother had died somehow. Which was sad, to be sure, but it was only one episode and not the dramatic point of the movie, and the Disney people had handled the tragedy with gentleness and tact, as I recalled. The ending I remembered vaguely as uplifting. There were several memorable secondary characters, a mischievous rabbit with a foot spasm named Thumper and a winsome skunk named Flower. Nothing very promising; certainly nothing dangerous.

I did remember it as having been a visually thrilling movie, however, filled with gorgeously painted scenery—endless northern forests, fields of wildflowers, falling leaves, snow and ice, lofty mountains, and turbulent skies—lyrical pictures of a world not unlike the one that I had grown up in and that actually surrounded

us now in the Adirondacks. A world I hoped to honor and celebrate
with my granddaughter.

It opened with a trailer for *The Little Mermaid*, a preview.
We winced and waited. This stuff is inescapable. Perhaps Sarah
thought the trailer was the opening scene of the new movie; or
the final scene of the movie we had just removed, a lingering
afterimage.

No matter. From the first frame, *Bambi* was of an entirely
different aesthetic and moral order than *The Little Mermaid*. We
approved of this. We may have been forced to deprive our granddaughter of the pleasure of watching the story of Ariel, the free-
swimming mermaid who surrenders her beautiful voice, becomes
a bimbo in a bikini—Barbie with fins—and lands her prince, but
we had given her instead the story of *Bambi*, which, from the scene
unfolding behind the credits, we realized would be a story about
love between mother and child, with possibly an early Green theme
tossed in—the enemy, the outsider, would be Man, we could see.
The central image appeared to be that of the Edenic garden before
the arrival of the wars between the species. Nice. We approved.
And where *The Little Mermaid* had opened like Andre Agassi's
wardrobe, a frantic disco-dance of primary colors, of garish neon
red and orange and fluorescent green and purple, the colors and
rhythms of *Bambi* were soft and muted, opening slowly like the
wings of a butterfly in shades of pale green and blue-gray, shifting
to rose to speckled sunlight. This was a visual lyricism we could
understand and value, one we wanted to share with Sarah.

It's the slow dawning of a spring day in the deep forest. Behind
the images, the voices of a male tenor and chorus, hymnlike, rise
up singing. . . .

My obligations to oversee the moral education of my granddaughter met, I was free now to sit back, relax, and watch the movie
for myself, and suddenly I was gone, lost inside the world of the
movie, and found again inside my four-year-old self. It was a

startling transformation, instantaneous and complete. I was at once and once again a country child on the cusp of boyhood, a creature just emerging from the polymorphous envelope of infancy and facing for the first time the beginnings of a terrifying, bewildering male life with others. An owl returns to his huge oak from his nighttime haunts, and flocks of birds waken the rest of the world with song. The dappled forest floor fills with parents and their newborn babes—quail, mice, squirrels, rabbits—all performing their morning ablutions, breaking their fasts, when a bluebird, fluttering from tree to tree, excitedly brings the news, "It's happened! It's happened!" What's happened? we all wonder. "The prince is born!" the bird exclaims. "The prince is born!"

Everyone hurries to what can only be called an adoration scene, a crèche, practically, in the thicket, where a lovely large-eyed doe nudges her newborn fawn into view. It's straight from the New Testament. Like a benign Dr. Johnson, Friend Owl, urging reverence, explains to the excited onlookers, especially the agitated, somewhat bewildered young: "This is quite an occasion. It isn't every day a new Prince is born."

Indeed. And that is why this dawn is different from all other dawns. The story of stories, your own story, if you happen to have just figured out this week that you yourself are a new prince, has begun.

The irrepressible Thumper asks what we all want to ask but don't dare. "Whacha gonna call Him?"

"I think I'll call Him," says his mother, in a voice that can only come from the mouth of a madonna, ". . . Bambi." (Not Jesus, but, to these ears, almost; or, more likely, what I heard was, "I think I'll call Him . . . Russell.")

After we have paused and admired the mother and child, the adoration is appropriately terminated by Friend Owl, and we cut away and move through the tangled woods to a slowly rising shot of a powerful stag on a mountaintop in the distance. It's the magnificent Hartford Insurance stag in profile, silent on a peak in Darien, nobly examining the horizon. The Father. Our gaze has gone from the son to the father, from adoration of the young prince to contemplation of the old. Time and destiny have entered the story.

Strong stuff. At least, for me it was. In seconds, the movie had shattered my personal time, had broken it into bits and swept away all the intervening years in which I had struggled, and mostly failed, to live out the story of Bambi, returning me to the moment when the story first took me over. I suddenly remembered (oddly, remembered with my right hand, which began to move, as if holding a pencil or crayon between thumb and forefinger) how for years I had obsessively drawn that hugely antlered male deer, the old prince of the forest. Seated now on my living room sofa next to my granddaughter and wife, I reproduced the drawing invisibly in air, just as I had done over and over again when I was a boy—a single swift line that traced the outline of the noble stag, covering brown paper grocery bags with it, filling schoolbook margins and endpapers, drawing it all over my notebooks, even in wet sand at Wells Beach and in new snow in the backyard.

The story of Bambi, subtitled in Felix Salter's book "A Life in the Woods," is both simple and amazingly complete. From birth to death, it describes and proscribes the territory of a male life in a sequence that follows exactly the Victorian and modern middle-class view of that life properly lived. It's a rigorous, wholly believable, moral story. Believable because, although it has no irony, no sly winking inside jokes between knowing adults, it has an abundance of humor. And while, as everyone knows, it has heartbreak aplenty, the movie, as few of us remember, is nonetheless not sentimental. It's downright Darwinian. *Bambi* has danger to be faced, great peril, obstacles to be overcome; and, at crucial moments, the movie shows us death. Both kinds—death that is sudden, violent, and inexplicable and death that comes late and is unavoidable, natural, necessary. It has sex, to be sure, but no

10   Hollywood sleaze, no puritanical prurience—males and females are simply drawn to one another, where they go mad with procreative desire ("twitter-pated," Friend Owl explains) and rush off to couple with one another and quickly produce offspring, all done with pleasure, great good gusto, and not a single salacious nudge or apology. No one, after all, wears clothes in this movie. In fact, the pleasures of the body—eating, sleeping, bathing, sport, and sex—are presented as straightforwardly satisfying and natural as in *Tom Jones*.

    Bambi makes all the stops on the life-circuit, and does so in a rigorously structured, comprehensive, and rhythmically patterned way, as precise and inclusive as a Catholic mass or a cycle of myths. Which, of course, makes it feel universal. And from that feeling proceeds its moral imperative. *Bambi* may be agitprop, but it's agitprop of a very high order.

    Not for everyone, however. Recently, a friend of mine took his son to see the movie in a Manhattan theater. My friend is a large and gentle feminist of a man; his son is a bright six-year-old boy, older perhaps by several lifetimes than I was when I first saw the movie. In the scene that follows the death of Bambi's mother, when Bambi's father arrives at the thicket and, basso profundo, says to him, "Your mother can't be with you any more . . . ," my friend's son asked, "Didn't the father help the mother?" My friend had to say no. After all, the movie said no. "Then we'd better get out of here," the boy said, and they did, father and son, barely a third of the way through the movie.

    On Manhattan's Upper West Side in 1990, *Bambi*, the boy's story, was not *their* story, that's for sure. Not the way it had been mine in the middle 1940s in small-town New Hampshire. My father had a rack of antlers and was absent on a hill, too—a plumber working all week on the construction of the weather station at the top of Mount Washington, coming home only on weekends, taking up my mother's time with his needs and watching over me from

a vast, powerfully masculine, fixed distance. "Were you a good
boy this week? Did you do all your chores? Did you obey your
mother, take care of your younger brother, learn the ways of the
forest?"

There are the usual differences between the movie and the
book that generated it, *Bambi: A Life in the Woods,* by Felix Salten,
translated in 1928 by Whittaker Chambers, of all people, with a
wry foreword by John Galsworthy ("I particularly recommend it
to sportsmen . . ."). The story has been simplified, streamlined,
slightly sanitized. But there is, to me, an amazing and shrewd
faithfulness to the overall structure of the book (everything is cyclic
and occurs in triplets—three acts, three seasonal sequences, three
distinct stages of life) and to Salten's realistic description of "a life
in the woods." His is not a kind and gentle woods; it's nature with
fang and frost, with hunger and hardship, with violence that is
natural and necessary (there are carnivores in the forest, after all)
and the perverse, gratuitous violence of Man the Hunter. And
although there is much in Salten's novel concerning the relations
between the genders that is explicit and didactic, in Disney's movie
that same material is implicit, is dramatized, and is no less the-
matically central or seductive for that. Quite the opposite.

At bottom, they are both, novel and movie, moral tales about
the proper relations between the genders, told for boys from the
Victorian male point of view. In the book, after having seen a
passing pair of grown male deer for the first time, Bambi asks his
mother, " 'Didn't they see us?'

"His mother understood what he meant and replied, 'Of
course, they saw all of us.'

"Bambi was troubled. He felt shy about asking questions, but
it was too much for him. 'Then why . . . ,' he began, and stopped.

"His mother helped him along. 'What is it you want to know,
son?' she asked.

" 'Why didn't they stay with us?'

" 'They don't ever stay with us,' his mother answered, 'only at times.'

"Bambi continued, 'But why didn't they speak to us?'

"His mother said, 'They don't speak to us now; only at times. We have to wait till they come to us. And we have to wait for them to speak to us. They do it whenever they like.' "

And a little further on, his mother says, " 'If you live, my son, if you are cunning and don't run into danger, you'll be as strong and handsome as your father is sometime, and you'll have antlers like his, too.'

"Bambi breathed deeply. His heart swelled with joy and expectancy."

As did mine. Hunkered down in my seat in the darkness in the Scenic Theater, and now here, forty-six years later, in front of a TV screen in my living room, I was on both occasions located at precisely the age when a child can be most easily colonized by the gender-specific notions of his or her culture, the age when the first significant moves toward individuation are occurring at a recklessly fast rate and in the explicit terms of one's inescapable biology.

At that moment, at the telling of one's story, one's heart cannot help swelling with joy and expectancy. Just as, earlier, Sarah's heart, perhaps, had swelled at the telling of Ariel's story in *The Little Mermaid*. And was apparently not moved in the slightest by the telling of Bambi's and mine. For this was, as she surely knew, a boy's story, and thus was not for her, was irrelevant, if pleasantly distracting. For, after all, the birds were pretty, the thump-footed rabbit funny, the shy skunk sweet, and there was the excitement of the forest fire, the scary presence of the hunters. All that seemed more than mildly interesting to her, but in no way capable of changing her life.

She needed *The Little Mermaid* for that, I'm afraid. I have no regrets that my wife and I kept it from her, however. And though it probably would have done me in the long run no good at all, I wish that someone—my uncle Bud Eastman, maybe, or a kindly grandfather conscious of the pain, confusion, and cruelty that come as soon as a boy marches into such territory—someone, had taken a quick look at the opening scenes of *Bambi* that Saturday afternoon and had said to himself, This movie is only going to drive the kid deeper into sexual stereotyping. It's going to validate the worst attitudes of the adult world that surrounds him. It's going to speed the end of his innocence.

"Let's get out of here, boys," he might then have said to me and my brother Steve and cousin Neil. He'd have needed to know back then only what my friend's six-year-old son knows now. "Let's go down the street to Varney's for an ice cream soda," he might have said, "and come back next week for a Zorro double feature, or maybe for Gene Autry, the Singing Cowboy. Let's come back when they're showing a movie that *won't* change your life."

◪

THE LAST TRAIN FROM MADRID

WAR CARDS, PURPOSE, BLAME, AND FIRE

Donald Hall

y father was too young for the Great War, not fifteen when it ended, and both of my grandfathers were too old. Their fathers fought in the Civil War—archaic blue figures stiff-bearded in photographs—but in 1937, when I was eight, Gettysburg might have been Agincourt or Marathon. As the new war came closer, I understood that my father felt guilty about missing 1914–18; but I understood that he wanted to miss the new one as well. Everyone was nervous, the Depression hanging on and war approaching. I was an only child, alert to my parents' anxiety. My mother was thin and attentive. She came to Connecticut from a remote farm in New Hampshire, and as I grew up, I became aware that she felt lonely in the suburbs; she paid more attention to her child, in her displacement, than she would have done if she had stayed up north with her sisters.

Sometimes she took me on excursions to New Haven—Saturdays during the school year, weekdays in summer. We walked up Ardmore Street to Whitney Avenue and waited for the bus that came every ten minutes to roll us four miles down Whitney and drop us at Church and Chapel outside Liggett's across from New Haven's Green. While I tagged along, she shopped at Shartenberg's and Malley's. When we had done shopping we ate lunch at a place where I ordered franks and beans—two grilled hotdogs and a tiny crock of pea-beans dark with molasses; dessert was Jell-O with real whipped cream or dry yellow cake with white frosting; lunch cost thirty-nine cents.

Then we went to the movies. We saw a first-run film, a B-movie, one or two shorts, previews of coming attractions, and a newsreel. I remember for certain only one film that I saw in 1937, but I'm almost sure that I watched Spencer Tracy in *Captains Courageous*; maybe Paul Muni in *The Life of Emile Zola* and *The Good Earth*; probably *Lost Horizon* and *A Star Is Born*, maybe *One Hundred Men and a Girl*. The only movie I remember for certain, after fifty-some years, is *The Last Train from Madrid*. After we took the bus home to Ardmore Street, I put my toy soldiers away forever and burned my war card collection.

In 1937 we boys wore long woolen stockings that tucked over the bottoms of corduroy knickers as we walked to Spring Glen Grammar School. There were no school buses. Children from my neighborhood took several different routes to school—for variety, or to avoid a bully or an old best friend who had become an enemy— but we always passed the Glendower Drug Store because it was only two short blocks from school. If we had change in our pockets, we spent it there. For a nickel, we bought big candy bars or flat pieces of gum creased into five sticks and pink as a dog's tongue. With the gum came cards that illustrated our different obsessions: of course there were baseball cards, and I seem to remember cards for football as well; I remember G-man cards, each of which illustrated a triumph of law and order as J. Edgar Hoover's agents flushed out Dillinger—shooting him in the lobby of a movie theater—or Pretty Boy Floyd. Although G-man cards were violent, they resembled the Society of Friends alongside another series that we bought and collected. We called them war cards, and they thrived in the bellicose air of 1937.

For then the war in Spain shrieked from the front pages of newspapers along with the Japanese invasion of China. In 1937 Stalin kept discovering to his astonishment that old colleagues had betrayed him; he shot seven of his best generals that year, doubtless a great advantage when Hitler invaded. In 1937 Trotsky found his way to Mexico, Amelia Earhart disappeared into the Pacific, the UAW invented the sit-down strike, Neville Chamberlain asked Hitler's cooperation in the interest of peace, the *Hindenburg* exploded and burned in New Jersey, Pierce-Arrow shut down, George Gershwin died, Orson Welles and Joseph Cotten appeared on Broadway in *Julius Caesar*, and thousands of American progressives joined the Lincoln Brigade to fight fascism in Spain. Half never returned.

Even in the fourth grade we knew about Hitler, whose troops and planes fought with Franco against the Loyalists aided by Stalin's troops and planes. Germany was the continuous enemy, less than twenty years after the Armistice of 1918. We were good, brave, loyal, outnumbered, and victorious against all odds; they were evil, cruel, cowardly, vicious, dumb, shrewd, and doomed. *We knew who was right and who was wrong.* (My father's mother's family had emigrated from Germany to New Haven in the 1880s, which was confusing.) In 1937 everyone—parents, teachers, even children—understood that there would be another war and that America would join it sooner this time. Isolationists and pacifists campaigned against war, but everyone knew that war was inevitable—whether it was or wasn't. A phenomenon like war cards, as I remember them, makes it seem as if we were being prepared; as if *they* made sure that we grew up expecting to become soldiers, accepting the guns and the bombing.

At least no one—so soon after the Great War—had the temerity to present war as a Cub Scout expedition. When we went to the movies, we saw a newsreel and sometimes even "The March of Time." The late 1930s was endless parades in black and white, soldiers marching, weapons rolling past reviewing stands; I remember refugees panicked on the narrow roads, all their possessions piled on donkeys, ancient trucks, or small bent backs. I remember the bombing and strafing of refugees. Ominous deep voices doom-spoke while the screen showed airplanes in formation, or artillery pieces recoiling with little puffs emerging from muzzles like speech balloons in comic strips. I remember Hitler addressing rallies, immense crowds of identical figures *Sieg-Heil*ing—robots of outrage and blood that jerked with a single will.

War cards used a lot of red ink. On the back a short text described a notorious occasion, and on the front an artist illustrated what happened. I remember one card which showed a Japanese bomb hitting a crowded Chinese bus, maybe in Shanghai: bodies coming apart hurtled through the air, intestines stretching between the separated parts of a human figure, headless bodies littering the ground. I don't believe that these cards were clearly ideological; in the United States, there were two ideas about war in Europe—get in or stay out—and these cards seemed neither isolationist nor interventionist. (As I recollect, the cards claimed to be educational, illustrating the Horrors of War.) Of course, it occurred to me later, there wouldn't be much blood for us if we stayed out. Blood was the whole matter; blood was the food on which our boyish death-love nurtured itself.

We loved our war cards, chewing gum as we walked home to add a new one to our collections. If it was a duplicate, we could swap, maybe the exploded bus for a card that showed the shelling of a boat. We collected war cards as we collected ourselves for war.

18   I loved airplanes in 1937 and read pulp stories about dogfights over
the trenches. I loved the pilot heroes of the 1930s—Wiley Post,
Amelia Earhart, later Wrong-way Corrigan. When I imagined myself going to war I joined the Lafayette Escadrille, flew Spads, and
shot down Fokker triplanes. I remember visiting the New Haven
airport—later, it must have been—and seeing camouflaged fighter
planes and bombers, including the mighty B-17, or Flying Fortress,
which in retrospect resembles an ultralight. I remember watching
parades on Memorial Day or the Fourth of July: tiny tanks clanking,
soldiers marching with Springfield rifles and wearing Great War
helmets.

Then I saw *The Last Train from Madrid*. Did it really change
my life? As I commit it to paper, the phrase sounds exaggerated,
melodramatic. I never registered as a C.O. (Nor did I serve in the
military.) Although I worked in Ann Arbor with the movement
against the Vietnam war, I was never a leader. Neither did I spell
"America" with a *k*. It was war horror that filled my chest, not
political commitment: a horror is not an idea, as a shudder is not
a conviction. My horror, I think, started with this film. Certain
connections of war retain the power to make me burst into tears,
especially the random slaughter of civilians. It is hard to remember
the outrage people felt over Guernica—after London, Dresden, and
Hiroshima—but Picasso's painting registers the shock and incre-
dulity. I remember, in late adolescence after the war, trying to read
an essay that told how French mothers had struggled, dreading air
raids in 1939, to fix their gas masks onto the tiny heads of their
babies. I could never finish the sentence.

In September 1990 I saw *The Last Train from Madrid* again,
fifty-three years after I had watched it as an eight-year-old in the
Paramount Theater in New Haven. Over the years, I had thought
of the film often, and assumed that it was anti-fascist or popular
front. It is no such thing. The film that I watched in 1990 is
astonishingly without political ideology: its single import is the

randomness of war horror. Clichés and stereotypes provide a plot, but it is impossible to take the plot seriously. As contemporary reviewers mentioned, the film is derivative—*Grand Hotel* on wheels—and its romantic framework hurries into irrelevance, leaving behind an expressive, almost expressionist, music of nightmare. I do not mean to say that *The Last Train from Madrid* is a good film. It is bad art: the plot is improbable and the motivation incredible; the writing is ghastly, from clumsy exposition to the flattest clichés of dialogue. Yet it terrified me once; and it retained much of its terror fifty-three years later.

The film begins with loud scare sounds and the hurtling image of a locomotive pulling a train. A radio newscast tells us that tonight the last train will leave Madrid, after which—we understand—the city will be overrun by the nameless army that besieges it. The army lacks not only name but idea, and its only purpose is death. As characters speak of the train's terminus in Valencia, on the other hand, that city becomes pure symbol: the destination is Arcadian peace in a countryside antithetic to the city of panic, chaos, and violent death. Naturally, everyone wants a seat on the train. The plot of the movie turns on separate and intermingled stories of people seeking passage on the train—their stratagems, their failures and successes. At the end, the train steams out of Madrid carrying some of our people and leaving others behind—not only behind but dead; in the film's emotional terms, *behind* means *dead*.

As the film begins, a noble young officer (noble because he is handsome and stands straight; noble because he is Anthony Quinn) listens to impassioned pleas for passes and in his dutiful nobility refuses them. We dwell on an old lady, well played, who begs and is refused. Most of our central figures are couples, two-by-two like the ark's animals: the romantic interest, which I doubtless ignored in 1937. It remains easy to ignore in 1990: none of it feels authentic, only partly because Dorothy Lamour (beloved of two leading men) plays her part with the expressiveness of a Malley's mannequin.

Lew Ayres is in love with Olympe Bradna, Robert Cummings with Helen Mack—and none of it matters. There is no genuine feeling between men and women. Love between two men matters more—Anthony Quinn and Gilbert Roland, who swore blood brotherhood as soldiers in Africa years before. This male loyalty is stereotypical—*Beau Geste* stuff—but it provides the strongest human bond in the film, its power only less than the forces of panic and dread. Quinn will betray any government or any commanding officer to remain loyal to his blood brother. In all of *Last Train*, we find no economic or political or social ideology; instead, we find the exaltation of private affection and a dream of pastoral peace in the midst of history's nightmare. Doubtless such dreams are conservative; they are not fascist.

A slaphappy American journalist (Lew Ayres) picks up a girl in the countryside (Olympe Bradna) who wants to get to Madrid to see her father before he is executed by firing squad. (Naturally they fall in love; this pair makes it to the train.) She sees her father, he is executed—and we never receive an inkling, not a *notion*, of what he did or stood for that led to his execution, by its nature dreadful because it is in cold blood. The killing feels wholly arbitrary because no motive is supplied or suggested. In this film's eerie political emptiness, execution by firing squad becomes merely *ordinary*—a repetitious daily event like sunrise or the six-o'clock news. In real life, the execution, which would have appeared unjust to some observers, would have been a purposeful political act. It is presented in the film as without purpose or meaning.

One soldier at the execution is tenderhearted and will not fire his gun: Robert Cummings. For his compassion he will be sent to the front. He runs away and falls in love. Now, the plot of this falling in love is astonishing. It begins as we see two strangers parting, a man and a woman whom we do not know. We understand that they have just made love, and that she is a prostitute. They seem fond of each other, happy, making plans for their next en-

counter, and as the man walks into the street we spy his shape   **21**
down the sight of a rifle; then a sniper shoots him dead. Although
we may assume that the sniper waited for this particular man, no
detail supports the assumption; we know nothing of this man or
his killer or why anyone would want to kill him; we know nothing
about the shooting except the brute fact. Like the execution, this
street killing—idyll destroyed by bullet—presents itself as wholly
random and arbitrary.

It is this young woman with whom Cummings falls in love,
and she with him—immediately. After Mack and Cummings drag
her dead lover's body into her flat, they talk; Cummings wants
the dead man's pass for the last train. Soon enough, they scheme
a double escape. During their brief courtship, these characters in
their dialogue establish the farm in Valencia to which the train will
deliver them—erecting the Arcadian alternative to Madrid. The
dialogue is typically hackneyed. "This war can't go on forever,"
says Helen Mack as her ex-lover stiffens in an adjacent room. (She
has just said: "A moment ago he was so happy.") Toward the end
of the film, as Mack and Cummings ride a wagon toward the train,
it becomes her random turn to die. This time there is a hint of
purpose; the killers want to hijack the wagon to get to the train
themselves. However, it is arbitrary that Mack is the one to die—
unless, under another agenda, she dies because she is not a virgin.
(Possibly, she should die for her dialogue.) Cummings makes it to
the train alone.

In fact, there are few deaths in *The Last Train from Madrid*.
Channel-surfing the television, happening upon a Chuck Norris
special, you will see more carnage before you can switch channels
than you'll observe in eighty minutes of this film. I remembered
one more death from 1937. While the train remains in the station—
only people with passes admitted on board—guards move through
the cars rechecking passes. As they demand papers from everyone,
our anxiety mounts, because they approach a vulnerable protag-

onist. Suddenly, looking at one man's pass—a stranger to us—the guards ask him to step outside. He looks nervous; he tries to run— and they shoot him down. They kill him *on purpose,* aiming their guns, yet they kill him *for no reason* that we understand.

Murderous paradox drives the film: malignity exists everywhere, yet most of the time it appears motiveless. To the psyche, all these deaths are as arbitrary as death by bombs from the sky. One air raid takes its place at the center of the film, a riot of civilian panic, people running and frightened. The soundtrack plays fear music, camera shots are quick and angular, and in one quick shot nervous pigeons scurry.

In Robert Frost's "Design," he writes about the malign coincidence of an invisible spider haply arranged to kill a fly; the poet asks what could have caused this coming together except for "design of darkness to appall." Then he qualifies the question in a further line: "If design govern in a thing so small." In *The Last Train from Madrid* we are surrounded by fear of imminent death, but, horribly, we lack design. As humans we wish or need to understand the cause or to place blame—on an enemy, on politicians who betrayed us, on the cupidity or moral squalor of a person or a class of people—because blame implies purpose, and it is our nature to wish to understand causes for our misfortunes. We search for anything that we may hold responsible for our fate: God, our political leaders, the Devil, the planets in conjunction at our births, the sins of our fathers, Muslims, biorhythms, Queen Elizabeth II, or a witch's curse. The film suggests that design may not govern in a thing so small as human life and death.

Print at the beginning of *The Last Train from Madrid* scrolls its neutrality; this movie will not uphold or defend either side of this war. When we read of battles in old histories, we study the motives of each side, although the cause may mean little to us. What we keep is not the ideas behind conflict but stories of heroism, cowardice, and suffering. "The river ran red with blood for seven days," we remember, not, "Thus Centerville retained its passage to the Danube," but we always understand that there appeared to be reasons for blood. By omitting ideology, *Last Train* purifies war from its particular historical contexts into eternal anonymous suffering. The film scrolls war's utter panic and sorrow. Oh, sorrow, sorrow, sorrow—the ripe life cut by hate without purpose, by anger lacking reason, by murder without blame.

◣

How did my mother happen to take an eight-year-old to such a movie? Microfilm of the New Haven *Register* explains. The newspaper printed paragraphs of studio puffery that wholly misrepresented the film: "With but two pictures to her credit, both of which were outstanding successes, Dorothy Lamour, the glamourous brunette, one of the season's most sensational 'finds,' moves into the ranks of the screen's charming leading ladies. The event takes place in *The Last Train from Madrid*, the romance laid in war-torn Spain." I find it breathtaking to read this notice of the film that horrified me. "In this story Miss Lamour appears as a beautiful patrician girl, who is the beloved of a young lieutenant in the government forces and his best friend." When I read Frank S. Nugent's *New York Times* review I am almost as astonished. He notes the lack of politics in this "glib little fiction," but for Nugent also there was no horror. "True, it speaks of the Spanish revolution, but merely as Hollywood has, in the past, regarded the melodramatic turmoils of Ruritania and Zenda." He called the film "a pre-tested melodrama which should suit the average palate," and in his conclusion makes a joke: "Its sympathies, neither Loyalist nor Rebel, are clearly on the side of the Ruritanians."

Frank S. Nugent was not eight years old. Was Nugent's cynicism more appropriate than my horror? At eight, I ignored the silly romance at the film's center and registered only the panic of unmotivated murder. When I returned home after the Saturday

24   matinee, I packed my lead toy soldiers with their flattish Great War helmets into a shoe box and tucked it deep in the long closet of my bedroom. I performed the ritual with so much solemnity that I might have played taps for background music. By this time I felt not panic but a sadness that would not relent, which may have derived from another melancholy that absorbed me that weekend. The film opened in New Haven on Saturday, July 10, 1937, while Amelia Earhart was missing over the Pacific. I remember playing outside the house, keeping the window open and a radio near the window; I remember a report that the navy had spotted her plane on an atoll; I remember the correction of the report. In my mind's eye, Amelia Earhart circled continually, high in the air, the hum of the Lockheed's engine distant and plaintive, gas almost gone, the pilot in her leather helmet peering for land as she circled . . .

It must have been a month or two later, maybe a cool September day, that something on the radio or in a headline reminded me of the film. Spain and China were in the news. On that day, alone in the house, I carried my war cards down to the cellar. I was not allowed to open the door of the coal furnace, but I opened it anyway and threw the war cards onto the red coals. At first they smoldered and turned brown and I feared that they would not burn, would give me away when my father came home and fixed the furnace. Then one card burst into bright yellow flame, then another, then all of them together flared briefly in the shadow-and-red hellfire of the furnace on Ardmore Street.

◰

SHADOW OF A DOUBT

FAT MAN AND LITTLE GIRL

MEG WOLITZER

n retrospect, it seems an unlikely pairing: the obese master of suspense from England and the thirteen-year-old girl from Long Island. But Alfred Hitchcock was my hero when I was an adolescent, and his movies stirred me in a way that I, who had been raised in the sixties on the pabulum of *The Parent Trap* and *Thoroughly Modern Millie,* had never been stirred before.

Every Saturday afternoon in the suburb where I lived, someone's mother would chauffeur several girls to the local mall and deposit us in a G-rated movie for the afternoon. The movies themselves were good-natured and thin, and we watched them obediently, for this was all that was available to us. The only movie theater within walking distance of my house had "The Sound of Music" blazing from its marquee for more than a year.

Our parents, however, had a much wider range of choices at

their disposal, and at night they left us with sullen babysitters and went to see R-rated movies such as *Goodbye, Columbus* and *Bob & Carol & Ted & Alice*. From my limited perspective, an R rating signaled to me that a film had to be pornographic. I imagined that the world was divided into two separate planes: G and R. On the G plane, which I occupied with my friends, life was unnaturally buoyant and easily comprehended. It never occurred to me that it might be possible to feel a thrill of affinity for characters in a movie. The questions raised by G-rated movies (Could Hayley Mills, playing identical twins separated as infants, manage to reunite her divorced parents? Should Julie Andrews leave the convent?) had nothing to do with the substance of our lives. Meanwhile, on the R plane, which was occupied by my parents and their suburban-sophisticate friends, the world was densely sexual and elliptical. On-screen, grown men and women tangled together in oversized beds, losing themselves in an ineffable frenzy of desire. I didn't know at the time that movies could fall into something other than either of these two categories. I hadn't yet seen my first Alfred Hitchcock film.

I came to Hitchcock's films in an odd but somehow appropriate way. One summer afternoon, bored and alone in the house with a friend, I played a frenetic game of hide-and-seek in the basement. Sliding behind a rusty old cabinet in a corner, I gashed my hand open. There was no pain, only a surprising fountain of blood, and I was wordlessly startled. Weeks later, when my parents were giving a dinner party, one of their friends commented that the scar on my hand bore a close resemblance to the cartoon profile of the director that appeared during the opening credits of "Alfred Hitchcock Presents." At subsequent dinner parties, I would proudly hold up my palm for inspection. The scar became a conversation piece, positioned somewhere between the ability to wiggle one's ears and bearing the stigmata.

While the adults were all well versed about Hitchcock, to me he was nothing more than a droll, pear-shaped man in a suit who introduced the black-and-white mysteries that my mother liked to watch on television each week. I would sit beside her dutifully during the show, bored and tapping my foot in time to "The Funeral March of the Marionettes." But now my hand was indelibly embossed with his imprint, and I decided that I ought to see at least one of his films.

I'm not sure which was my first Hitchcock movie; I only know it was fast-moving and well done—perhaps *To Catch a Thief* or *North by Northwest*. But whichever one it was, it affected me enough to make me decide to seek out all of Hitchcock's films that summer. Suddenly I was combing the television listings in the newspaper and convincing my father to drive me to an obscure revival house on the outskirts of the suburbs for a showing of *The Man Who Knew Too Much*. That summer I learned that movies could be something other than inane or titillating; they could also be dark.

Hitchcock was always referred to in print as the "master of suspense," and in fact he seemed to have absolute mastery over audience anxiety, plotting when to make us sit up straighter and tighten our jaws, when to make us clap our hands over our mouths. His films pulled responses from audiences by addressing their small, unnerving fears, then widening the aperture of those fears. Of course, the same can be said of the most primitive horror movies, as well as of high art. But Hitchcock seemed to combine a self-conscious sensationalism with a patient and sophisticated beauty. The long close-up of a dead Janet Leigh's eye in *Psycho*, accompanied by the steady, pointless beat of the shower; the word "Froy" written on a dusty train window by an old woman who is about to disappear in *The Lady Vanishes*; the man's hand held up to reveal a missing finger in *The Thirty-nine Steps*; each of these static images is crucial to the story of its respective film, and yet each can hold the gaze in much the way that still photography can.

As you're watching any of these images, you know how hokey it is and that you're meant to find it so. The director has clearly had a grand old time dishing out each representative shot. Knowing how much pleasure he must have taken in planting these arch and chilling moments is part of the pleasure of watching.

During my Hitchcock marathon I saw the best of his movies, such as *Strangers on a Train* and *Notorious*—and the worst of them, such as *Topaz* and *Torn Curtain*. That summer I learned to distinguish between good and bad. My tastes began to develop; I brought an unschooled but nonetheless critical judgment to what I saw. Somehow I knew enough to remain unconvinced by *Marnie*, and somehow I understood when Hitchcock was striving for something intriguing yet missing the mark, as was the case with *Spellbound*. Then there were the films that worked, such as *The Lady Vanishes*: a stylish and crisply British creation that starts off witty and slowly becomes seized by a creeping sense of urgency. For a while *The Lady Vanishes* was my favorite of all Hitchcock's films. I hadn't yet seen *Shadow of a Doubt*.

Hitchcock once maintained that this film, released in 1943, was his favorite. When I saw it for the first time, thirty years after it was made, it thrilled me in a way that none of his other films had. But the director and I are in a minority. To this day, when I praise the film to friends, I am often met with a vague response. My friends murmur that they don't think they've seen it, and they wonder if perhaps it was the one that took place in New England and starred a very young Shirley MacLaine. They talk about *their* favorite Hitchcock movie, which usually turns out to be either *Rear Window* or *Vertigo*. I always leave these conversations astonished that *Shadow of a Doubt* has somehow managed to slip through the cinematic cracks into neglect. As a suspense film it is first-rate, and as a psychological drama it is unsettling and often moving. But there is no shower scene to be found here, no sky eclipsed by a swarm of birds, and no smoky blonde like Grace Kelly or Eva Marie

Saint to provide a little stimulation between killings. Unlike any   **29** other movie in Hitchcock's body of work, the emotional core of *Shadow of a Doubt* rests within an adolescent girl.

Movies that address the complex emotional lives of girls are rare. There was often a syrupy quality to the girls' movies I saw when I was growing up; the young heroine tended to be as chipper and wide-eyed as a Keane painting. It hardly mattered that those of us watching the movie were starting to undergo a sea change. At thirteen we were beginning to sour *en masse*, as though there were some unwritten expiration date to our childhood exuberance. The self-conscious darkness of adolescence set in; the sky above our junior high school seemed eclipsed, as if by a swarm of birds.

But darkness, at least as depicted in the movies, is usually no place for adolescent girls. Movies have always tacitly segregated the sexes, and when the sides are drawn, darkness is invariably a male province. This is not the case with *Shadow of a Doubt*. The plot, which bears repeating here, concerns a teen-aged girl named Charlie, who finds life in small-town Santa Rosa, California, dull and predictable. Her well-meaning American family (the screenplay was co-authored by Thornton Wilder) cannot help her shake her teen-aged moodiness; in fact, their good intentions serve to make matters maddeningly worse. The only person who can help is her beloved uncle Charlie, after whom she has been named. Young Charlie decides to post a telegram to her uncle, only to find that *he* has just sent a telegram to her and her family, saying that he is arriving imminently.

The beloved uncle turns out to be a slim, secretive dreamboat with silky ties and an armload of lavish gifts for the whole family. He manages to be both exciting and safely avuncular, and as such is a perfect unconscious object of desire for his niece, although the element of safety is eventually stripped away. Over the course of the movie, enough clues are dropped to make Charlie slowly grow suspicious of her uncle, until finally she must face the fact that he is in actuality the notorious "Merry Widow" murderer, a man wanted for strangling rich, elderly women. She is the only one to see the truth; the rest of her family is permanently swaddled in their own *Our Town* brand of innocence.

When young Charlie's mother is asked what Uncle Charlie does for a living, the best she can do is to gesture with her hands and describe her brother vaguely as being "in business—the way men are," delineating the chasm between male and female, or, more to the point, the chasm between male experience and female knowledge of that experience. For young Charlie, this split is infuriating. And for me, watching the movie for the first time, it was as familiar as my own life.

Throughout my childhood, I had always suspected that boys were doing something better and more exciting than anything I would ever be allowed to do. In *Shadow of a Doubt*, Hitchcock taps into the relentless curiosity that girls feel for the male province. Charlie playfully accuses her uncle of harboring a secret, and while this is in fact true, she has no idea of the horrible nature of his secret. What she does understand is that there are layers to her uncle's life, and she is doggedly determined to uncover them.

Charlie's desire reminded me of how desperate I was for information. What went on in the boys' bathroom? my friends and I wondered. In the boys' camp across the lake at night? In the offices where our fathers worked? Inside the hearts of the boys and men we knew? We formed a cluster after school and whispered our speculations about all things male. For most of us, maleness was hopelessly alien, a great mystery that would not be solved for years, and even then—when we loved and lived with men—only partially. As grown women, each of us would invariably experience moments of looking across the table at our husbands and lovers, and thinking: Who *are* you?

In the film, Joseph Cotten's character is "exposed" as the "Merry Widow" murderer, and a pat sentence or two about a

childhood accident that left him bedridden is used to explain his
pathology, but this feels like a capitulation to Hollywood's insis-
tence on safe closure and easy answers. Beneath the explanation
Uncle Charlie is left thoroughly untouched and unknowable. Hitchcock maintains the stance that we cannot know one another in any
real sense; even spiritual twins cannot make the leap from soul to
soul.

This question of otherness entranced me at thirteen in ways
that extended beyond the boundaries of gender; it also applied to
the schism between adult and child. In the absence of experience,
I found my parents' universe of dinner parties and cocktail shakers
and R-rated movies inexplicable. I began writing short stories that
summer, often about experiences beyond my own life. In my sub-
urban bedroom with its stuffed animals and white furniture, I wrote
of blind girls and Vietnamese orphans. I wrote with bravado and
a huge lack of knowledge. As an adult, I'm certain my knowledge
has expanded, but my bravado has in some ways declined. Finally
I know what it is I can never know.

Jane Austen wrote that she never created scenes in her novels
in which only men were present, because she had no idea of what
they spoke about when women weren't around. It is this urgent
longing to uncover the truth about the Other that Hitchcock ex-
plores so successfully in *Shadow of a Doubt*. Much of the power
of the film certainly comes from the performances. As Uncle Charlie, Joseph Cotten is a slow-voiced, edgy stud. As his niece, Teresa
Wright is convincingly tremulous and full of feeling. Hitchcock
doesn't hesitate to give her a complexity, to move her beyond the
seemingly simple borders of her own girlish bedroom and into
something darker and eventually more threatening.

A few years ago, I read Donald Spoto's biography of Alfred
Hitchcock, and learned that the director apparently hadn't a clue
about women. There are many examples of this ignorance throughout the book, but two moments in particular come immediately to

mind: When an actress in one of his early films couldn't go in the water during a beach scene, Hitchcock was told it was because she was menstruating, but the director had no idea of what that meant. And during the filming of *The Birds*, Hitchcock was so taken with his star, Tippi Hedren, who did not return his obsessive feelings, that he apparently terrorized her during rehearsals with a flock of clacking, sniping birds. Hitchcock was an anomaly who blustered ahead, sometimes exploiting his outsider status with brilliant results. On-screen in his famous cameos, he lumbered past, seeming to enjoy the joke of his own awkward presence, or at least turning it into a joke before anyone else could.

After reading Spoto's biography, I began to seek out Hitchcock's movies again, just as I had done at thirteen. It was easier now, since VCRs had been invented and I was able to watch his films in sequence. This time I was struck by how wrongheaded and often offensive was his screen interpretation of women. Of course, misogyny and sheer ignorance about women abound in the movies, both then and now, but many of Hitchcock's films contain a distinctly perverse brand of naiveté. *Marnie*, featuring Hitchcock's beloved Hedren, is absurd in its portrayal of a woman with a sordid and repressed past. And *Psycho*, for all its blunt, memorable horror, portrays Mrs. Bates as a shrill, oppressive harridan—one of Bruno Bettelheim's schizophrenogenic mothers—thus neatly blaming (and tacitly excusing) Norman Bates's murderous violence toward women.

Yet *Shadow of a Doubt* gets it right. For once Hitchcock not only approximates a realistic interpretation of what it means to be a woman, but actually manages an unexpected protean turn as an adolescent girl. During the opening scenes, while Charlie still believes her uncle's secret to be something wonderfully exciting, she never once takes a guess as to what it might be. Instead, a complicated series of expressions crosses Teresa Wright's face, and we understand that her longings are coupled with a certain painful

hesitation. This uneasy combination of fantasy and timidity seems   **33**
to me a brilliant distillation of the female adolescent experience.
It's this distillation that I must have responded to when I saw the
film for the first time, and it's this experience, so seemingly foreign
to the fat man with an almost willful ignorance of all things female,
that Hitchcock got unmistakably, unaccountably right.

Or, perhaps, not so unaccountably—not if these unarticulated
desires were Hitchcock's own. The man who knew too little about
the inner lives of women, and who remained permanently suspended in a state of preadolescence, felt most at home exploring
presexual longings. My favorite Hitchcock film (and, at one time,
his) is informed by a longing that is immature, touching, and
inevitably unsatisfied.

Many of Hitchcock's films are narrowed by the director's
limited sensitivity toward adult drives, but in the case of *Shadow
of a Doubt* this lack only serves to bring him intimately close to
his subject. Nearly a half century after it was released, the movie
still resonates with felt life. And nearly twenty years after I first
saw the film, finally I understand what the master of suspense could
possibly have had in common with a thirteen-year-old girl who
bore a thin white scar on the palm of her hand.

◪

HORROR /
SCIENCE FICTION

PREMATURE
BURIAL

JAYNE ANNE PHILLIPS

'm ten years old in 1962 and my hometown is still pretty. It's a college town, the county seat, in north-central West Virginia. It seems more a college town than a coal town, though in fact it is both—home to a private Methodist college where Bible classes are required curriculum, home to a network of rural deep mines connected by two-lane roads. In fifteen years the mines will begin to close, give way to strip mining that will ruin the land even faster, fill the air with fine black dust that subtly changes the colors of the houses. The coal trucks will cease their circuitous routes and lumber right along Main Street, breaking the pavement, scattering coal dust and sick exhaust through downtown, past the grade schools, out toward Interstate 79, where they'll carry away what little the state has left. Strip miners aren't really miners; they're heavy-equipment operators from out of state, and the only

38 local businessmen who survive will become their suppliers. Everything else will dry up, and the town will go down. But in 1962,
there is no strip mining, no interstate highway, no fast-food chains
or malls. Stores are owned by men whose fathers owned the stores,
and restaurants are run by women in their fifties who have worked
in the restaurants for thirty years. The town listens to the mine
report before the national news and the local radio station begins
its broadcast on snow days with lists of shifts: *These shifts will
work . . . Century No. 2 . . . Nitro . . . United Bethlehem . . .
Hundred . . . Ludlow 1.* The miners are employed; paid well for
compromising their lives. Every twenty years or so there's a cave-
in or an explosion, men trapped, women camped out above ground
to pray. Veteran miners are habitually short-winded, but most of
them are smokers and the term "black lung" is not yet common
usage. The streets of the town are clean and the teen-age sons of
the miners drive new pick-ups up and down Main Street on Saturday nights, conducting a kind of class warfare with the boys from
town, who drive Mustang convertibles and date the most popular
girls. Everyone goes to church on Sundays. There are the First and
Central Methodists, Central and Southern Baptists, First and Second Presbyterians; past the city limits, out closer to the mines, are
the Pentecostals and Holy Rollers. There's one large Catholic
church, near the hospital run by nuns. In deference, the schools
serve fish sticks every Friday. There are no Jews. There are three
or four black families in the town and they're all related. Their
children are well accepted by their same-sex peers but, funny thing,
the teen-agers don't date and no one even wonders about it. The
larger world, the world that might question the social and economic
drift of the town, just doesn't exist beyond the mountains and
valleys and small skies. We see that other world in *Life* magazine,
on TV, and at the movies.

The movies are beautiful. There are two theaters. The Kanawha is the bigger one and sits at the bottom of Kanawha Hill,

nicknamed "Quality Hill" in the twenties. The branches of hundred-year-old oaks and elms meet heavy-leaved over the wide street where the grandest houses have already been given over to fraternities and funeral homes. The Kanawha signals the edge of the tiny downtown, its giant *K* blinking alternating stripes of blue and violet neon. The lobby is art deco inside, not much of a lobby at all, just two big ascending corridors to the right and left on either side of the candy counter. The smaller Colonial is on Main Street next to the Dairy Queen. The old-fashioned marquee is lit by tinkly pink lights, the cave of its dim rococo interior papered in wavery pink and green scallops. The Colonial is popular with teen-agers because it has a balcony, accessible from the lobby along a steep tunnel of twisting, carpeted stairs. Mr. Winkler, the wizened owner, takes tickets by the big double doors of the theater and won't let little kids up the balcony steps. We sneak up when his back is turned. Later, when we call our parents to pick us up, Mr. Winkler stands with us in the little office that smells of his cigars, hugging us, saying what good girls we are, stroking our chests through our cotton sweaters or bulky winter coats. He hugs us from behind while we dial numbers on the old black telephone. We jostle to evade his grasp but not one of us thinks of mentioning his embraces at home. We don't talk about anything that happens at the movies, so why would we talk about him? We talk about which clothes we want to wear or which TV shows we want to watch, and we watch a lot of TV because TV is still a sort of innocent miracle in regressive, West Virginia time. It's as though we were living in the late forties rather than the early sixties. Most people have had TVs for only a few years. Often we watch TV as a family, Perry Como sitting on a stool and tapping a glass with a teaspoon: *Catch a falling star and put it in your pocket.* But kids go to the movies alone, dropped off at the door to meet our friends. We girls sit in groups of five or six across; we never know what exactly it is we're going to see until we sit down and watch, and the scary movies are delicious because we scream in unison and get right down on the floor, writhing and peering through our fingers. We're nine or ten years old, growing up together at the movies before we have to think about boys; only the dim buzz of parental struggle at home shadows the intensity of our own politics. We love Vincent Price in *The Last Man on Earth.* We are terrified when he walks down the steps of a big white public building that resembles the Lincoln Memorial, dodging the undead with his inimitable scowl. We cover our eyes, giggle nervously, hide in each other's arms. And we love *The Phantom of the Opera,* that great moment when he swings across the opera house on a vast crystal chandelier as the audience gapes, and his feat seems wholly believable in the world of this theater, where it is always dark and the dark is filled with sound, and the only reality is the colossal picture on the screen. In fact, this world seems more real to us in many ways, more the way life should be, than what we see in our town, in the county around the town, where in fact bad things happen. Despite crowded Main Street and employment in the mines, there is grinding, entrenched poverty, poverty that a pittance of monthly welfare checks does nothing to alleviate. We don't know much about it, it's a secret we take in by osmosis in Murphy's Five and Ten Cent Store on Saturdays, where we gather by the record rack to listen to 45's. We see the families standing inside where it's warm. The women have dead eyes and their children's hair is uncombed. Their skin is alabaster white, blue-veined, and they haven't been able to get clean. The kids are dirty in an old, dry way; they are dark between their fingers, and their wrists are cuffed with shadow. The delicate bracelets of lines on the backs of their wrists are etched with dirt, as though someone had taken a pen with a very fine point and traced each tiny cross and whorl. Their eyes are not dead. They look—what, exactly? They look startled. Their eyes are wide with apprehension. I look at them and wonder what they've seen; I know the world of the town is not what it seems. The movies are exactly what they seem, but the world is not like the movies.

My mother is a first-grade teacher in the town and tells me how some kids come in off the buses so hungry that she has to take them to the school lunchroom and find them something, anything, to eat before she tries to teach them. She collects odd mittens and gloves from neighbors and matches up same-size rights and lefts for the kids from the country, so at least their hands will be warm. Some of them are too proud to wear those mittens and their hands are chapped and mottled, almost mauve, when they finish the long bus ride to school in town. Every fall the churches donate warm clothes to the welfare office, but the clothes, if they show up on the kids at all, get dirtier and dirtier, and wear out before winter is over. My mother says the parents cash the welfare checks and drink the money. She says it's the mothers in Murphy's with the children waiting for the fathers to finish drinking at the bars. She says some of the mothers break down and take off, or they break down in a different way and go to the bars with the men. Then it's the older sisters waiting with the children, sisters who are not much older than me. Soon they'll quit school, if they haven't already, and be taken up by some man who probably already has a brood of kids. They'll live in a hollow like the one they grew up in, places with names like Mud Lick, Sago, Volga, a cluster of buildings around a coal tipple, the wood-frame houses fanning off, far apart, up dirt roads. Those roads are beautiful in summer, and the creeks are still full of catfish, but in winter the cold is brutal. The little houses are heated with coal stoves, easy enough to keep going, but someone might forget or not be home or be drunk. I hear my mother discuss this or that story with other women: *That poor baby got too cold to wake up—they were keeping it in a cardboard box on the floor,* or *Mother of five, just sat down on her own subzero porch, couldn't take it anymore.*

I don't know how the women know these stories. I know my friends and I don't see the country kids at the movies. But I think about them in the dark, inevitably, as though they are ghosts mixed up in the light of the overwhelming image flickering over us. I fantasize a tall man in black like Vincent Price, evil enough to meet any evil, slitting the screen with a big knife, and letting those children in. He lets them into a world of velvet gowns and jewels and pink cravats and sparkling glasses, operas and great houses and British accents. Then I don't have to think about them anymore, and I can watch the movies, one after another, every Friday night and every Sunday afternoon.

I see Doris Day and James Bond and John Wayne but what I'll remember most from these years are the B-grade horror films of Roger Corman—not the creature films, but the opulent versions of Poe. The fog machine is always working overtime and the air is billowy with clouds. I'll realize later that Corman's luxuriantly gothic (and inexpensively produced) sets were the stuff of a girl child's dreams, and I'll know too that I remember certain images because of my real life—not because the images changed me, but because they were haunting, inverted metaphors of things that were true, things too frightening to think about as a child. What about those houses with slanted porches up the dirt roads, the houses where women and babies freeze? What about my own family, how shaky things seem, how hard my capable mother seems to work at school, at home, coping always with my father's anger and resentment. What does it mean: *buried*? The frequent, gothic burials in Corman's films are relatively speedy events; here in our town, there's daily life—a long, slow process. There is no screaming, no hugging or group catharsis, for the observers or the participants. I suppose my friends and I are both, though at least we are town kids—we won't wake to find our mothers frozen on a broken-down porch. My brothers and I really are town kids, definitely, I tell myself. Though we live out a rural road, the road is paved and we're only a mile from the city limits. More important, my family is well thought of—my mother's people were wealthy once, owned a lumber mill, went broke in the Depression. My father's established and owned the non-Catholic hospital. Later he

owned a concrete plant, but that is gone now. This winter my   **43**
parents have had to cash in their children's savings bonds, and my
father is working for the local Chevrolet dealership, selling used
cars. Cars don't sell in the cold weather, my father tells me, and
sometimes when we get home from school with my mother, my
father is already there, frying potatoes for supper in the big iron
skillet. He always drives us into town on Friday nights for the
movies, which cost fifty cents. I occasionally pretend to have lost
one of my quarters; he grimaces and looks pained, shakes his head,
but it's only pretense. He digs into his pocket for another coin,
chuckling. Lately I realize the ritual has gained importance for him,
and I remember to do it each time. Tonight he drops us off at the
Kanawha to see something called *Premature Burial.* When I read
the title on the marquee I think maybe the film has to do with
babies born too soon, but when I see the poster in the lobby I
realize I'm on familiar ground. My friends buy popcorn but I
purchase a Sugar Daddy, a rectangular caramel sucker on a stick
that I can warm to the shape of my mouth and taste throughout
the previews and well into the feature itself. My friends have names
like Susie, Kathy, Janie, Joanie, names that are just not serious,
and we all settle in, pretending to be what we're supposed to be,
and then the lights go down.

Corman characterizes *Premature Burial* as one of his less
successful efforts. It may have been a formulaic low point in his
career, but, seeing it twenty-five years later, I think it must have
been great fun to make. I'd always remembered Vincent Price in
the role of Guy Carrell, scion of a dwindling Victorian family,
rattling around with his drab sister and assorted servants in a
mansion on the foggy moors. But it's actually Ray Milland, who
doesn't steal the film as Price would have. He leaves that to the
female leads, who do suitably restrained but campy versions of the
spinster sister, Kate, and the love interest, "sweet, beautiful, gentle
Emily." Milland is distanced, rather vague, obsessed with the idea

44 that his father had catalepsy and was buried alive. He's certain that he's inherited the illness and will meet the same fate. We girls take it all in, slouched down with our knees propped up on the seats in front of us. We first see Milland dressed in black top hat and cape, grave robbing at night in a cemetery with doctor colleagues. They are decidedly unlike our fathers, standing there in their evening clothes as Sweeny and Mole, the whistling gravediggers, unearth a casket in a hole below them. They are rich men watching poor men work, but they all look so funny in their formal attire as dirt flies around them that we snicker into our hands. Music swells as the lid of the casket is wrested off and slammed into the face of the viewer, its inside streaked with blood. We stop snickering. Close-up of a shrunken corpse that does in fact resemble a fetus, its hands upraised like knobby, foreshortened limbs. The grave-diggers continue to whistle the excellent, beautifully timbred version of "Molly Malone" that will haunt Milland throughout the movie. It has already occurred to me that my own father is haunted, but I don't yet know why. I've observed that some of my friends' fathers hold the power in the family matrix as my own father does not. Even so, they seem disgruntled; they don't converse much with their daughters. When we see Emily, a daughter herself in the film, her auburn hair is upswept and her snowy cleavage is concealed in a hooded velvet cape. She is driven in her carriage to the mansion of the suffering Milland, who's decided not to marry her because his imperfect genes forecast disaster. I immediately think he is referring to the children of their union rather than to the hardship of his own demise, and I think of the man who lives in the house next to the town jail, just across the parking lot from the theater. He's a grown-up man with the mind of a boy; my mother has told me he's a mongoloid, which reminds me of the country of Mongolia, and he does look Oriental, ancient, with his jowls and his wrinkled, down-sliding face. Doglike, he sits at the window staring toward the traffic on Kanawha Street, his face pressed to the glass. I've never seen him outside and I've never seen his mother, but she couldn't be anything like the glamorous Emily, who pronounces herself unafraid of disaster. Maybe she is more like the drab sister, Kate, who is clearly the villain—wrenlike, embittered, dressed always in black, her little mouth clamped into a straight, disapproving line. But the drab, dark sister turns out to be the honorable one; Emily is after the house and the money and is typically, underhandedly feminine: she's hired the gravediggers to whistle the song and appear at second-story windows. She's "set her cap," as my mother would say, for the handsome, sincere Dr. Miles Archer. Miles has invented a tabletop contraption with cords and clamps, the better to observe the contractions of electrically stimulated frogs, but his real interest is the human mind. They are all here for the wedding—not the frogs, of course, but the good doctors and all the other elegant guests—and so is the noisiest lightning storm on record, with claps of foreshadowing thunder drowning out the vows. At the reception in the great hall, Emily goes to the piano in her wedding gown to play "Molly Malone," whose strains precipitate Guy's swoon into a sleep of dread.

Now Guy lies in funereal repose on his baronial bed. It resembles my mother's high, antique beds, but when my mother feels dreadful, she lies still on the narrow couch in the living room, and my father is not home. She has a blinding headache and can't open her eyes. She lies with her arms straight down at her sides and directs me to press down on her forehead with both hands, press down, hard, harder, don't stop. In the moments when my muscles begin to ache and I have to rest my arms, she groans, so I start again, pressing on her forehead, pressing as hard as I can. I am thinking about my mother while I watch the movie, her form supine in the house on the rural road, her smooth forehead just the size of my two hands, and I see Guy awaken with a plan. The quality of my attention changes. Soon Emily summons the helpful Miles to view the mausoleum Guy has designed to curb his fear.

46   It's a sort of Greek Revival–style temple with all sorts of built-in devices. Guy himself narrates its wonders and demonstrates with obvious pride: there is a tasseled cord to pull which activates a sliding door in the stone wall, a coffin whose lid is fitted with tools, whose push button instantly pops the top and sides apart. There is a bell to pull for help from the house. One may have to wait— there are books, periodicals, food and drink, and a gramophone to provide the soothing effects of music. If help doesn't come (or no one cares to answer), a gate automatically opens in the wall. A pull cord drops a rope ladder to a door in the roof. Then there is the dynamite in a gold box ("a recent invention by a Swedish chemist called Nobel"). If all else fails, there is poison in a silver chalice. Afterward, Emily takes Guy walking in the fog and dark, where he hears the gravediggers whistling and runs through thorns and brush in a panicky search to find some physical presence responsible for the sound. The tune gets louder and faster like an ether dream. Guy faints alone on the moors and has a nightmare. He wakes up in his coffin but the button doesn't work and the tools are gone. He cries out noiselessly in the eerie blue light of the box, finally upsets the coffin with his struggling and breaks it open. The food, of course, is spongy with mold. The velvet rope has rotted and the escape gate is jammed; the rope ladder falls from the ceiling in strands. A tarantula crawls over the box of dynamite, which crumbles to dust in Guy's hands. Rats scramble everywhere. He pulls the chalice from its cobwebbed crevice and begins to drink, and the worms in the cup tumble right into our faces. Girls to the right and left of me have their faces in my neck, but I'm staring straight into the image. Here is a movie about a foiled escape, and I am already plotting mine. I must succeed, not fail; the escape is not only mine, it is hers—my mother's—because I am her and she is me, and my escape will be her escape, the only escape she will ever have. I am plotting our escape, not by thinking or planning, it's too soon for that, but by looking, watching, perceiving even the smallest useful detail, and remembering—what? Everything, everything that matters. This is love. This is who and what I will be.

But Emily's love is false. She convinces Guy to blow up the mausoleum, scares him into a cataleptic seizure, watches him buried (in a coffin with a window, no less). Secretly, though, her heartless father has him immediately dug up as a research specimen. Freed, he goes on a bit of a rampage and does away with all the villains. He actually buries Emily alive in his own grave and is holding Miles off admirably when Kate, the honorable sister, puts him out of his misery with one quick, clean shot.

There is no clean shot in life. There is Kanawha Street, shimmering with rain and darkness when we walk out of the lighted theater. And there is my father's big white Ford, floating like a boat on the rain-slicked blacktop, wipers clacking, motor idling, the headlights sending two long beams through the dark. I see rain falling in the light he makes, and the oily puddles at my feet are faceted with color.

The honorable sister in my family is me. I'm the only sister—for years, I think I have no choice. But no, actually I choose to be honorable. I'm the one my mother will confide in as she exits the marriage in careful stages, moving us to a house in town, moving her bedroom to the basement of that house, asking my father to leave the year the children are all off to college. She has a graduate degree now and a demanding job in administration. For some years we live parallel lives, living alone with our dogs, doing our work, except I move at least once a year, establish a number of intense relationships, experiment in every way. My mother wishes I'd encounter a Dr. Miles Archer, but I'm moving too fast, I take no prisoners, sabotage any rescue. When I'm thirty, I buy my own house. Shortly after, I'm the one holding my mother's hands in the radiologist's office when he clips the X-rays to light boards and touches the white spots with his pointer. "Here," he says, "and here, and here, and here." We try one thing after another: radiation first, then stoic acceptance, then, when I'm pregnant with my first child, chemotherapy. She has to leave home in a wheelchair, move in with me on the East Coast. My son is born, and the drugs help her for a while, then they fail. Now we are really terrified—there's no putting it off. I begin to understand what premature burial means, I begin to understand about foiled escapes, and anguish. When my mother dies in her room at my house, I'm the one who is with her, and my husband is there, and so is the young black woman who helps us at night. She's from an isolated place, like me, where there is warmth and lush vegetation and wrenching poverty, where there are town kids and country kids and just one or two theaters. She tells me, in her lilting island patois, that we've all done well.

But my mother's death is not like death in the movies. My husband, who is, in fact, a doctor, tells me later she wasn't there when it happened, but I know she was, trapped inside. I know how it will all stay with me, nothing buried, nothing even out of sight. For years, I'll find myself staring right into the image that changed my life.

At the cemetery I stay alone while the cremation takes place. It is a raw November day, banked, melting snow, very misty and foggy. I sit by a half-frozen pond in my raincoat while smoke ascends from the crematorium chimney. This is the oldest section of the cemetery; the stones are Victorian and dramatic. It's so foggy that I can't see the road beyond the wrought-iron fence, only dimly hear the sluicing sound of passing traffic. I have patterned my adult life on escape and redemption, escape being flight, movement, self-reliance, redemption being the circle back, the writing, the saving of a version of events that is emotionally real, that can't ever recede or be lost. Escape is no longer possible; I no longer believe in escape, and there is too much at stake now to simply rely on myself. It's as though I hold my child in my arms and

move in an inexorable spiral toward the eye of life and death. When   **49**
I was a child and watched someone else's dreams at the movies,
the stories were shadow plays. *You and I were very close once.*
You stood aside and let them bury me alive. I shall not bury you;
that sorry task I shall leave to the earth, and the darkness, and
the terrible pounding of your own heart. Stay where you are,
Miles, this has nothing to do with you. My beautiful, treacherous,
perfidious love . . . She's dead. Thank God. There are no shadows
in this white day. The smoke of my mother's transformation is
dark as it meets the air, climbing in curls, but the color lightens,
drifts, disintegrates in the fog, completely taken up.

◪

THE THING
THE REAL THING
CLARK BLAISE

error works the same way lust, suspense, slapstick, and heroism work: by attacking the outer edges of our naiveté. Older than eleven, and I would have found *The Thing* a joke. Older than fourteen (well, in my case seventeen), and *Gilda* would have turned into shameless mush. Older than twenty, and *Jules and Jim* would have been sentimental Eurofantasy. It's not the film—acting, production, direction—exactly, it's the time we first saw it, how fully it seduced all that we were capable of giving.

It's rare now, at fifty, for me to find a picture that engages all I want to release. The naiveté is gone. Now I even write films, but I watch them like baseball games, a superior amusement I appreciate but expect to walk away from unchanged. The beauty of pictures, though, is that you can always go back and be captured by the moment you first saw them, be the child, the adolescent, the would-be sophisticate.

I can't remember where I saw *The Thing*, but it was still somewhere deep in my eleven-year-old innocence. We lived in six different cities that year, starting in Florida and ending in Ohio. In one of those cities, I entered the theater, as was my habit, about twenty minutes into the showing. Movies ran continuously and were meant to be barged into, and be figured out on a fundamental level: *Which of these guys is going to die first?* If we date our maturity from various first times, then the first time we checked the movie schedule in advance and waited in line is one of the big ones.

Probably I entered during one of the earlier scenes—the briefing room, perhaps, where Scottie the journalist and Sparks the radio man and Pat the captain and hero are trying to get the word out. It doesn't take long to determine the situation; they've dug something out of a flying saucer.

Sputter, sputter. Must be interference, Captain. A storm's coming up. Keep trying, Sparks. Right, Captain.

We've dug out an alien! An ugly son of a bitch, too. It's lying there in the cold, in its slab of ice, under a blanket guarded by a dark-haired, weak-chinned expendable who is reading a book. How like an eleven-year-old's sense of the world. They've discovered something weird and terrifying, and when they try to talk about it, their voices sputter. Orders come down from Anchorage: Secure the perimeter, do not disturb the site, do nothing till you hear from us. The generals in Anchorage are no more effective than homeroom teachers who've been called out of class. *Stay in your seats, no talking.* That's the art of terror and the secret plot-twist in nearly any picture, comedy or drama: The trusted authorities, the parents, the lovers, are busy. They wash their hands; you get dirty. No one believes you; you must act alone. *That's nice, dear. Now wash your hands for dinner.*

I could not have seen it in New York or Cleveland, where my parents looked for work and I was left in a bedroom with model planes and a tube of glue, hiding from truant officers. It couldn't have been in Winnipeg, with its *Other-Victorian* moralism. My cousins and I had to stand outside the theaters in Winnipeg and beg adult males to pose as our fathers to take us inside. Winnipeg was struck with polio epidemics every summer, and my mother was a cautious Canadian opposed to swimming pools and movie theaters for her late-born, only child.

It must have been Springfield, the Ozarks town where I first rode my bike in the middle of the street, and where uncharacteristically I joined the Y and learned to swim. Springfield turned a dutiful, repressed, fat little boy into a daredevil. Because of the bike, I had access to the city. I found a comic book store and a stamp dealer, and Saturdays were my own. I discovered the Mulligan Movie House, where three Westerns and at least three serials kept half the boys in Springfield cooped up each Saturday. The trouble with such an attractive probability is that the Mulligan Movie House wasn't really a theater. They served popcorn in brown paper bags. It was just a large garage with no slope for better viewing, no aisles, and folding chairs to move around and sometimes throw, and I remember seeing *The Thing* in a place I couldn't turn my back on, backing up the aisle as I left. So maybe I first saw it in a proper Springfield movie house, or a few months later in Cincinnati, in the Avondale ghetto where we settled.

The Thing is a movie for a sheltered eleven-year-old boy initiating himself into independence. Bruno Bettelheim has psychoanalyzed the classic children's stories, the "Hansel and Gretel"'s and "Snow White"'s, seeing them as passages out of childhood, Oedipal fantasies, parri- or matricides, and narrowly averted filicides. *My parents are trying to kill me. My father is a monster. I can trust only myself. Watch the skies. Watch the skies!* There's a daddy aspect to *The Thing*, the nightmare behind every door, the monster regenerating itself in the dark, the creature you should have left sleeping in his block of ice. It reminded me of Sundays in my childhood: Where's Daddy? Let him sleep.

The Thing works, in retrospect and upon re-viewing, because of verisimilitude. There's a good reason—Howard Hawks produced it and a reliable contract professional, Christian Nyby, directed. The sets are cheap but not tacky: a barracks is solid old *Stalag 17* stuff. The special effects are minimal: a black cloth over the ample torso of James Arness; some studio snow and a wind machine. The terror comes from timing and shadows. In 1951, we didn't have to watch (and listen) as slimy alien growths crinkled from their hosts' bodies. We were not involved then, as we seem to be today, in shocking an audience back into childhood terror purely on the level of special effects.

In addition, the characters are credible: a stock World War II ensemble. The journalist, Scottie, really is cynical—he's even against the American army—and his cynicism is justified. The hero, Pat, is something of a take-charge fly-boy, never out of his white scarf and bomber jacket, who goes through brief periods of frustration with a minimum of contemporary angst. (To see how times have changed, think of the equivalent character, played by Kurt Russell, in John Carpenter's 1982 remake. By 1982, the monster is—like the "Body Snatchers" of a paranoid age—palpable and shape-changing; he is one of us, not an external evil.) The scientist is bearded and a bit of a cliché, an appeasing proto-comsymp willing to sacrifice American lives for possible "scientific communication," but the hero's love interest is bright and witty, a self-reliant brunette (not a googly blonde to catch the monster's eye and turn an ankle in the mandatory chase) who's obviously spent time in the captain's bed in a different time and place, and walked away from it with a smile but no pain, no stigma, and no bitterness. No *film noir* here; this is the fifties. In other words, it's a clean horror story: us against it, human against alien, good against evil, life against death.

But back to the film. Twenty minutes in, and ticking.

54   In the best Hollywood tradition, the blanket under which the thing is hidden, is—unknown to the guard—electric, and the heat is accidentally on, and the ice is melting. (A nice touch, I think now: the 1950 Arctic base is nearly done in by an electric blanket.) A witty bit: electric blankets, lazy susans, Mixmasters, Studebakers and televisions and blenders and portable radios—everything my father used to bring home from his trips on the road—the 1950 marketplace-promises we fought the Nazis and commies for, doing us in. How long before the folds of the blanket begin to twitch?

There! (Mass intake of audience breath).

The guard (an expendable) pays no attention, his back is to the monster. We know that shot; an exposed back is irresistible: it's the killer's, or monster's, point of view. Never has a slow shadow, angling toward the chair, falling over the guard's back, his shoulder, then finally across his book, been used to better effect. Slowly, the guard drops his hands. He knows. The temperature in the theater has just dropped twenty degrees. He straightens his back. He turns his head, degree by degree, as his fingers curl on his gun belt . . . That classic take—haven't we seen it in Karloff's Mummy and Frankenstein movies, in Chaney's Werewolf and Lugosi's Dracula, in the Cat People, the Zombies . . .

There's no greater horror than a slowly advancing shadow over an obliging expendable's back. Even in our world of million-dollar gizmos, who needs a spaceship, mechanized gremlins, slimy rubber masks, when you've got an Arctic barracks, a storm, and a monster inside? The horror works because everything's in perfect scale. The monster's threat doesn't exceed the collective will and ingenuity of the defenders; he's strong and brutal but no Godzilla. We have an outside chance of winning.

Speaking (or remembering) as an innocent but imaginative eleven-year-old, I can say *The Thing* stuck with me because of its seamlessness—no nutty premise requiring a suspension of disbelief like Dracula, the Mummy, or the Werewolf; no gratuitous, wacky-lens gigantism like Mothra, Godzilla, or a dozen other undersea, atomic-mutant threats to Tokyo; and no shadow political allegory like the Body Snatchers, those smooth-talking pod-people out to pirate our gene pool. *The Thing* played to our anti-*Chinese* communist, Korean War anger, which was far closer to the spirit of Iwo Jima than anything since. *You got an alien monster problem here? Zap it with a million volts.* *The Thing* is the last of the World War II adventure movies, the bridge to the domestic anticommunist agenda.

The implacable, generic evil of a nonhuman enemy was a match for an eleven-year-old boy just testing his independence and his boyhood, let alone his manhood. *The Thing* is really a displaced frontier fable, a cowboys-and-Indians, us-against-them bit of backs-against-the-wall patriotism. The Monster has no weapons, only fang and claw and a stupendous birthrate.

In other words, The Thing is not a fallen Transylvanian count or an Alpine doctor or an Egyptian priest. She (after all, her severed hand, the one torn off by sled dogs, reveals a seed-pod) has no humanity, no Karloffian cultured side, no Lugosian viscosity. She's just stashing drained bodies under the Bunsen burners and planting her seeds in plasma. The thirties had given us ambiguous villains suffering from acute social demotion (count to casket-sleeper, high priest to catacombs guide, research scientist to ghoul); the late forties gave us *film noir* and the terrors of female sexuality ("Where did she learn this stuff? It wasn't from me!"). Then came Korea and the commie scare. Nineteen fifty-one fed our nostalgia for real villains, a Hitler from Outer Space. When I was eleven, it was as much horror as I could bear, believe, and retain. Even the sight of the alien's hand, the closest thing we get to a special effect, was terrifying. In pieces, the monster was more convincing than when fully intact.

◢

Looking back now as a man of fifty, I think how appropriate science fiction is to its national obsessions. Horror for the Japanese

56   appears to be alien gigantism of any kind (Godzilla, Mothra, Americans?), mega-terror through magnification. From that mythic horror, a microchip industry is born.

For the British, the aliens appear to be disagreeable dinner guests, social boors of suspect pedigree who demand acceptance. Like the various good doctors (Jekyll, Frankenstein) or counts (over-rich, oversexed and over here?), they are fallen aristocrats or grasping *arrivistes* who really don't know their place. Some of these visitors can, on occasion, be made ashamed of themselves, taught their manners. If we Stand Up for Our Values, the Alien Threat will be vanquished. (The original American "Star Trek" strikes me as a fancier version of the "Dr. Who" premise: superior force can be outsmarted. One clever leader and his intrepid team can sail into the universe armed with deftness and no nightsticks, with little more than gentlemanly integrity and a talent for debate.) And if we can't outfight them or outsmart them, as H. G. Wells reminds us in *The War of the Worlds*, we've still got an ally in the common cold, or in salt water, as in *The Day of the Triffids*.

It seems to me there are three distinct blends of horror science-fiction. In the first, the villain is human, perhaps even noble, but genetically flawed. They are accursed, they *want* to be like us, but they cannot. Clearly, this is a literary form, Romantic in origin, capable even of tenderness. It's too subtle for an eleven-year-old, and I'm sorry that contemporary taste has sunk to such low levels that the sturdy archetypes survive only in low parodies of the teenage werewolf and "Freddy" variety.

In the second, the villain is nonhuman and implacable; it can only be stopped. It is somehow beyond good and evil: it aims to kill us, eat us, use our carcasses as seed-pods, rape the planet, and move on. The spaceship is a refitted meat locker. No moment of eye contact, King Kong to Fay Wray. There is no human core to reach, no appeal to pity, compassion, or exception to be made.

Clearly, *The Thing* belongs in this uncomplicated, two-dimensional genre (we won . . . *this time*), and I responded to it only because it was so well done, so suggestive, realistic, and low-budget. So, in a word, sincere. And of course, it lends itself to parodies of the Schwarzenegger school.

What is, finally, the ultimate horror? The killer who looks and acts just like us, who seduces us into his madness, or the visibly deformed monster who lurks behind every door? These are the enduring archetypes of terror. As a child, I responded to the second; as an adult, I assent to the first, reluctantly.

Predictably, modern cinema has given us a hybrid: inhuman savagery with a bland human face. This is *The Bad Seed, Psycho,* and *The Manchurian Candidate,* shorn of pop psychology, infused instead with killer microbes. This is Norman Bates with alien DNA. The formula for contemporary horror is murder from within by body-snatching shape-changers. We know they're out there, but we don't know who they are. We—the last human (Kevin Mc-Carthy in the original, Donald Sutherland in the remake of *Invasion of the Body Snatchers*)—can't communicate the experience because "they" (the doctors, the journalists, the politicians) are the first to capitulate. We are Everyman, sure of his own humanity, but unsure of anyone else's, and that uncertainty eventually forces us to blow away our best friend, our wife, our lover. This also became the focus of John Carpenter's 1982 remake of *The Thing,* with its progressive derangement of the Kurt Russell character, the reduction of the cast to one black and one white and a flame thrower, the Wagnerian smoldering set as the cold and death set in. The original injunction, shouted by Scottie to the world, "Look to the skies!" becomes a sullen, silent waiting out of death. The knowledge and experience will die with the characters. What it tells us about our own uncertainty, the narrow ledge we tread between sanity and madness, good and evil, human and clone, self-confidence and manipulation, is a rough diagnosis, a dark reading of contemporary life.

◸

Did *The Thing* change my life? No movie, singly, ever did, and cumulatively I'd have to say the onslaught of fifties boy-girl films, with their mixed codes of idealized innocence, mysterious wholesomeness, and leering sexuality, fed expectations of desire that left a deeper, more permanent psychic doubt. What junk we Americans are fed on! What useless expertise we accumulate! When I think about my schooling, my movie going, my sports addictions, I'd say there's not a single elevating experience in my childhood or adolescence, nothing that I could say fed my cultural acquisitiveness, my sensitivity, my fund of timeless knowledge.

Yet that simple, low-budget sci-fi horror flick did something no other movie ever did. It split my childhood in two; it exposed a layer of dread that I couldn't shake and still haven't shaken; it infected a novel I wrote called *Lunar Attractions* (1978), and it led me always to ask, when I write, what is the ultimate horror in any encounter? A twitching hand on a laboratory counter, a jerking in the folds of an electric blanket, a running shape in the snow on fire with sled dogs hanging from its arms, a shadow falling over a drowsing guard—these are literary, not technical, accoutrements of terror, and they stuck with me.

I'm permanently locked in the second level of terror, not in the shape-changing world of the Body Snatchers, but in the primordial world of claws behind doors. *The Thing* ruined me for Spielberg's conciliatory visions, and for the triumphant logic of "Star Trek." It disabused me of the need for explanations—I really don't care why Freddy stalks Elm Street, why zombies roam Pittsburgh, or what attracts poltergeists. I'm still not comfortable, when I think about it, sleeping alone in large houses, walking dark streets, or swimming in mountain lakes, and I know it's because of something out there—the shadow—in the water or behind a tree. When I'm alone, the world is an animated and dangerous place to be, not because of criminals and serial murderers (the "things" of the present time), but because once when I was eleven, I saw the proof.

There are far worse things awaiting man than death.

—Dracula

DRACULA
THE VAMPIRE'S SECRET
JOYCE CAROL OATES

he images to which memory accrues!

In this timeless and utterly silent void, very like the pit of darkness at the bottom of the brain that opens, in sleep, to draw us through, there moves the somber, elegant, impeccably groomed figure of Count Dracula—stark white face, gleaming black hair, demonically luminous eyes. And there is the large, hawklike, dreamily fluttering bat, no ordinary bat but a concentration as of intelligence or will. And the graceful ballet of white-gowned female figures, Dracula's trio of beautiful mute wives who, like their master, arise from their coffins when the sun sets. The conspicuously setting sun too is a strong image, if more abstract—the surrender of day's (reason's?) power to control, or at least to keep at bay, the forces of evil—evil "nature"—that surround us. And of course there is the potent image of Christian sanctity, the Crucifix, from which Dracula and his vampire disciples shrink as if it were not **61** merely metal but a blinding beacon of light.

Dracula as film and *Dracula* as novel: the "triumph" of Christianity over, as we say, the forces of evil. (Are all horror stories thus constructed, to provide us with this "triumph"?—the classic stories, at least, before even genre became self-reflexive and postmodernist.)

In Tod Browning's *Dracula,* in which the celebrated European actor Bela Lugosi made cinematically immortal the mythopoetic figure of Bram Stoker's Dracula, all is enacted against a background of utter soundlessness: except for the sweetly seductive opening bars of *Swan Lake* as the credits come on, the film has no musical score, no distractions from its spare, poetic, highly charged dialogue. (The film was made shortly after sound came to moving pictures; the further concept of providing sourceless music as background, to disguise a too-silent theatrical atmosphere, had not yet occurred to filmmakers.) In this, *Dracula* more resembles a dream than most surreal or fantastic films, since—I assume I speak for all of us?—our dreams lack musical accompaniment. Dreamlike, too, and eerily suggestive of that stylized, unvarying ritual that is the Catholic mass, is Dracula's every movement, premeditated as a dancer's, or, indeed, a Catholic priest's. The unfolding of fantastic events as if they were decreed by Fate is ideally suited to such silence, for rational comprehension is hardly the point here, only this emblematic experience, both primitive, as life feeding on life is primitive, and sophisticated, for, unmistakably, Bela Lugosi in evening dress and cape, the most studied and articulate of villains, *is* sophisticated. As Werner Herzog has said, what is film but an "agitation of mind." To subject it to intellectual analysis, let alone academic analysis, may be to misapprehend its true nature, and to endanger our openness to its magic.

Yet analysis is always a temptation, especially analysis many years after an initial experience. It may tell us, along with things we want to know, some things we don't.

◪

Seeing this classic *Dracula* for only the second time in my life, a remarkable sixty years after it was made and released, and nearly forty years after I'd first seen it, in the long-razed Rialto Theater in Lockport, New York, I am struck at once and during the days following by a storm of images—emotions, haphazard and teasing shreds of memory—it has stirred. Perhaps for many of us, for Americans of my generation most of all, it is film, thus the visual/aural, that has the power of Proust's madeleine to summon forth memory? Not the privacy of narcissism, the taste in the (child's) mouth, but the communal awe of the darkened, hushed, churchlike movie theater, especially those movie theaters of old, which seemed to us places of legitimate wonder, and, indeed, were built to promote that fantasy; that swoon of expectation. *Dracula* plunges me into an obsessive consideration, not simply of the film, and the now-mythopoetic Dracula, and the novel of 1897 (which I first read in the early 1950s, no doubt immediately after having seen the reissued film, and have subsequently "taught" in university courses, and have written about, in an essay titled "Wonderlands"); not simply of the ingenuity of its bold conceit (which has to do, in short, as, for instance, Lewis Carroll's Alice books do in their entirely different way, with the nightmare evoked by Darwinian theories of survival of the fittest and natural selection, morally repugnant to Victorian traditionalists), but of countless seemingly forgotten personal matters, anxieties of my own, and revelations, too, small quirky bits of no possible interest to anyone but myself, or perhaps my parents; indeed, incomprehensible to anyone else. (For instance, it is fitting that I saw *Dracula* at the Rialto Theater, not the Palace: the Palace, on Main Street, formerly a vaudeville house, had loges, velvet draperies, mock-Egyptian ornamentation, even a pastoral mural on its high, high ceiling, and **63** was, in a modest way, "palatial"—but the Rialto was small, unglamorous, in its later years frankly shabby, back off Main Street on the corner of Pine and Walnut, a place of second-rate Hollywood movies, reissues, cowboy and Tarzan serials, children's Saturday matinees that transformed the place into a monkey house. The Rialto was, in every sense of the word, *back-street*.) Perhaps because I've seen the film during a period of personal stress, when, as it's said, "ego defenses" are lowered, I feel unusually vulnerable to such incursions from the unconscious, from that shadowy region of the brain where our oldest memories reside.

The most striking insight the film has left me with—though now that I've seen it, how transparent, obvious—is that the figure of Count Dracula as played so coolly by Bela Lugosi *is* priestly; his formal evening wear, high starched collar, ankle-length black cape suggest the vestments of a Catholic priest, as do his carefully choreographed movements, the precision with which he pronounces words, enunciates syllables, as if English were a language foreign to him—as of course it is. And what resonance in this, for, in Catholic ritual, the priest celebrating the mass drinks "the blood of Christ" (diluted red wine) out of a chalice, as the congregation prays, in the moments before the dramatic (to some, those who truly believe, intensely emotional, sometimes intimidating) sacrament of Holy Communion, during which the communicants come forward to the altar rail, kneel, clasp their hands, tilt their heads slightly backward, shut their eyes and open their mouths, and, discreetly, extend their tongues an inch or two so that the priest can place the consecrated wafer on it and murmur, in the past in Latin, *Hic est corpus Christi:* This is the body of Christ.

We were instructed to allow the wafer to dissolve—never to chew it.

We were instructed it *was* the body of Christ, who had died on the cross for our sins.

We would be instructed, in time, if our curiosity had a theological bent, that, indeed, the communion wafer must not be
confused with a mere "symbol" of the body of Christ; it *is* the
body of Christ: that's how we Catholics distinguish ourselves from
Protestants, forever.

As I've indicated, if you were a Catholic, especially a young
Catholic, who unquestionably believed in this miracle—in technical
theological terms, the "transubstantiation of the Eucharist"—going
to communion was not a casual matter. Not only must outward
behavior during the hours between Saturday's confession and Sunday's communion be strictly regulated (you must fast, for instance,
from midnight onward, regardless of how late a mass you attended
on Sunday), but your every thought, and this means micro-,
nano-, and wholly involuntary thoughts, must be regulated. A
single impure thought, profaning communion, could plunge you
into mortal sin; if you died in a state of mortal sin you would go
to hell, where your soul would be in torment forever.

Did I ever believe—*can* anyone believe—such things? I am
tempted for romantic reasons to argue that, yes, I did believe, I
was a true Catholic in those days, but in fact I remember myself
too skeptical even as a child, a habit of mind I've inherited from
my father; in church in particular I was too restless in my thoughts
to pay strict attention to the mass—church was a place for cinematic
daydreams, an enforced calm. I could never make myself seriously
believe that, in taking communion at the altar, beside the other
communicants, I was being given the body and blood of Christ:
this is a gulf, trivial to the non-Catholic, immense to those who
have grown up in Catholic surroundings, that separates me as a
former Catholic from other former Catholics, including my husband, who did believe.

Not that Roman Catholicism is the only religion in which
"ritual cannibalism"—vampirism?—is or has ever been practiced.
It is simply the most elaborately reasoned of religions, the most

politically powerful and traditional; the most "aesthetic." The very religion against which the Middle European "Nosferatu" (Romanian for "un-dead") of legend defined themselves, in opposition, as damned souls, or souls that would be damned, if their Christian adversaries could catch them unprotected during the day, in their coffins, and drive stakes through their hearts.

◪

My other insight into the probable reason that *Dracula*, the film, made such a strong impression on me as a child has to do with the fact that Bela Lugosi, in his ethnic exoticism, somewhat reminded me of my maternal step-grandfather John Bush, who had emigrated from Budapest to the Buffalo-Tonawanda area around the turn of the century. ("Bush" is an Americanization of "Büs," which is Hungarian for "melancholy." No, no relation to the Presidential Bushes.) Beyond this, all resemblance ended, for my Grandfather Bush, a blacksmith and a steel-foundry worker, a man particularly fond of hard cider, was hardly a figure of Austro-Hungarian nobility; his crude, candid, guileless manner was rather more that of the proverbial bull in the china shop than that of the demonic-priest Dracula.

My grandfather never saw Bela Lugosi on the screen, so far as I know—never went to the movies at all. Unlike my Grandmother Bush, he was able to read English, but his reading was constricted to the newspaper. At the time of the reissuing of *Dracula*, though only in his sixties, he was a worn-out, prematurely exhausted man, soon to die of what would now be called an occupation-related condition (emphysema). It was Grandpa's wedding portrait that suggested his ethnic kinship with Lugosi, the set of the eyes, the heavy arched brows, the thick stiff black hair, a portrait taken when he was in his early twenties, and dashingly handsome, Magyar exotic.

This old wedding portrait, long lost, of which I find myself thinking, so strangely and sentimentally haunted by, these days following my viewing of *Dracula* on our VCR.

◤

Anyone opting to see a movie after forty years risks discovering that the movie will prove disappointing, if not embarrassing. I'd worried that *Dracula* as a film of 1931 would be too dated to justify discussing it in the speculative terms of an essay.

Not at all. The film is riveting throughout, intelligently and shrewdly constructed; it certainly deserves its classic status, and Bela Lugosi his fame (as a yet more sinister, because wholly unsympathetic, brother-rival to Boris Karloff's immortal Frankenstein). In terms of contemporary cinema, of course, Tod Browning's film is excessively melodramatic and stagey—the presentation of visual horror, in contrast to the more subtle psychological horror which prose fiction can render, is notoriously difficult. Yet, in a darkened movie theater, with an audience, if such an audience might exist, unfamiliar with the vampire legend, how much more effective than on the screen of one's household television, where all images are domesticated, thus diluted. My initial response to the film is surprise that it moves so swiftly—too swiftly? Did early audiences catch the vampire exposition flung out at them by frightened Transylvanian peasants on the eve of Walpurgis Night? In a mode very different from the mock-Gothic, systematically digressive Stoker novel, narrated from the viewpoint of numerous diarists and letter writers, the film reveals its secrets within the first five minutes, so that there is never any suspenseful doubt about the nature of Count Dracula: we soon see him and his three wives, dressed as for a formal evening, rising from their coffins amid a nervous scuttling of rats and spiders. (These creatures are shown fleeing the vampires!) What an eerie yet elegant sight, and how disquieting it would have been, years ago, to a child unfamiliar with the conventions of vampire lore: for, if there is anything "forbidden" about

adults in the night, in their beds, in privacy and secrecy, the vision   **67**
of Dracula and his wives rising from their coffins would con-
firm it.

A technique Tod Browning uses throughout the film, no doubt
for economy's sake, is nonetheless very dramatic: we see the initial
movements of an action (Dracula rising from his coffin, for instance), then the camera cuts elsewhere, then back, and now Dracula
is standing composed, as if he'd been there all along. His later
metamorphoses from bat to man—a bat hovering in the opened
French windows of a young woman's bedroom—are even more
striking.

The subliminal message is: Blink just once, and the vampire
is already *there*.

The film *Dracula* differs substantially from the novel *Dracula*,
having been adapted from a play, by Bram Stoker, now apparently
forgotten; the film is rather sharply truncated in terms of plot
development, not rushed exactly, but with an air, in the concluding
minutes especially, of incompletion. In place of Jonathan Harker
visiting Castle Dracula for business reasons, we have the less fortunate Renfield, who is quickly overcome by his sinister host, and,
by way of a bloodsucking scene we are not allowed to see—the
screen fades discreetly as Dracula stoops over his fallen prey—is
transformed into a slave of Dracula's for the remainder of his life.
Back in London, after the storm-tossed Channel crossing, Renfield
becomes the "zoophagous" patient of the asylum director, Dr.
Seward; the man is mad, exhibiting the grimaces, grins, and
twitches that are the cinematic clichés of madness, yet he is mys-
tically enlightened, and even, at times, eloquent: his impassioned
talk of life, life devouring life, life drawing sustenance from life,
is a distillation of Darwinian theory, disturbingly contrary to Christianity's promise of spiritual redemption/bodily resurrection. In
the film, Renfield eats flies and spiders to provide him with "blood";
in the novel, he catches flies and feeds them to spiders, feeds his

spiders to sparrows, and, one day, astonishes his keepers by eating the sparrows raw, and alive. Renfield's finest scene in the film is a speech of radiant madness, made to Dr. Seward and Van Helsing, a report of Dracula's Luciferian promise to him: " 'Rats! Thousands of rats! All these will I give you, if you will obey me!' "

Once Dracula has relocated to London and becomes acquainted with, and attracted to, the beautiful young women Lucy Westerna and Mina Seward, Dr. Seward's daughter, the story is an erotic fantasy in which the Stranger—the non-Englishman—seduces one too-trusting woman, and then the other, beneath the noses of their male keepers. (The men are Dr. Seward; Mina's fiancé, Harker; and the scientist Van Helsing, an early prototype of the "wise scientist"—as distinguished from the "mad scientist"—without whom horror and science-fiction films could not exist.) The erotic triangle is a recognizable one: the "good" (i.e., gentlemanly, proper, Christian) man and the "evil" (i.e., sensuous, duplicitous, ethnically exotic, un-Christian) man compete for Woman (i.e., virginal, Christian, and of the right social class). Woman per se is naturally passive, childlike, maybe a bit stupid; the contest is solely among men of varying degrees of enlightenment and courage. Van Helsing emerges the victor, saving Mina for his friend Jonathan Harker; in another mode of the fantasy, Van Helsing would marry beautiful Mina himself.

In the novel, Lucy Westerna's seduction/victimization/gradual death is the focus of much narrative concern; in the movie, the young woman is dispatched quickly, after a single visualized nocturnal appearance of Dracula in her room. Lucy's subsequent career as a vampire (who preys upon small children) is sketchily treated, and the extraordinary scene in the novel in which Van Helsing and his friends drive a stake into her heart, in a lurid, prurient mock rape, is omitted entirely. (So violent, brutal, erotically charged, and, indeed, horrific a scene could scarcely have been filmed in 1931, though it would be a delight for our special-effects movie technicians to prepare today.) So abstract is this *Dracula* in its **69** depictions of vampire assault and ritual vampire-killing, so greatly does it depend upon dialogue summary, it might be possible for an uninformed or a very young viewer to miss the point altogether. What *are* those people in evening dress doing to one another?

It is the subtle, suggestive, disturbing *appeal* of the vampire that makes of the Dracula legend a very different fantasy from, for instance, that of the werewolf or the golem (Frankenstein's monster being a species of golem), whose grotesque physical appearance is sheerly repugnant and could never be construed as "seductive." The most insidious evil is that which makes of us not victims, or not victims merely, but accomplices; enthusiastic converts to our own doom. The way of the vampire is the way of an absolute addiction—for the taste of blood one might substitute virtually any other substance, legal or otherwise. One of the special strengths of the vampire, Van Helsing warns in the film, is that people will not believe in him—"rational" people—but it is primarily women who resist believing in his evil; like Lucy Westerna (whose name is transparently obvious—she suggests "Westernization," rebellious female doubt of patriarchal tradition), who becomes a vampire, and Mina Seward, who, but for the zeal of her male protectors, would have succumbed to the same fate. The beautiful blond actress Helen Chandler plays the role of Mina in the film as convincingly as one might do in so circumscribed a context; her one animated scene, when she is infused with a bit of Dracula's rich, centuries-old, Transylvanian blood, shows her surprising and exciting her staid English fiancé with an unexpected erotic intensity otherwise absent from the film. The struggle is not really between the forces of good and evil, nor even between Christianity and paganism, but between "propriety" and "the forbidden."

Dracula is, on the surface at least, a resolutely chaste film. If lovely female bodies are violated by Dracula, the actions are never visually depicted; no skin is punctured; the "two small holes" said to be discovered on the throats of victims are never shown. In the novel, Dracula's wives speak lasciviously of their bloodsucking as "kisses"—the most voluptuous scene in the entire novel occurs in Castle Dracula, as a beautiful young female vampire stoops over to "kiss" the semiconscious Harker ("I closed my eyes in languorous ecstasy and waited—waited with beating heart")—but in the film Dracula's power seems primarily that of the master hypnotist, eyes gleaming, fingers outstretched like talons, capable of bending others to his will. His stylized movement as he bends toward a victim's throat only symbolically suggests a kiss, and only a psychoanalytic theorist, committed to seeing sexual imagery in all things, could argue that the vampire's "kiss" is a metonymical displacement for rape, or any physical, genital act. Is the vampire's "kiss" simply a "kiss"?—not on the lips, which might signal both complicity and adulthood, but on the throat, as a child is kissed, blessed, with no expectation of a response? Certainly the vampire legend, like many such classic horror legends, has about it the air of the nursery. At their cores, these are cautionary tales for the infant in us all.

I note in passing how truly oblique this 1931 *Dracula* is: in a film in which blood is so crucial, no blood at all is ever shown on-screen, except when Renfield, in Castle Dracula, accidentally cuts his finger as Dracula stares hungrily.

◪

The true horror of Dracula, as I've suggested, lies in the man's will. He has an uncanny ability, which Bela Lugosi makes credible, to mesmerize his victims, thus to make them want *him*—this, one of the vampire's secrets, that the virtuous victim, who is us, can so readily be transformed into the evil accomplice-disciple. (As movie goers are "seduced" by screen actors and actresses—otherwise, why movies at all?) Not mere destruction of the sort that other, ugly, "monstrous" villains threaten, but the awakening

of desire in the victim; an unholy, loathsome, yet clearly enormously exciting complicity in being damned. Civilization is a structure of artfully coded taboos, and taboos entice us to violate them,
if for no other reason than to rebel against our parents, teachers,
spiritual leaders who have indoctrinated us, or tried to, into the
accumulated wisdom of the tribe. There is a yet more pernicious,
because so romantic, sense that Dracula's interest in a woman is a
consequence of her beauty. The most beautiful woman is the most
desired woman, the most desired woman is not killed, but made a
bride: this is her (and our?) reward.

71

It's a matter of social class, too. The hapless little flower girl,
a street vendor, is a victim of Dracula's, but unlike Lucy and Mina,
she is merely killed. No mystery why.

The wish that desire of a brutal, primitive, Darwinian sort be
rooted in physical attractiveness, thus in our individuality—this is
surely one of mankind's most tragic, because infantile and enduring, fantasies, the secret fuel of sadomasochistic relations, in life
as in art. To be raped—to be murdered—to be devoured—because
we are *irresistible*: what solace! That we might simply be devoured,
as Renfield devours his flies, for the "life" in us, and at once
forgotten, is too terrible a truth to be articulated.

Art, by its selectivity, is always a matter of fabrication: thus
its great value, its solace. *Lie to us*, we beg of our cruder fantasies,
collective no less than private.

◪

"There are far worse things awaiting man than death."

Dracula's enigmatic remark, made in Dr. Seward's drawing
room, passes virtually unheard in that context, though it is perhaps
the most disturbing idea in the Dracula legend. In other versions
of *Dracula* (notably Werner Herzog's 1979 remake *Nosferatu the
Vampyre*) the isolated and tragic nature of the vampire is explored;
the vampire is less villain than suffering victim of a curse; an

oblique kinship is suggested between Dracula and the rest of humanity—for aren't we all blood drinkers? carnivores?—don't we all, in a myriad of ways, prey upon one another? This, the vampire's most startling secret, allows us to feel a tug of sympathy for Dracula, seeing that he is not really immortal or supranatural, but trapped in flesh, condemned to forever feed upon the warm blood of living creatures. Tod Browning's film is of course a conventional one structurally, and does not explore this theme. As the film moves to its prescribed ending, scenes are accelerated, condensed; there is a chase scene of a sort, Dracula with Mina in his arms, Van Helsing and Harker in pursuit; as Dracula lies helpless in his coffin, Van Helsing, unassisted, quickly dispatches him with a stake through his heart, and the story is over. Fear has been aroused, fear has been protracted, fear is now banished: THE END *is* truly the end.

Herzog's brilliantly cinematic remake is of the 1922 classic of the German silent screen, F. W. Murnau's *Nosferatu*. After writing this essay, I arranged to see the Murnau film, which is a remarkable work—a German translation of the very English Stoker novel into gothic-folklore terms, set in Bremen's oldest quarters, with an opening sequence in Dracula's castle that makes comparable scenes in Browning's *Dracula* seem stagey and low-budget by contrast. The Murnau Dracula is a bat only partway transmogrified into a man, and is both comic and terrifying; where in Herzog he acquires a tragic grandeur of a kind, in Murnau he is simply a monster, and subhuman. Set beside this powerful work of 1922, Browning's *Dracula* would be a distinctly inferior accomplishment were it not for Bela Lugosi's performance, which sets a standard beside which all other vampire performances must be measured. (Frank Langella's *Dracula*, of 1979, is, as I recall, a sensuous-sophisticated remake, in which the vampire is distinctly human, accursed like the Flying Dutchman, and romantic in his fate. The break with the earliest Dracula, that of Murnau, is complete.)

Strange, and revealing of the habits of mind to which we are all heir, that images which may endure in the memory for decades can be discovered, upon a re-examination, to have been strung like beads on an invisible yet always palpable "plot"—the tyranny, not just of genre, but perhaps of film generally. Its great, raw, even numinous power resides in *images*; its weakness is virtually always narrative, *plot*. There is a new theory of dreaming that argues that dream images are primary, culled from the day's experiences or from memory and imagination; the dream itself, as a story, is a pragmatic invention to string together these images in some sort of coherent causal sequence. If this is true, it argues for an even closer relationship between film and dreaming than film theorists have speculated upon.

◤

I should probably confess that, contrary to the spirit of this collection of essays on film, I can't really claim that any film made an impression on me commensurate with that of the books I read as a child and a young adolescent; it's likely that had I somehow never seen a movie at all in my entire life, my life would not be very different from what it has been and is. Had I never read a book, however—that's unimaginable.

Yet movies, composed of images, among these images the enormously inflated faces of men and women of striking physical appearance, have the power of lingering in the memory long after all intellectual interest in them has been exhausted. Nostalgia is a form of sentimentality; sentimentality is overevaluation; the "overevaluation of the loved object" is Freud's deadpan definition of romantic love. To be haunted by images out of one's own remote past is perhaps a form of self-love, which is after all infinitely better than self-loathing. We seem, once we pass the approximate age of thirty, to be involved in a ceaseless and bemused search for the self we used to be, as if this might be a way of knowing who and what we are now. For me this contemplation of a 1931 *Dracula* first seen sometime in the early 1950s, when I was twelve or thirteen years old, seen again now when I'm fifty-two, has become a kind of conduit into the past, which deflects me from analyzing it in purely intellectual terms; I'm tugged by memory, as by gravity, to the old Rialto Theater there at the corner of Pine and Walnut streets in Lockport, New York, as if these early memories were fated always to be stubbornly rooted in time, place. Especially place.

As it happened, my father, Frederic Oates, worked through high school in the display departments of both the Rialto and the Palace theaters, helping prepare the marquee and lettering signs (in watercolor, on a black-lacquered and easily washable surface— the era of mass-printed cardboard posters hadn't yet arrived), and he tells me a fact that seems astonishing: both theaters, in a city of only about twenty-five thousand inhabitants, changed their bills *three times a week.* And these bills were double features, plus a newsreel and a cartoon or comic short. So we're speaking of quantity, sheer quantity, in those pre-television, pre-Depression years. He tells me, too, as explanation rather than apology, that he'd soon grown to be bored by movies, since he had to see each new bill three times a week, in order to prepare publicity; and since the display department was in the theater, in fact, in the Rialto building, he had to listen to film dialogue again, again, again, to the point at which the entire phenomenon must have seemed—and here I am speaking for him, supplying my own metaphor—horribly like the *maya* of Oriental religion, the ceaseless flood of diversionary dream-shadows and delusions that constitutes life at the surface of being, not spiritual life, at the core. So, as an adult, he stopped seeing movies entirely, rarely watches television, and spends as much of his time as he can reading. Only once, in my memory, did he overcome his revulsion for the medium and see a movie— *On the Waterfront,* in 1954, at my urging, and because the movie had drawn so much praise. (Did he like *On the Waterfront?*—well, it was "all right.")

Perhaps it's simply the case that where romance isn't operant, **75** our susceptibility to dreams is lessened. We see through them. We can't detect our own images in them. Our human propensity for "overevaluation" shifts elsewhere.

◪

DRAMA

A man goes to bed with Rita Hayworth and wakes
up with me.
—Rita Hayworth (born Margarita Carmen Cansino, 1918)

My mistress' eyes are nothing like the sun.
—William Shakespeare

GILDA
"THE ZIPPER"
LEONARD MICHAELS

ita Hayworth stars in *Gilda*, but she isn't seen for the first fifteen minutes, while the friendship of two men, played by George Macready and Glenn Ford, is established. Macready saves Ford from being robbed on the docks of Buenos Aires, then hires Ford to manage a gambling casino owned by Macready. They become trusting, affectionate pals in a nightlife society where women are marginal. Then Macready leaves on a business trip to the "interior." When he returns, Ford hurries to Macready's mansion and is surprised to learn about a woman whom Macready has just met and married. The woman is heard singing, a muted voice in the interior distance, in a bedroom, in the depths of Macready's mansion. Macready leads Ford toward the singing, into the bedroom, to meet the woman, and—cut—Rita Hayworth lifts her face to look into the camera and see who is there. In this gesture, with all the magic of the word, Rita Hayworth "appears." She is bathed in light, seems even to exude it like a personal quality, like her wavy hair, her voice, and the flow of her body when walking or dancing.

She looks into the camera, into me, my interior, and I see that the friendship of Macready and Ford is in trouble, for this is the beautiful face of betrayal, jealousy, murder, suicide, war. It is the face of love from Homer to Shakespeare to the 1940s.

Like other actresses of her day, Rita Hayworth had mythic power and could carry a movie without a male star. I thought she carried *Gilda* despite George Macready and Glenn Ford. To my view, they were of slightly repulsive dramatic interest, but I was about thirteen when I saw the movie. I took it as seriously as life. How could Rita Hayworth get involved with guys like that?

Macready, playing a Nazi agent who lives in Argentina, walks rigidly erect, carrying a sword cane. He looks frosty, pockmarked, and desiccated, like the surface of the moon. There is something priestly about him, a lofty, ascetic air. Ford, playing a lowlife hustler who cheats at cards and dice, has a soft, dark, sensuous look, sensitive rather than intelligent. He smiles and wiggles around Macready in a flirty way. Wiggly and Rigid form a love triangle with Rita Hayworth, very degrading to her, since she is way out of their league; but then she is repeatedly humiliated in the movie. She seems to ask for it, even to need it badly; once she actually crawls at Ford's feet. Humiliation, essential plot matter in Hollywood and novels, is probably basic to fiction generally. Even the cherished story of *Alice in Wonderland,* in which a girl falls into a hole and is then repeatedly insulted in mind and body, has to do with humiliation. When I saw *Gilda,* I didn't wonder if there was a universal need for such subterranean experience.

Much dramatic tension is created when neither Rita Hayworth nor Ford tells Macready—who is made suspicious by their instantaneous, mutual hostility—that they already know each other, that, in fact, they were once lovers. Not telling Macready, they betray him. Ford thinks he is being loyal to Macready, protecting his peace of mind, and he is angry at the intrusion of Rita Hayworth into his paradisiacal friendship. He says, in a voice-over after Macready presents him to her, that he wanted to hit her, and he also wanted to hit Macready. Ford is bitterly frustrated and confused. I disliked him, but I suffered his anguish.

Trying not to succumb to Rita Hayworth's charms, Ford becomes increasingly self-righteous and more rigid than Macready. There is an excruciating moment when Macready, concerned not to look like a jealous husband, tells Ford to pull Rita Hayworth away as she dances with another man in Macready's casino. But she will not only dance with other men, she will go out with them. She doesn't love Macready, she fears him; and yet she makes him jealous of Ford, just as she makes Ford jealous of her and other men. It emerges that her licentious bitchery means only that she loves Ford; he loves her, too. They are trapped in a viciously delicious game of mutual detestation which becomes the main plot. It complicates, in a feminine way, through flamboyant gestures and shows of feeling. The subplot, full of male violence—guns, fist fights, crime, war—is turgid and easy to forget. You might say the movie is sexually structured, the woman (feeling) on top.

Rita Hayworth, with her amazing blond light in this dark movie (where almost everything happens in rooms, and even the outdoors seem indoors), suggests that dark and light are Manichean opposites—dark is evil, light is good. Gray represents confusion of good and evil. I certainly didn't think this when I saw the movie in the Loews theater on Canal Street, on the Lower East Side of Manhattan. I didn't think anything. I felt the meaning of things, especially the morally murky weight of the gray-lighted bedroom scene where Rita Hayworth asks Macready to unzip her dress as she lies on a bed. She says more than once that she has trouble with zippers, a helpless girl imprisoned in the dress of a grown-up. Zippers, a major erotic trope of forties movies, represented a man's access to a woman's body, despite her invisible, metal teeth.

I didn't want Macready to unzipper Rita Hayworth's dress. I didn't want Macready to touch her, though she is married to him, and she herself invites physical intimacy. Macready had told Ford he is "crazy about her," so his heart is in the right place. Nevertheless, I didn't want him to touch Rita Hayworth. I knew he didn't really love her; didn't even feel desire or lust, only a sickening idea of possession, and a mysterious need for betrayal. Why else would he hire Ford, a known cheater, as his most trusted assistant? And why else would Macready marry a woman—even Rita Hayworth— he has known only one day?

Macready flaunts his frightening sword cane, which he calls his "friend," but he moves in a delirium of masochistic self-destruction, and he is finally stabbed in the back by his "friend," literally the cane, metaphorically Ford. Macready gets what he deserves, which is what he wants, including sexual betrayal by Ford. Despite Ford's furious resistance to her, he gets Rita Hayworth, which is what she wants. Everything seems to work out, to balance and close, but not for me. I left the movie haunted by images of Rita Hayworth, yearning for her.

She had so much beauty and vitality that I assumed she would recover from what Macready did after unzipping her dress. Whatever it was, it wasn't good, but I supposed it happened a lot in Hollywood, where men go about touching women without feeling love, and—utterly unbearable—there are women who want to be Macreadied. Thus, in the religioso movie darkness, I saw Rita Hayworth request her own humiliation by the ascetic, priestly, frightening Macready. Zip. She is sacrificed and apotheosized. I had to remind myself that *Gilda* is a movie, not real life, and George Macready is a fine actor; also probably a nice guy.

No use.

The creep touched her.

I understood that real life is this way.

Nothing would be the same for me again.

I wanted to forget the scene, but it had happened as if to me, and was now fixed in my personal history, more indelibly than World War II. Only an instant of zipper business, yet it colored my love for Rita Hayworth with pity and grief. She lay there, utterly still and vulnerable, and Macready leaned over her the way kids play doctor, an eerily erotic game.

Seeing this was like a criminal privilege, though I was only sitting in a movie theater, doing nothing but looking. But I looked. I didn't shut my eyes. Unspeakable pleasure was aroused in me, in my head or heart, that secret, interior, moral theater (as opposed to the public showplace, the Loews Canal) where movies dreamily transpire, differently for each of us. I disapproved of the sensations, the pleasure—it wasn't due to anything nice—but pleasure and disapproval feed on each other. Rita Hayworth will be all right in the morning, I thought. It won't matter what Macready did, even if it was shameful and sad. What I felt was, perhaps, felt by millions.

Today, these feelings are considered sentimental, quaint. They have lost force and spontaneity. We still have them, maybe, but they no longer have us. Macready did it to Rita Hayworth. So? He didn't rape her. The scene ended. I didn't have to watch Macready actually do anything—not that it would have been possible to film Macready in bed, doing things to Rita Hayworth, without destroying the movie. The remake of *Gilda* will, of course, show Macready doing everything, but it must be remembered that *Gilda* was released when feelings—like clothing styles, popular dances, car designs—were appreciated differently from the way they are today. Perhaps feelings as such had a far higher value. Movies didn't have to show naked bodies, fucking, paraphilia, or graphic mutilation and bloody murder. Techniques of suggestion were cultivated—the zipper, for example. Less was more—except in regard to words. There were long scenes brilliant with words. We didn't so much use our eyes, like roots digging into visible physical bodies for the nourishment of meanest sensation. The ear, more subtle than the eye, more sensuous than sensual, received the interior life of persons, as opposed to what is sucked up by the salacious eyeball.

Later in the movie, Rita Hayworth asks again for help with her zipper, during a nightclub routine, as she does a striptease dance. Several men hurry to oblige and help her become naked. Ford notices, goes into a tizzy, stops things from going too far. He slaps her. His hand doesn't wither and rot. Not only is there injustice, but there is no justice. I feel so sorry for her, not to mention myself, poor kid, having to grow up, to know such things. Rita Hayworth is never seen disrobed in the movie, though it is threatened more than once. The atmosphere of dark repression and mysterious forces—the mood or feeling of the movie—might be destroyed by the revelation of her body. It scared me as she began her striptease dance in the nightclub. I didn't want everybody to see her body, or even to see that Rita Hayworth had a body. (The length of her beautiful left leg—I nearly died—is fleetingly exposed by a slit in her dress, as she dances.)

Two years later, I had sex for the first time, and I was taken by a weird sorrow riding home alone in the subway, as visceral odors lifted from my hands, reminding me that I'd fallen a few hours ago with my girlfriend—both of us virgins—from Heights of Desire into bodies. (Religious movements, West and East, have cultivated a practice of dreamily disembodied, extended, nonorgasmic sex, as described in John Donne's poem "The Ecstasy.")

In plain sight of Ford, who is obliged by his job to watch her, Rita Hayworth flirts with other men and says, "If I were a ranch, they'd call me the Bar-Nothing." She thus tortures Ford, showing him—in the desires of other men—the body he can't let himself have. Ford watches. He tries to seem angry, then blurts out that Rita Hayworth can do whatever she pleases. It doesn't matter to him. He says he will personally deliver Rita Hayworth to her other men, then pick her up like "laundry" and return her to Macready. In effect, everything Rita Hayworth does with other men will be determined and controlled by Ford. Impassioned and irrational, Ford doesn't know what he means.

My moral notions, already disturbed, were further disturbed—the hero talks like this? I was being introduced to deep stuff, subterranean forces, years before I understood what was happening to me, or maybe the world in the forties. It had to do with sex—hardly anything doesn't—but I didn't know about sex. I believed something more important was at stake. I saw Bad presenting itself—in the form of pleasure—as entertainment; and I was being made to know that I was susceptible to the pleasure of Bad, if for no other reason than that Bad was in me, like Gog and Magog.

Was the experience indeed pleasure, not merely a strong sensation, like the electrical excitement of an idea, or the effect of a novelty, or a demonic, masturbatory fantasy? If it was a real feeling, could I be violated by it, my own real feeling? Could it happen to anyone? If so, could anyone ever be a good person?

I continued to wonder, without words to analyze or describe it, about the distinction—in real life—between pleasure and its innumerable imitations. Saint Augustine says, "The love of this world is fornication against God," and that's that. For me, the question was: If I felt something I believed was bad, but it felt good, would I want to fornicate against God again and again? And would I then despise other pleasures, assuming other pleasures remained to me? Had Macready unzipped me, too? In Flannery O'Connor's masterpiece "A Good Man Is Hard to Find," a mystical murderer says, "It's no real pleasure in life." I wondered about real pleasure. What is it?

Ford's antiheroic, homoerotic hysteria, basic to the dramatic effect in *Gilda*, is virtually explicit when Rita Hayworth suggests that a psychiatrist can tell Ford that he likes the idea of Rita Hayworth as "laundry," or dirty—that is, doing things with other men. I didn't understand this in feeling or thought. Is sexual infidelity— deserving of death in the colorful Mediterranean community I came from—what Ford likes? I didn't see his angry, tyrannical show of controlling power as a refusal to acknowledge that he is the hapless creature of dark impulses. Rita Hayworth understands what's going on in Ford, but Ford never gains an understanding of himself. Instead, he becomes sadistically determined to punish Rita Hayworth for his inadmissible need to see her do what he likes her to do.

Gilda—written by a woman, starring a woman, produced by a woman—suggests that women know better than men, what men are looking at, when men look at women. They know that such looking—a function of blindness—is not seeing. In effect, Rita Hayworth exists fantastically for Macready and Ford within the so-called male gaze. She is constituted by their looking, a form of ideological hypnosis, or blindness, or stupidity, perhaps crucial to the perpetuation of human society as it currently exists. In the movie, the male gaze keeps two men fixated on a woman rather than on each other. Outside the movie, in real life, Rita Hayworth was the fixation of millions of men in the armed services, their favorite pinup girl. An erotic icon, she kept our boys straight.

In Gilda, Rita Hayworth famously sings one song several times. (I later found out her voice is dubbed; also, her hair is dyed, her hairline is fake, her name is Margarita.) The refrain of her song is "Put the blame on Mame, boys." Mame (Freudian pun intended) is responsible for cataclysmic occurrences—the Chicago fire, a terrible snowstorm, etc. (She's hot, the city burns; she's cold, "for seven days they shoveled snow.") The song ironically implies that boys, who are exquisitely tortured by the capricious dominatrix, want to imagine that Mame has tremendous, annihilating power. I could see the amusement in Rita Hayworth's eyes as she pretends to sing, and I loved her for that, her peculiar quality of spirit. Not quite playing the role, she is more real, nearly accessible, more heartbreaking.

Ford abandoned her in the "interior" when he ran out of money. To express the audience's contempt for him, the attendant in the men's room of Macready's gambling casino, a comic, philosophical figure, lowly and godlike, twice calls Ford a "peasant." Ford lacks aristocratic sensibility, or class. But Rita Hayworth gives him an opportunity to transcend himself by choosing her over his career as Macready's thing. He doesn't choose her until the end of the movie, when he supposes Macready is dead. Ford thus remains a peasant, or at best a grubby careerist who takes his work more seriously than love. The movie ends. Poor Rita Hayworth goes off with Ford. A grim winter night, streetlights, traffic—the shock of the real—awaited me.

I went down Madison Street, passing under the Manhattan Bridge, then turning left on Market Street, walking toward the East River, until I came to Monroe Street and turned right. These directions, these streets, restored me to my life. I passed the tenements with their Italian grocery stores and candy stores, and I passed my old elementary school, a huge, grim, soot-dark Victorian building, P.S. 177. From the Church of Saint Joseph, at the corner of Cherry and Market streets, I heard a bell tolling the hour. The church stood opposite our first-floor apartment in a building called Knickerbocker Village. Walking down Monroe Street, I approached the wavering light of Friday-night prayer candles in our kitchen window. The shadow of my mother, against the window shade, moved from refrigerator to stove. Everything as it should be. Italian ladies with shopping bags and baby carriages. Italian kids sitting on the stoops of their tenements. This was real. Anything too different—like a blond woman who might bring the solidity and value of this neighborhood into question—wasn't good.

The darkness of the movie, like a darkness inside me, contained nothing real, but there was a faint glow of *Gilda* within it, and I felt tumultuous yearning for Rita Hayworth—the woman, not the actress. I yearned to bring her home, where she would descend, or lovingly condescend, to sweet reconciliation with the ordinariness of my life, even its banality and boredom, which I believed was good. The good. My mother, cooking a good dinner in the small but good kitchen of our three-room apartment, would be embarrassed. She would apologize to bad Rita Hayworth for not having prepared a more sumptuous dinner, but I hadn't given any warning. "Do you like borscht? It's good. Do you know, Miss Hayworth, the good doctor who delivered your bad baby is my good cousin from Canada? When he told me that he delivered your bad baby, I almost fainted. Maybe you remember him. Tall. Curly hair."

It was like this for me, in a day when love was praised and much desired, even the terrible anguish it was known to inflict. As for Rita Hayworth—dream of heroes, five husbands, millions of servicemen—she was love, catastrophic, wild, impossible to domesticate. So much of her life was public, spectacular imagery that it is hard to suppose she also had a real life, or to suppose that her feelings about Rita Hayworth were not the same as ours.

◩

GONE WITH THE WIND

GUILT AND
GONE WITH THE WIND

VALERIE SAYERS

ll movies were guilty pleasures in my childhood.

In the mid-fifties and sixties, Beaufort, South Carolina, had two drive-ins, on the two roads out of town, and one real movie theater downtown: the Breeze, with seating for whites downstairs and a "colored" balcony upstairs. With the exception of *Cleopatra*, which ran for a whole week and occasioned a line extending two blocks down Bay Street—the first movie line I ever saw—the Breeze usually only held movies for two or three days, so you had to be either quick or lucky if you wanted the pleasure of a good air-conditioned movie on a hot day.

My family depended on luck and the Legion of Decency guide. If a movie was okay by the Legion, we strolled into the Breeze (downstairs) whenever it was convenient—I don't believe it ever occurred to us to inquire what time the feature started. Unless we accidentally stumbled in at starting time, we saw the movie from a midpoint, puzzled over the plot, watched it through to the end, started all over again, and left whenever we could all tear ourselves away. The experience gave me a strong taste for disjointed narrative.

Disjointed or not, the movie had to be approved. Once a year at Saint Peter's Church my family stood with the rest of the congregation and took the Legion of Decency pledge that meant no *Peyton Place* or *Irma La Douce* or *The Carpetbaggers* for us Catholic children. I was limited to (and, hoping to win the Piety Award in my very large and very pious family, for a while only *wanted* to see) movies the Legion had rated A-I (Morally Acceptable for All) or, when my parents were feeling daring and expansive, A-II (Morally Acceptable for Adults and Adolescents). Walt Disney movies were A-I, and so were musicals like *The King and I* and *My Fair Lady*. You couldn't take anything for granted, though. Doris Day movies might be A-I's, A-II's, or even A-III's (Morally Acceptable for Adults Only), so you had to consult the list, printed in the *Catholic Banner*. By the time I was eleven or twelve, and my classmates were going to see *Tom Jones* and *Dr. No*, I pored over every new edition with lust in my heart and newly resented obedience on my mind.

The juiciest parts of the Legion of Decency list were the A-IV's (Morally Acceptable for Adults, with Reservations), the B's (Morally Objectionable in Part), and the C's (Morally Objectionable in Full). Just reading the titles in the C section was guilty enough pleasure. And there were enough posters for racy movies—one midway between our house and downtown, one right on the turnoff for my catechism classes—to make me confess looking at them.

ME: Bless me, Father, for I have sinned. I don't avoid the movie posters.

YOUNG, SYMPATHETIC CURATE: I'm sorry, I don't think I
understand.

ME: The posters for the B-movies. There's one on Pigeon
Point Road and one on Ribaut Road and I know I should
avoid them as an occasion of sin, and I always *mean* to
avoid them, and most of the time I close my eyes when we
get to those corners, but sometimes I don't, I just look.

CURATE: So you're confessing that you *look at the movie
posters?*

ME: (Shamed. Mortified.) Yes.

CURATE: (Amused.) But that's not a sin!

ME: Sister said not avoiding the occasion of sin could be a
sin itself. [She actually said that looking at the movie posters *was* a sin, but I didn't want to rat.]

CURATE: (Giggling. *Giggling.*) I'll talk to Sister about that.

I was sure that the curate, holy as he was, had never really
looked at a movie poster himself, and—not knowing about the
cleavage exposed and the legs visible through thigh-high slits—
could not even imagine what very large occasions of sin they were.
The nuns were more practical. They looked once, and they knew
what they saw. It had to be a sin, and yet I wasn't allowed to
confess it anymore. The only solution seemed to be not looking:
I went for six months staring straight ahead or screwing my eyes
shut when the family station wagon passed by the movie posters.
Years later I saw a study indicating that among all religious de-
nominations of Americans questioned, Catholics reported the greatest guilt over sexual matters, and also the greatest amount of sexual
pleasure. The confirming image that came to mind was my childhood self, squished between my siblings in the back seat of the car,
squeezing my eyes shut at the corner of Ribaut Road where the
new movie poster was displayed: happy, happy, happy.

But movies were not morally dangerous only because they
were sexy and might fall into the wrong category on the list. Even
those bland A-I's and A-II's of the fifties and sixties, even *The*

Parent Trap and *The Unsinkable Molly Brown*, showed a world so gloriously materialistic that it was threatening, a world of martini glasses and lipstick smears and good clothes and late-model cars. The first movie I saw at the Breeze, when I was a very small girl, was *High Society*. For years I chased the image of tipsy Grace Kelly, holding up her woozy picture to compare her with holy cards of Saint Claire and Saint Agnes and Thérèse of the Little Flower. I was torn: movie opulence was charming, movie opulence was grotesque. When I coveted all that sunny slick movie glamour, I betrayed those wispy-looking saints and I betrayed my family. We were certainly not poor, but we lived in a crowded modest house and rode in an old car. On Saturday mornings my father wrote out checks for hospitals and schools and orphanages in Vietnam or the Belgian Congo or the Philippines.

My mother took us to the movies (*Please Don't Eat the Daisies*, A-I, I guess) the day she delivered her seventh child. Delicious agony for me: I wanted the movie family's house, their clothes, their one-liners. A childhood of movies, even A-I movies, was a childhood of all that my parents taught us was not important. Boats. Blondes. Minks. I can remember seeing two movies of abiding seriousness when I was a child—*The Diary of Anne Frank* and *Francis of Assisi*—and they both sent me running up the aisle in terror. But when I saw Audrey Hepburn or Cary Grant, they held out from the screen the possibility of the cohabitation of wealth, or at least worldly sophistication, and happiness. That was a distinctly threatening proposition for a child raised on the Sermon on the Mount—at least, one who wasn't willing to believe the priest about what was a sin and what was not.

Perhaps in my discomfort I was closer to a Protestant Southerner. Catholics—drinkers, smokers, dancers; guilty enjoyers of sex, evidently—found it amusing to laugh at our dour white Protestant neighbors and the Southern version of fundamentalism. Catholics were so much fun that even our clergy were portrayed

by the likes of Bing Crosby and Ingrid Bergman. My parents loved
the movies, the more sophisticated the better, and I believe they
enjoyed them without much ambivalence. They had a sense of
perspective, but I was a moral absolutist. Pleasure, money, sophistication. Poverty of spirit, humility, sacrifice.

Guilt.

◤

I was torn, too, about my identity. Today I say without hesitation that I am a Southerner (I overlook my twenty years' res-
idence in New York), but as a child in South Carolina I was not
so sure. There was not a moment of my childhood when I did not
see the town of Beaufort, stretching out as it did into salt marshes
and creeks and pine woods, as home. But I was the first of the
seven children in my family born in the South—my parents and
three older sisters were all Yankees—and though there were plenty
of other transplants in a town like ours who called themselves
Southerners, there were times I wanted to dissociate myself completely: not from the place, which I loved, but from what "Southerner" was coming to mean to me.

Beaufort was and is a beautiful, strange little town. It's got
plenty of live oaks and Spanish moss and palmetto trees, and it
looks enough like a movie set that several movies have actually
been shot there. It sits on a breezy subtropical sea island between
Savannah and Charleston, full of history: the Yankees occupied it
early on during the Civil War, so the grand old antebellum houses
are preserved intact, and so is an abiding interest in that war and
its aftermath.

When I was growing up there, Beaufort's population was only
seven or eight thousand, but it shared with the bigger coastal cities
the effects of exposure to other worlds. Military bases dominated
the town's economy, so it was not isolated: not a cracker town, as
we called the arid little cities upstate. There were more Catholics

and Jews in Beaufort than there were in those other towns, and there was even early integration on the marine bases.

But Beaufort itself was completely segregated: the schools and the churches and the doctors' waiting rooms and the beaches and the Breeze Theater. Wealth was confined to the grand houses and the big plantations, but poverty was amorphous and stretched out through the town and the sea islands. Extended families lived in rough little shacks with wax paper or oilcloth taped over the windows; tuberculosis ran rampant among the Negroes (or, more commonly, "nigras"). You'd see a pair of dark eyes over the ticket seller's head at the Breeze: a boy waiting to buy his ticket and slip up the back stairs to the balcony. You didn't have to be wealthy to have a "colored maid," because they were paid so little, or to have a "gardener," a position often filled by elderly men who had already spent a lifetime working in the fields of some white land-owner, and now fussed over some white matron's azaleas. White people amused themselves by talking Gullah.

In the fall of 1963, when Beaufort was still segregated, I found myself in a schoolyard debate with a friend from an old Southern family. The subject was integration. It may have been the only time in my life when a political idea came to me whole: I remember a peculiar delight that day that I was able to argue with such vehemence for integration. I had been hearing my father make the case for years—he was a great admirer of Kennedy and King—but until that moment on the playground I don't believe I'd ever given the issue five minutes of thought. All of an instant, at the age of eleven, I was passionate.

The debate spilled over into the classroom. The whole year long, while we were still absorbing the murder of Kennedy and the bombing in Birmingham and the beatings of freedom riders, we worried about integration and segregation. The argument always climaxed at the subject of intermarriage: the greatest horror white seventh-grade schoolchildren had been taught to imagine.

Mis-ceg-e-na-tion. The teacher taught us how to pronounce the **95** word.

Our curriculum that year was South Carolina history, and history fired us. When the teacher had us write papers defending or attacking the institution of slavery—*slavery*, in 1963—many in the class defended it. The climate was right, they said, the slaves were treated well and were better off than they would have been if they'd been left over in darkest Africa to starve. We were taught to call the Civil War the War Between the States, because there could be no civil war between two sovereign nations. Charleston was sixty-five miles away, but we could see Fort Sumter from where we sat at our school desks: we could see cannonballs piled by the guns in the Battery. Boys possessed of a paralyzing shyness became garrulous on the subject of battles their great-granddaddies fought.

Now, I was certainly not the only white seventh grader in Beaufort, South Carolina, proposing that we support integration. There were plenty of others in the class who argued on my side in those long debates, Southerners and transplants alike, but I became the self-appointed speaker. Mired as I was in the confusion between childhood and adolescence, integration looked simple, and it became for a short while the focal point of my identity. In 1963, in Beaufort, South Carolina, you were an integrationist or you were a segregationist. There was no need to waver, as I did with the movies, over questions of comfort and sacrifice, pleasure and guilt. No need to torment myself over whether I should sneak a look at the movie posters. Here, at last, was a moral issue that was clear: politics without sex (and one that required no sacrifice on my part, since all I did was appoint myself chief debater. It was black children, not white, who had the courage to integrate the schools of South Carolina).

I was so relieved to have this moral issue to embrace whole-heartedly, and with so little responsibility, that when the rest of the girls in the seventh grade read *Gone with the Wind*, I was ready to spit disdain. A novel of the Old South (gag). A novel of the ultimate Southern belle, Scarlett O'Hara, whose name I had been hearing all eleven years of my life (puke). A novel of slavery. Unthinkable that I should ever crack its pages. The least I could do for civil rights.

◪

It seems to me that Margaret Mitchell's book is tied to the movie *Gone with the Wind* by a more tangled skein than holds any other American novel to any other American movie. When I was small my Yankee mother (who was tickled by all extremism in Southern manners) loved to tell us of her subway commute through Manhattan to Wall Street the year *Gone with the Wind* was published. Everyone, she said, lugged the big book around, and everyone was so loath to look up from its pages that commuters were likely to miss their stops and find themselves in Brooklyn. Long before I was old enough to read the book I was picturing actresses desperate to play Scarlett O'Hara, picturing the casting arguments among those New Yorkers on the subway who knew lines of dialogue verbatim.

We did not have *Gone with the Wind* in my house, but when I visited friends I might see a copy right next to the Bible—in fact, there were only two books that counted in some Southern homes. When I was old enough to read it, I enjoyed boycotting it, but still its pull (after all, New Yorkers didn't resist) was a temptation. The romantic mythic South of *Gone with the Wind* that intrigued my mother when she was riding the subway in New York mirrored for me the South I lived in, the South where I was out of place and real Southerners—the slow-moving waitresses down at Harry's Restaurant, the friend preaching states' rights as if she were John C. Calhoun himself, those boys reliving the Civil War—were all right at home.

And, as it happened, I was only a few years behind the other girls reading *Gone with the Wind*. The first African-American entered Beaufort High School the year after Kennedy was killed, and by the time integration was more or less achieved I was old enough to have a sense of irony. I didn't know the word "kitsch" and wouldn't have thought to use "camp" (hadn't read Susan Sontag yet), but I justified reading *Gone with the Wind* with a new-found sense of detached amusement. A few years earlier I thought reading it would be treachery. Now reading it would be (I can hear my teen-age voice) *fun*.

Though maybe I wasn't as detached and amused as I thought—I was sucked right into Miss Mitchell's Hoover of a book. I was fourteen or fifteen when I finally checked it out of the library, and I read it in three days, taking meal breaks with some reluctance. When I ran across one of Miss Mitchell's horrid vacuous little asides about slaves or slavery, I held in my breath or sucked in my cheeks. But a book is easily chopped up for analysis, and I was ready to dissect that novel the way we dissected frogs in biology class. Here was a narrative passage full of the racial attitudes of the day, ready to be underlined and cackled over, then dismissed; but over there were scenes of Scarlett O'Hara and Ashley Wilkes and Rhett Butler made flesh. I was shocked by how very appealing I found the flesh in the pages of that novel, but *I* could separate the wheat from the chaff.

And Scarlett O'Hara, to my mind, was the wheat. My adolescent self swallowed her wicked white soul whole. Margaret Mitchell peels back the layers of Southern manners in her novel, but remains a perfect lady narrator herself (down to her unctuous descriptions of "pickaninnies"). It's Scarlett O'Hara she unleashes as the incarnation of willfulness, so selfish that an adolescent reader can dismiss her as model and, from a superior moral position, enjoy her all the more. For *this* adolescent girl, in the South in the sixties, when the purpose of female existence still seemed to be the suppression of all natural instincts, and the definition of slut might have been "she who walks down the street smoking a cigarette," Scarlett was the perfect protagonist to deny and enjoy.

I knew my moral and intellectual identification was supposed to be with Ashley, who loves poetry and means to free his slaves anyway; and my emotional identification with Rhett, the dauntless lover (though he shoots a nigger for being uppity to a white woman—underline that part and throw it away. Isn't even believable, anyway). I was used to identifying with men in books and I certainly didn't buy any of that Melanie Hamilton–Great Lady business. But for all the romantic hokum that surrounds any of her scenes with Rhett and Ashley (or maybe, at my age, because of all the romantic hokum), I could buy Scarlett. Ignorant and petty, hopelessly conventional as a simpering Southern belle, she nonetheless rebels against all other Southern proprieties. Freed from the need to "identify" with a "heroine," I could take as much pleasure in Scarlett's ruse with the green drapes (or her stealing of her sister's man, for that matter) as I could in my own small rebellions. (And in my case, there was the bonus pleasure that Scarlett is a Catholic Southerner with no spiritual depth whatsoever. No possibility of ambivalence.)

Up to that point in my life I'd been hearing so much drivel about the brave foolhardy Confederacy that I had been resisting any more knowledge about the Civil War than I needed to pass the social studies test, but when I read the novel I was suddenly hungry for the news from the front that reaches Scarlett in Atlanta or at Tara. As for the book's picture of plantation life and slavery, I discarded those images from my moral imagination as they appeared on the page. There are perhaps two or three real slave characters who have some substance in *Gone with the Wind*, yet most of the slaves, and the whole economic system on which their existence depended, are as unbelievable or as invisible as they were in real life, or in my seventh-grade social studies class. But depictions of slavery come in passages, and I was eliminating those passages from my consideration so I could enjoy the good stuff, the Grand Passion and Scarlett's fall.

I cannot possibly separate that first reading of *Gone with the Wind* (not to mention however many subsequent readings there were) from my first viewing of the movie. Like those subway riders my mother described to us, I became so immersed in the life of the book that I lived it for a while, ignoring all that was unpalatable. And when I finally went to see the movie (at the Breeze, of course), I brought along with me all that painstaking accumulation of detail Miss Mitchell brought to her characters and her setting and her events. If *Gone with the Wind* had been a slide show, I probably could have made the still pictures move in my imagination.

◪

The movie of *Gone with the Wind* was reissued in 1967 and reached the Breeze in 1968, around the same time as *Bonnie and Clyde*, *The Graduate*, and *In the Heat of the Night*. I'm not sure exactly when my family started shrugging our collective shoulders at the Legion of Decency list, but movies were suddenly *about* something, and I was shedding my guilt for lusting after materialistic movie sets around the same time the women of America were shedding their girdles and bras.

At Saint Peter's, the pastor gave us a sermon on *Cool Hand Luke* (Paul Newman as Christ figure), and at Beaufort High School, Mr. Ellis told us that the medium was the message. I thought I saw a new moral tension in the edgy acting of Newman and Hoffman and Poitier and Dunaway. But what did I know of scripts that ignored the boundaries of genre, of idiosyncratic direction? I had been confined to A-I's all those years, A-I's I watched from the middle. Now boys took me to the movies on time and let me know that most people watched from the beginning.

And now that there were new movies to watch, I finally got around to *Gone with the Wind*. I may have been the last teen-ager in Beaufort to see it. It had certainly been around before—my A-I family may have thought me too young, but other parents, Southern parents, had brought their children to see it in Beaufort and in Savannah and in Atlanta, too. When I finally went to see the movie, it was with that same teen-age sense of fun that sent me to the book, but in a much higher fever of teen-age romance. I went with a boy I loved like crazy, but there was a complication: he wasn't the only object of my affection.

When I settled in to watch *Gone with the Wind,* I was prepared for weepy mush and especially for grand spectacle. Hadn't I been hearing my whole life about the dying soldiers in the streets of Atlanta, about how the camera pulls back and takes your breath away? Hadn't I been hearing about Rhett's drive through Atlanta, the city burning and toppling around his buggy? I expected the movie—especially if it were to compress that huge book—to concentrate on the big scenes and to make even the most intimate scenes full-blown.

Like the novel, the movie puts its emphasis on story first. *Gone with the Wind* has a straightforward narrative (occasionally interrupted by visual schmaltz: those long shots of Tara, the icky orange Technicolor glow suffusing Rhett as he takes his wartime leave). There's a real visual unity in all those shots framed by windows and stairways (the greatest collection of stairs ever assembled for the screen), but the style is at the service of the characters, the actors. *Gone with the Wind* may have been an epic movie to everybody else who saw it, but for me it was all acting. The big scenes—the bazaar, the hospital, the burning of the city—set me up all right, but all those opulent interiors and aftermath-of-war scenes were what I expected.

What I wasn't prepared for was the emotional wallop my sixteen-year-old wavering romantic self was in for. What I didn't fully expect was Vivien Leigh as Scarlett O'Hara. Of course I'd seen stills of her, and I knew that I would have to ignore what the novel says in its opening lines, that Scarlett O'Hara was not beautiful. And I was disappointed when I first saw, or rather heard, Scarlett on-screen, framed by the Tarleton twins. She looks right, even if she is beautiful, but her voice is wrong: the accent's offhand enough, but she's too tart, too fast. Southern women—Southern *ladies*—do not speak quickly. It took about ten seconds to overlook that objection; by the time the Tarleton brothers have told her about the visitors to Twelve Oaks, and she's said, "Melanie Hamilton, that goody-goody," I was completely taken.

It's one of those performances you can fall in love with—and I did. It's a performance that depends on intensity, Leigh's intelligence transformed into Scarlett's cunning and shrewdness: I loved the way she narrows her eyes, or raises that right eyebrow. Scarlett is self-centered and shallow, but in Vivien Leigh's flesh she is also charming and so contemptuous of the society around her that I thought she was sent as a personal metaphor for my own contemptuous adolescence in the South.

Immediately, I was all caught up in the performance, and I experienced a mounting sense of confusion as I watched Scarlett being laced into her corset for the barbecue, Scarlett dancing the Virginia reel, Scarlett slapping Prissy. I had been able to read the novel and pick out its acceptable parts, but a movie, seen in a theater, in the dark hush, is a continuum. (Of course, videos have already changed this experience profoundly; being able to press "rewind" and "fast forward" indefinitely means that any ordinary viewer can analyze the movie in its considered and reconsidered scenes.) But a movie on the big screen hurtles forward, and on this ride I could distinguish no narrator's voice (didn't even consider those impossible titles), nor even necessarily a director's vision. I vaguely knew there was more than one director involved, but it would be years before I would read which were the scenes directed by Victor Fleming, which by George Cukor, which by William Cameron Menzies. At the time I was not interested in directors, because

Vivien Leigh, as far as I was concerned, was the one pulling out the throttle all the way.

Part of my teen-age self acknowledged the sheer theatricality of the performance, the romance and exaggeration of the costumes (the hats!) and lush interiors. But another part of me, miserable over my romance, chose to identify completely. Was this boy I sat with Rhett Butler or Ashley Wilkes? He had a little of the formal idealist in him, a little of the reckless lover. Which was he? The wrong answer meant a lifetime of misery. I was sixteen. Scarlett, skirts spread out around her, is sixteen when the movie opens. Reading the book, I did not have to identify with selfish unread Scarlett to luxuriate in her downfall. Watching Vivien Leigh, beautiful and intelligent and subtle and still so wickedly selfish, I could not resist seeing the parallels between Scarlett's life and mine.

And I could not believe that I would sink to such a cheap identification, that I would fall—even for a few hours in a movie theater—for such Southern-belle sap. What was most horrifying was that it was not only cheap romance I was swallowing, but also the same picture of slavery, that very legacy of the South that had kept me from seeing myself as a Southerner. Now the politics of the Civil War was competing with Grand Passion, and as the movie sped along (all that compression of years, of momentous historical events—Gettysburg reduced to the casualty lists at the railway depot), I became more and more miserable. It certainly never occurred to me that some multiplicity of vision was confusing me. What did David O. Selznick and all his hirings and firings mean to me? Besides, Leigh's Scarlett provides the unity that was irresistible to me. And if I couldn't resist it, what else was I condoning?

The most painful moments for me, at that first viewing, were all the scenes with slaves. When I watch *Gone with the Wind* today, I still flinch when Big Sam insists, in that amiable childlike voice, that he be the one to call it quitting time, and when Pork—the most obsequious character in the entire movie—scrapes and bows, and when the little slave girl fans the plantation girls stretched out for their afternoon naps. Of course, there are actors in *Gone with the Wind* who breathe real life into their slave characters. Hattie McDaniel may mug, but her presence is strong and genuine; she is the picture of anguish as she tries to tell Scarlett her mother is dead, the picture of strength as she nurses her after her miscarriage. And there's a wonderful moment of release when Scarlett threatens to sell Prissy South—at last, the malevolent mistress reveals herself—and even better is the split-second look of contempt Prissy throws her from the stairs. But all those other compliant "Yes, Miss Scarlett"s and "Thank you, Miss Scarlett"s form a background chorus of falsity.

And as soon as the falsity appears, it disappears. This is movie time dashing along, and almost every scene comes back to Scarlett. Her presence had me hooked, and ashamed to be hooked. The other characters revolved around her: I was willing to love Leslie Howard and Clark Gable for her sake, but Howard's Ashley is just too weak, even if he is subtle and dreamy; and Gable's Rhett didn't thrill me so much as he embarrassed me, especially in Part Two, when he beams a good deal. His worst line is probably "What a woman!" accompanied by a humiliating grin, but by the time he gets to "Observe these hands, my dear," Vivien Leigh is playing against him as he *should* be, and he's close enough. He looks right, anyway, and at sixteen that counted for a good deal with me.

And if Clark Gable looks right, so do Dr. Meade—just perfect—and Mrs. Meade, and India Wilkes and Miss Pittypat and Cathleen Calvert and Mrs. Merriweather and Frank Kennedy. I could not forgive Sidney Howard, or whichever of the screenwriters was responsible, for doing away with Scarlett's first two children, but the writers did a remarkable job of keeping so many of the novel's supporting characters and giving them good crisp dialogue even when they are stereotypes (Big Sam. And Belle. And the ultimate stereotype, Miss Mellie, with whom I guess nobody could have done much more than Olivia De Havilland did.)

By the end, when Scarlett's miscarriage, Bonnie's accident,

Melanie's death, and Rhett's departure are all crammed together into the final moments, I was sobbing. I tried to differentiate scenes—slavery and hokum and cheap appeals to my most girlish romantic self—but it was no use. If the novel was a vacuum cleaner, the movie was a freight train.

When I had finally broken down and read *Gone with the Wind*, I read a book suffused with Southern manners, a story narrated by a Southerner who knew all about tradition and exaggerating history so your side comes out noble. The very pace of the book, its careful slow telling of every detail, is part of the South I knew. I felt at home in it, or at least as if I were at a neighbor's, at home enough to fling it across the room if I got mad at it.

But *Gone with the Wind* the movie is not a Southern film at all, no matter how well all those British actors finally speak their parts. It can't be Southern—it has to move too fast, and cover too much ground, and it has to do it without the mediating voice of a narrator, or even a single director. Its production values threw me off-guard and made me feel I was small again, watching a big slick world.

And Scarlett O'Hara was somebody I was chasing the way I once chased tipsy Grace Kelly. I knew all about her ambition and selfishness and her wanting to tell everyone to go to hell. Now, for days after, I pictured Scarlett as Vivien Leigh: Scarlett pretending she doesn't know which way the hat goes, Scarlett holding her hands out in the jail cell for Rhett to kiss, Scarlett calling out "You look mighty pretty, sweetheart," to Bonnie just before she dies. I'm sure I took to raising one eyebrow and narrowing my eyes, and I certainly thought the whole world was in love with me.

I went to see the movie again, before the week was out. And yet again, a few weeks later. (It was exhausting, but I pretended otherwise.) Soon I realized that these repeated viewings were diminishing the impact of the movie, because with each viewing I could analyze it better, separate the parts from the whole. Each time I saw it, I could put it in better perspective—and so lessen my guilt.

Guilt does not have a big following nowadays, but I've always liked the definition given by my old high school English teacher: You feel guilty, he used to say, because you've done something wrong. As far as my teen-age self was concerned, with *Gone with the Wind* I had indeed done something wrong. Just as I was losing my ambivalence toward the movies, I'd fixated on *Gone with the Wind*, a movie that put years of struggle and misery into a few hours of costume drama with stirring background music. I might as well have been eight or nine again, confessing that I had looked at the movie poster. I'd got myself back in romance mode, and I was chasing after a high gloss I'd known to mistrust even when I was a child.

Most of all, I think I felt guilty because it turned out that I got excited over the same things everybody did: romance and escapism and especially Grand Passion. Just as I was beginning to discover real art, real movies and books and plays, it turned out that I had a pretty common mind, after all.

◪

I feel some little sadness when I watch *Gone with the Wind* on videotape now. Scarlett still shines, but Tara looks mighty hokey, and those orange skies are not any skies I ever saw in Georgia. It's not the kind of picture that should be reduced to a small format; like Belle Watling, its attraction springs from its excesses.

The way I'd really like to see *Gone with the Wind* again is back home at the Breeze. I'd like it to wash over me in a place where the big screen first brought all those threatening images of other lives, other possibilities. Now that I get to make my own list of acceptable movies, now that I'm not a wavering teen-ager anymore, I'd like to see it in that old movie house in the South, which is, after all, home.

I'd still be taken in by Vivien Leigh: she really is the radiant center of *Gone with the Wind*. And I'd still flinch whenever Pork says "Yes, Miss Scarlett." But I won't be watching it in the Breeze—it's gone the way of so many downtown movie theaters in this day of the mall. There were quite a few years of integrated seating, anyway, before the end.

And besides, I think I made my peace with *Gone with the Wind* the last time I saw it at the Breeze. Watching it, I could let all my worries about slickness and materialism and morality and civil rights and Southern manners come to the surface one last time before I left home. Maybe it was the last great guilty pleasure of my movie-going life.

◤

LOVE ME OR LEAVE ME

BHARATI MUKHERJEE

first saw America when I was twenty. Outdoors, even in New York City, the air must have been lambent with summertime the day that my seventeen-year-old sister and I flew into Idlewild, but inside the terminal, waiting in a long, nervous line of foreign students and tourists to be questioned by suspicious Immigration and Naturalization Service officials, the light felt interrogation-harsh.

"Let's go back home," my sister said. She was a veteran shuttler between India and the United States, having already put in a fall semester as a sophomore at Vassar College, and having rushed back, homesick, at Christmas.

We didn't turn around and get on an Air India plane that summer afternoon because we didn't want to disappoint our father. Coming to school in the States had been his idea, not ours. We

108 stayed in line and had our visas and chest X-rays checked by an official who was amused that I was headed for the University of Iowa.

"Know how to find Iowa on the map?" the man asked me. And when I lied, yes, he laughed, "Hell, I don't," and wished me good luck.

My sister got homesick again that winter, desperately enough to be sent back to India.

"It must be hard for you, too," my father wrote in each of his thrice-weekly letters. "But be brave. And before you know it, the program will be over." Meanwhile, he was interviewing Bengali Brahmin bachelors in order to find me the perfect groom.

The truth, which I couldn't share with my family, was that I was happier in Iowa City than in Calcutta. It was that time in my life when every song and film about love seemed to speak directly to me. I fell in love with, and married, a man who happened to be an American citizen, and scrapped all plans for ever going back to live in India.

If I had gone to graduate school in Paris or London, I might just as easily have fallen in love with a Frenchman or a Briton and made my life over very differently than I have in America. But in my family, my father, a very successful businessman, a devout Brahmin, and a benevolent patriarch who made all decisions, was also a contradictory man. He had no son; thus his financial empire could not be passed on. He wanted education and independence for his three daughters. (When would-be husbands later demanded dowries, he answered, "My daughters are all educated women. That is worth more than all the gold I could give them.") He was a progressive man in a traditional context; he saw in Doris Day an empowered woman.

He sent us to America, a country he himself had not seen, instead of to Europe, where he had been a happy graduate student, because he was in love with the world of Doris Day and all MGM musicals. He never spoke of "the United States." It was always

"America." To him America was a realistic-looking facade on an MGM backlot, where fantasies about young women achieving fulfillment and power could be acted out as they couldn't in tradition-bound Calcutta.

My father never missed Doris Day at the Metro Cinema on Chowringhee Avenue. He would call my sisters and me from his office on Thursdays—which was our day off from school, a neo-colonial establishment run by Irish nuns for Calcutta's most proper girls—to say that he had rearranged his schedule so that he could accompany us to the matinee show.

Though he savored every Doris Day film, even *Please Don't Eat the Daisies* and *Pillow Talk*, his favorite was *The Man Who Knew Too Much*. On jerky drives through the crowded city, in between yelling at the chauffeur to be more cautious and at the two bodyguards cramped in the back of our conspicuously large Dodge station wagon to be more alert for bomb-tossing, acid-splashing, communism-inspired thugs, he would sing "Que Será, Será." "What Will Be, Will Be" became for him more a mantra than a song; it synthesized a New World pleasure in risk taking with a fatalistic Hindu acceptance of disastrous outcomes.

The marvel that was my father's love for Doris Day will become clearer if I tell you that the neighborhoods we had to drive through to get from our home or from my father's pharmaceutical factory on the outskirts of the city to the Metro Cinema in midtown roiled with the fecund despair of the destitute and the permanently displaced. The Calcutta of the fifties—the Calcutta of my childhood—should have been heady with post-Independence hope and vitality. Certainly politicians promised every Indian boom times. But what choked the streets was the human debris from famines and religious riots. Even an oversheltered, overprivileged child like me was toughened enough by Old World cynicism (which, in those days, I accepted as a synonym for wisdom) to cut through jingoistic nation-building slogans. Though at school the nuns assured us that prayer would quickly bring Mr. Stalin and his Calcutta admirers to their senses, we could see and smell the "blood-dimmed tide" surging at our horizon. In that transitional decade, when preparations to flee the city seemed cowardly and prayer little more than escapism, Doris Day was an abstraction for democracy. A person with gumption—any person, even a ten-cents-a-dance taxi dancer like Ruth Etting—could turn her grim life around. The handicaps of caste, class, and gender could be overcome.

Doris Day was a physical curiosity. I don't think I'd ever come across a woman so tall, so big. And in those days, the only blond hair I expected to see was the Technicolor-bright cap of it on her Cinemascope-sized head. Most enforcers of the Raj—people who might have had natural or bleached yellow hair, British corporate executives and civil servants, for instance, the lighter-skinned Eurasians, even many of the Iraqi and Syrian Jews whom we'd thought of as "Europeans"—had left just before or just after 1947, when India became a sovereign nation. The bedtime stories my mother told me had been about teen-age Bengali freedom fighters rather than the traditional ones about gods fighting shape-changing demons.

I had thrilled to my mother's stories about schoolgirls raiding police arsenals or hiding pistols in dormitories. Fan worship of a British film star would have seemed to me treasonous regression. Doris Day, with her mighty shoulders and toothy smile, a woman who said exactly what was on her mind and said it in a nearly incomprehensible American accent with stereophonic loudness, was all right to love precisely because she was American. (In my neo-colonial school I had been forced to study British and European history, not the history of the United States and its various involvements, and so was slow to catch the ironies of undeclared imperialism.)

Brought up as I was to accept rather than to protest decisions made for me, Doris Day grew into an icon of spunk.

My father may have been in Europe on a business trip when *Love Me or Leave Me* finally came to Calcutta. Or perhaps he had seen the trailer for it the week before and decided that the Doris Day who sang "Que Será, Será"—*his* Doris Day—had to be kept separate from the gritty Doris Day who cocked a hip in a black sheath dress and burned the screen with "Ten Cents a Dance." Perhaps he saw the film on his own and decided that he had to protect us from the sex and sleaze it revealed about adult life just ahead. In any case, this was the only Doris Day film I didn't see or talk over with him.

Ten of us convent-school friends went to see it the evening our Overseas Cambridge School Leaving Certificate Examinations were over. I was fifteen. In three weeks I would start college as a sophomore. That I should be sneaking into my first "adults only" film that evening seemed deliciously symbolic.

I try not to think now how we must have appeared to the street people and beggars outside the Metro Cinema or how we might have appeared to Charles Vidor, the director, if he had seen us being chaperoned by servants from cars to the movie theater. We were ten adventurous but shockable young ladies dressed in our mothers' evening saris, with hair pinned up in elaborate chignons and smelling of sandalwood soap and jasmine. I remember I wore a peach-colored French chiffon sparkling with sequins.

I also remember that I walked into the theater (which always smelled of musty velvet drapes) expecting to be titillated, and that I walked out convinced I'd been uplifted.

What *could* I have discovered in a story about an obscure chorine in Chicago who meets a crooked nightclub owner and allows him to help her become a singing star even though it means denying or delaying true love? That the world was a rough place in which to be a poor woman with talent but without protection.

Early in the film, when Ruth Etting had to wear skimpy, spangled chorus-line costumes and put up with the teasing of less ambitious chorus girls ("Oh, I forgot. You're different. You're going places"), I identified with her totally. I, too, intended to go places, be somebody.

"You don't have to do a thing!" I mimicked her telling off Marty Snyder, played by James Cagney, my second-most-favorite screen villain. (James Mason was the first.) "I'll get it for myself!"

"It" was my own desire to be a writer and touch people with my novels.

I'd started my first novel at age nine and had published several first-person stories about Roman gladiators and Napoleon in local English-language magazines. But I was careful to hide from the nuns and from relatives and friends the forcefulness of my need for self-expression. They tolerated my "gift for the pen" (the mother superior's phrase) only because they regarded fiction writing as a womanly accomplishment, on a par with flower arranging or playing a musical instrument.

The Doris Day of *Love Me or Leave Me* sent me subliminal messages. When she pleaded with James Cagney to let her sing in bigger clubs in cities out of his reach, she pleaded for me. And when she begged, "I have to work. Don't you understand? I've got to. It's all I've got," I substituted "write" for "work." In Marty's admonition, "You're going to work here so you don't get so big," I heard my own community's censure of women who didn't accept their place.

Though my world was silken with privilege, I would have to choose, like Ruth Etting, between paralysis and ambition, between protection and pain.

My parents and the parents of my friends were nominally

patrons of the arts in that they bought or were given tickets to
events such as the premiere of Jean Renoir's *The River* (set in
Bengal) or charity performances by the Moral Rearmament Society,
but they knew no writers or filmmakers. They didn't attend screen-
ings at the foreign-film club founded by Satyajit Ray. Like them,
I hadn't heard of *film noir* at the time, and I certainly hadn't known
of screenwriter Daniel Fuchs, let alone read his proletariat novels
about Brooklyn Jews. I must have missed the neo-*noir* significance
of the first shot of Marty "The Gimp" Snyder standing in shadow
outside a garishly lit dance hall, lusting after a spirited blond god-
dess. I had to have missed the odd resonance of Marty's mumbled
"Mazel tov!" as Ruth, "Chicago's Sweetheart," went off to give
her first star performance. How could I have caught the ethnic
ambiguity of Snyder as a last name? Or that Fuchs's Chicago was
not that different from Brooklyn? What I did instead was to Ben-
galize Fuchs's Chicago-Brooklyn, just as I had, before the age of
ten, Bengalized the alien societies of my favorite Tolstoy, Dosto-
yevsky, and Gorky novels.

I accepted, more readily perhaps than I should have, that
Charles Vidor's film was about Ruth Etting. Ruth was its hero,
Marty its villain. But even the huge and wholesome Doris Day
couldn't quite sanitize her character's moral ambiguities. For a
decade the nuns had forced on us an annual course titled "Moral
Science" in which they presented right and wrong with absolute
clarity. But there on the Metro Cinema screen (from which I learned
more about the world outside than from the school-approved Victorian and Edwardian novels) was virtuous Doris Day assuring me
through song that "I can be good, I can be bad/ It all depends on
you . . . ," that it was not at all unethical for the Woman as Artist
to lie and cheat and use men on the way to stardom.

With one song she reduced the stern, solid truths of Moral
Science to fictions. She guaranteed us women who fancied ourselves
talented extraordinary absolution.

◪

"I've tried it without help," she explains to Johnny, her piano-playing faithful admirer, as she breaks a date. "I didn't mind it being hard. I just minded that it didn't work." And off she goes for a night of salacious fun with corrupt and ill-mannered Marty, who can pack her shows with his applauding friends.

The nuns had taught us that what mattered was how we played the game and not whether we won or lost. And my Hindu parents had taught us that after the householder phase of material comforts and family devotions we must prepare for phases of self-abnegation. But Doris Day, the oracle of the silver screen, busted those old truths in one evening. The end justified the means.

Doris Day's Ruth Etting was a woman whose virtue was not assailed by her manipulativeness with men. (I think now that if Rita Hayworth had played the role I might have been totally un-settled by Etting's self-justifications; I didn't see a Rita Hayworth film until years later.) The trouble was that I couldn't stop worrying about the walk-on chorines, the fatigued women in soiled leotards and snagged stockings. They may have had more talent than Ruth, but they were less calculating. The first time Marty Snyder visited her in her dressing room, Ruth had pegged him as a powerful man and seized rather promptly his offer of protection. She'd rejected a lifetime of cheap pick-ups. She was, as Marty might say, a smart cookie.

I did believe her when she declared, "I'm not a tramp!" Marty was accustomed to picking up whores, not artists who were having to pay the bills with taxi dancing, women he could get his faithful buddy, Georgie, to throw back into mean streets with a tip or a pat on the rump. Her sense of self-worth had been established within the first few minutes of screen time; even as a starving rookie taxi dancer, she'd kicked the letch who for his ten cents had groped when he should only have danced.

The woman artist combined smart-cookie-ness with integrity and innocence. I watched, amazed, as Ruth's self-righteous morality triumphed over Marty's street codes on the larger-than-life screen.

Marty himself was an ambiguous villain. In fact, he was more a raw force than a villain. In his crooked, dog-eat-dog world, his crook's-eye view made sense.

"I couldn't handle those people with kid gloves." That was Marty's convincing self-defense. "It's push or get pushed."

How could I fault him for initially assuming that Ruth shared his moral environment? When Ruth refused to weekend with him in Florida as payment for his having gotten her a big singing gig in his Chicago nightclub, he sized her up as a smart cookie holding out for more. "Ah, I get it," he rationalized. "She thinks it's a line . . . I say Miami, and she thinks it'll be Atlantic City."

I just couldn't summon up hate for him.

So he was a crook; so what? My schoolfriends and I—Calcutta's small, elite band of missionary-educated postcolonial adolescents, brought up on too much Oscar Wilde and Somerset Maugham—confused mordant wit and cynicism with sophistication. I persuaded myself that Marty was, in fact, an incompetent in the world of serious crime.

Marty won me over with his enthusiasm. How could I dislike a man who used "You've got a very excellent personality" as his line to a dancer in a dingy dressing room?

Like my father, an optimist, Marty could say lines like "You want to know what your trouble is, girlie? You got no faith in human nature," and mean it.

Marty trying to control his wife didn't shock me. In traditional, patriarchal Hindu families like mine, men commanded and women obeyed; to love was to protect. I understood that Marty slapping Ruth was Hollywood—not Hindu—shorthand for deplorable behavior and that Hollywood would deliver Marty his comeuppance.

To me, Marty was a bewildered, lovesick fool; a man of strength brought low by bravado or hubris. (At fifteen I could declaim soliloquies from Shakespeare, Racine, and Sophocles, and regularly used words like "hubris" and "catharsis.") Marty was a man who bullied and bossed because he lacked self-confidence. Without Ruth's total dependence on him, he became nothing. He was the guy from the wrong side of the tracks, the thug, the loner, who had built himself a fortune but not an identity and confidence. In his life the question "Who *are* you?" and the answer "They think I'm nothing" recurred with sinister regularity.

How could I know then—coming from an overdetermined, confident hierarchical culture in which everyone knew the most minute detail of everyone else's life, in which a family name revealed caste and region—that the ambiguously named, mysteriously unrooted Marty Snyder was, in his splendor, his power, his pathetic hollowness, an American archetype? And that the reading of such ambiguity, from the stagnant steadiness of the Calcutta upper classes, could be alluring?

Marty's crime was love, the kind of monstrously possessive, Othello-like love that turned the beloved into chattel. It was not that different and no more overwhelming than the love I both cherished and hoped to escape. In Marty's "Didn't I do wonders for her?" guilt made me imagine I was hearing a patriarch's lament.

By the time Doris Day finally sang "Love Me or Leave Me," I knew what the future held. Things would work out for me as a writer as long as I rejected both the Johnnys and the Martys. The Martys, the tiny tough guys with limps, were all trouble; they charged you up with unseemly passion and got you to break rules, take calamitous risks. The patient, long-suffering Johnnys appealed to your modesty and goodness; they shamed you into working hard, following rules, and waiting for a payoff that was more likely to be self-righteous liberty than stardom.

There was a cost. There was always a cost. Ruth didn't know

or couldn't admit that cost to herself. She hadn't *asked* Marty for "breaks." Marty had sensed her wants. He'd given; she'd grabbed.

That cynical lesson cut deep. As I left the Metro Cinema that winter night and drove through a city awaiting Marxist revolution, I hoped that when I started my life over on an MGM backlot made up to look like America, I'd retain enough of the worldliness of my Calcutta youth to be more honest with myself than Ruth had been.

◪

THE BOY WITH GREEN HAIR
FACING GRANDIOSITY

DAVID ROSENBERG

six-year-old closet intellectual, I viewed my first adult film, *The Boy with Green Hair*, in secret. It might as well have been Milton or Shakespeare—way, way over my head. The central character held me spellbound nonetheless, as if he were the defiant, magnetic Satan in *Paradise Lost*. By the time I was fifteen and spending my movie money on Freud's *Interpretation of Dreams*, I'd forgotten previous encounters with knowledge that seemed life-changing.

Now the earlier experience comes back. I had thought I was watching a horror movie. I misread *The Boy with Green Hair* as easily as fundamentalists can misread the Bible's literary core. Here was a movie that opened with an upbeat song and continued along like a musical, including a sing-along with four schoolboys and "Gramps." That just increased the mystery of terror for me: I

knew from the coming-attractions posters the boy's hair would
turn green. Could life be worth living if that kind of stigma could
attach itself to someone any fine morning? I never learned what
the boy did to deserve his fate; the secret was contained in a letter,
and when it was opened at the end I couldn't comprehend its words.

The film fully embraces the boy's story, presented in flashback—as told to a child psychiatrist, after the boy refuses to speak
to all other adults. He has run away from his last home to a nearby
American town where he's unknown. His mystery is signified by
a freshly shaven head, and his story will unfold backward toward
that transforming event. We learn early into the story that he's a
"war orphan" living with a "foster parent"—horror signs to me.

But I refused to understand (or did I?) that here was a boy
whose parents had been killed. I'd heard in my own brief life the
stories of those murdered in the camps. I knew the dread, though
I knew it only through a family ritual of naming faces in Old
Country snapshot albums. As I watch the film on videotape, the
faces of the war orphans the boy meets in a dreamlike scene in the
forest are the same faces he's seen earlier, in the pictures on refugee
posters at school. I freeze-frame the biggest poster now, from "The
United Jewish Welfare Fund," though I couldn't have read it as a
child.

The dread of being branded an outcast was already in me in
childhood. My first apprehensive day at public school I wanted to
change my name, knowing Jews "across the ocean" suffered for
names. Yet the particulars of the movie boy's orphanhood were
lost on me; I saw only the American boy I wanted to be: struck
with hair horror, yes, but bearing it with defiance. I had no idea
why I also felt defiant. I was, in fact, filled with fear that my mother
would not forgive me for watching this. Or worse—that I would
actually witness some forbidden adult act that would scar me forever. Looking back now, it's not hard to imagine what horror scene
I was afraid to witness: long before, even as an infant, I may have
crawled (I wouldn't stay put in my crib, I'm told) into my parents'

bedroom one night, unannounced, dumb with fear over the muffled groans I'd heard . . .

Especially now, as I watch the movie forty years later, the boy's particulars remain profoundly lost. All of the movie characters go through a frightful displacement—forced to represent something other than who they are by the taboos observed in 1948, the year of the film's making. It's as if memory of the Holocaust had to be represented by the incongruous lore of the Irish. In this freshest of post-Holocaust movies, the Irish in America are white-washed stand-ins for Jews, just like vaudeville whites wearing black-face, or a Jew, Al Jolson, black-faced in *The Jazz Singer*—in another era, before Hitler even came to power, yet a mere seventeen years before *The Boy with Green Hair*.

So, what are we told of the boy's martyred parents? Only that they tell him, in the letter, to "always remember and help others remember." They chose to die, to stay behind and "help others." This revelation at film's end, which helps the boy accept his fate, more surprisingly justifies his earlier fear that his parents abandoned him. It was this fear that could have given him green hair (as worry is said to turn our hair white), but when the boy stares in the mirror in disbelief his fear vanishes: green hair stands for his defiance of fate, and he wears it like the baseball cap of a losing team, proudly. He is loyal to himself, his uniqueness, come what may.

I was the little boy watching in the hat of the woebegone fifties Detroit Tigers. Yet strange hair represented a different universe to me, the one that put you in a concentration camp for being circumcised (that's how I heard it) and having a Jewish name. My terror stood apart from the headstrong boy, yet we were the same boy. Smarter than he, I didn't think a baseball bat beside my bed would be of any use against the dark of the Holocaust whisperings enveloping my childhood. I had living, comforting parents—but I felt they were helpless, useless as a club against the darkness within, and within our history. I was living closer to the real world than was the movie. Not that I knew it, though. I was terrified of what I didn't know, so I held on to the boy's stubbornness: I would survive, like him, by the grace of words. In his case, the letter; in mine, books.

Or, even before I was reading, the life of the mind. That mind which in high school carried around an unread paperback by Milton, a badge of defiance bulging from my back pocket. I little knew that inside *Paradise Lost* lived a Satan every bit as humanly defiant and conflicted. I couldn't understand what I read then, just as I couldn't understand the movie I carried around for years in my childhood head.

My father owned the American Popcorn Company in Detroit. Until I was eight, when I bought a paper route, I helped him deliver the beer-barrel-sized aluminum canisters of the day's freshly popped corn. Although I could not even get my arms around the cans, they were almost as light as air. I was delivered into the dangerous wide world of adults in the benign disguise of popcorn boy—into a network of darkness, from bar to bar to theater lobby. On weekdays the first shows began around 6:00, so when we delivered in the late afternoons after school I could walk under the sandwich-board posters of coming attractions, alone in the empty theater while my father talked to the manager in his office. The theater was dark except for spotlights on the sandwich boards. I fantasized the movies from these posters, though I'd never seen an adult movie. They—posters and movies alike—were like dreams, with incongruous things happening all at once: a car speeding off behind the ear of a woman with fear on her face, and behind the other ear a door half-opened, moonlight spilling onto her shoulder. I couldn't yet—or didn't—read the words. The first words of an adult kind I remember reading came later, a headline "extra" in the Detroit *Free Press,* glimpsed in the drugstore window on the way to school: ROSENBERGS TO FRY, something like that. The boy in *The Boy with Green Hair* poster caught my eye long before the movie arrived; I sensed I looked like him.

I sneaked my way in, hiding out in a men's-room stall after a Saturday kid's matinee. (I would later tell my mother I had fallen asleep—a more complex plot in my head than it sounds.) I was surprised the movie boy was older than me, about ten. Still, my obsession with him matched his own identification with an even older boy his classmates said looked like him, in a war-orphan poster pinned up outside his new classroom. In the pivotal forest encounter to come, when the poster faces turn into real children, this older boy tells him that the reason his hair has changed is to make the world listen to him. I understood little of it, but I assumed the worst—the one boy in tatters, the other with green hair. What could be worse than having everyone expect a grandiose statement from me; a child, I had nothing to say, and I wanted the freedom to grow up anonymously enough to survive my mistakes. I was so terrified, in fact, that I remembered the film as being in black and white, except for the green hair—the rest of the color washed out by fear.

An early, crucial scene in *The Boy with Green Hair*: Gramps has to demonstrate to the boy that nothing changes when the lights go out at night—and, even so, when the light is turned off the boy gropes beside the bed until his hand finds the trusty baseball bat. He's already ten. He was abandoned by his parents, I thought at six, and he still thinks a bat can help him?

◪

Why are we terrified of the first haircut? Little narcissists, we can't imagine parting with a part of ourselves. So the movie boy rediscovers his childhood's lost hair—in his own, newly green hair. He is grandiosely unique again, on a mission, and in the forest he learns what it is: the older boy explains that he must tell the world it's in danger of destroying its children. This, from the mouth of his older likeness, the war-orphan poster; green hair, he learns further, symbolizes hope, spring, and life's renewal. The words used among the orphans in the forest are exactly those the boy once overheard, as we watched him taking in—and only half understanding—adult conversation in earlier scenes of the film. For instance, a woman expresses her anxieties about nuclear war to the grocer in a store. In another scene, Gramps expounds, in a bit of a brogue, upon what green means to the Irish. So, with no specific clues, we already know the forest scene is meant to function as a dream; the day's anxieties are worked into a real but fantastic tale.

This is a dream like the movie itself, with the audience asleep in the dark. The story is a fable of a boy's life changing itself as it grows. If life itself is like a fable or a dream, the incongruous songs in the beginning of the film now make a kind of sense. Still, a mother dies in *Bambi*, a disaster-dream anchors *The Wizard of Oz*, yet in *The Boy with Green Hair* the mixing of musical with horror genres is uncanny. I found the previews of *Bambi* and *Oz* accurate when I was a child, while that of *Boy* mislead me. By not being made with children in mind, it reflected for a child his own fearful mystery of self-importance and weakness.

◪

Having heard I was writing on *The Boy with Green Hair*, a colleague told me that for her it was not a horror film at all. Older than I when she saw it, at eight, she accepted the boy's green hair as a gift. The hair promised the boy a future—releasing him from feeling sacrificed by his parents ("They didn't care about me, but only saving other children").

But at movie's end, I countered, and at the end of his story in flashback, his head is shaven and the gift of a new identity is gone. And that is how we find him at the beginning of the movie—before the flashback—unable to utter his name. The police detective says to the child psychiatrist: "This is Mr. Nobody. Doesn't have mother and father, doesn't go to school, doesn't know anybody at all." When he finally does speak, the boy (Dean Stockwell) will tell the psychiatrist (Robert Ryan) his entire story, the film proceeding in flashback, up to the greening of his hair and then the forced cutting, a prolonged scene as anxious as a child's first haircut. Yet to my friend, the film was a parable of the artist, who must make art to replace the lost grandiosity of a part of herself.

Still, watching the film again, I'm sickened by the haircut, as if it's dehumanizing: it cuts off the boy's speech as well. When he's finally tricked into telling his tale, his first words come out of hunger, tempted with hamburger and malted. And now I think of death-camp inmates, shorn of their hair—seeing again what I saw at six, the victim's terror. Confiding this to my friend, she suggests the artist's imagination is like a child's, a grandiose experiencing, memory entered into as intensely as a dream. She sends me back to my own life again.

When I became an adolescent poet I was not so much writing poetry as translating a memory of poetry, of how I heard the Hebrew psalms in childhood: a speaking to God, chanted gently, as if God liked rhyme and lullaby—as if He were my parents' fathers and was singing through them. I can remember standing no higher than my father's prayer-shawl fringes, watching him sing the psalms to himself in synagogue. In *The Boy with Green Hair*, the boy's memory of a world being destroyed (losing his parents) is turned into an atomic nightmare (he overhears adults discussing this). It's the child's drama—not the adult antiwar themes—that disarm us. I continue to think of poems as translations—even translations of a child's cries, just as the Bible's psalms will often cry out to mother and father, in between the murmuring and chanting.

As I absorbed my colleague's comments, I grasped how movies, in their return of childhood, can disarm the grandiose, blurring the line between dream and art. The boy in the movie, unlike Dorothy in *The Wizard of Oz*, never escapes from his difficult predicament. His transforming moment, when he learns from his double in the forest that his green hair symbolizes not "something you've done—but something you're going to do," is the artist's moment. By the end he won't need the green hair, only the mission itself: to pass on his parents' letter, their love for him embodied by it.

I'm still left with my own problem about the use of war orphan and smiling Irish euphemisms. In his film history *Behind the Mask of Innocence*, Kevin Brownlow recounts that in the 1916 film *The Children Pay*, as originally filmed, the character played by Lillian Gish finds her life ruined by her parents' divorce. In the version that was released, however, the divorce was censored—it was just too shocking a subject back then. Instead of having suffering inflicted upon her by her parents, Gish was portrayed as an orphan. Thirty years later, in *The Boy with Green Hair*, an orphan boy once again stands for the unspeakable. In 1948, the Holocaust is the unspeakable atrocity, a leap from an earlier time, when divorce could not be addressed directly. This need for displacement probably made a better movie out of *The Boy with Green Hair*; my anxiety now, just as when I was a child, is about the necessity for it. I was terrified by what I couldn't understand of the movie as a child. Now that I understand it, I worry that the plot (except for the boy's character, which makes *all the difference*) was too glib.

◪

A later, college equivalent to my high school infatuation with paperback classics came with art films. The luscious, dreamlike cover for the Signet edition of *The Interpretation of Dreams* was replaced by freethinking life styles and free-ranging directorial styles. *Hiroshima Mon Amour* cuts quickly to *Last Year at Marienbad* in my memory. I walked around campus one year carrying great films, not books, between my ears. You could tell by looking at me how heavy they were: my shoulders hunched, my eyes darkened behind shades, my hand holding on to my pipe for stability.

In my way, I wanted to punish the world for its insensitivity to my childhood; or, in another way, I wanted to punish my parents. I see now that the unconscious wish behind the movie boy's dream is not simply to work through the loss of his parents but to punish them for his abandonment. I punished mine by "withdrawing" my belief in them and projecting it instead onto a movie-screen-sized window of the world. In this world I was a hip, college-aged orphan, proud of every neurotic tic I could cultivate. Although I remembered it, I didn't come back to *The Boy with Green Hair* until recently. I thought it was probably unhip, back when I was in college, too freighted with social messages about war with a capital *W*. And the boy was too *obvious* an orphan. Now I can see that for my six-year-old self the revealed letter at the movie's end was as powerful as Freud and Milton were to be for me later. The letter's grandiose words washed over me as I studied instead the boy's listening face. He seemed also not to understand; it was the object itself, the letter and its envelope, that became symbolic of his identity as he lovingly pocketed it. In unconscious imitation, almost ten years later I would fold my latest poem into a shirt pocket, while in my hand a paperback of *Paradise Lost* nestled, a thoroughly worn copy—not from reading, however, but from carrying.

In childhood, I knew the secret of the letter, all right, even if I couldn't understand it. The boy's parents had abandoned him. There was no hint of a fable for me then. And even now, it's the realism that makes the film work for me—in spite of the director's more expressionistic intentions. Joseph Losey and his producer, Dore Schary, seemed to imagine their film deriving from Brecht and Weill (Losey had just directed Charles Laughton in Brecht's *Galileo* on Broadway; from there, he was convinced by Schary to try Hollywood). Hollywood may have intimidated Losey into building his boy archetype into a recognizably defiant adolescent, and that happy pressure makes the film resonate with realism.

The Boy with Green Hair takes a grandiose theme—fear of the family gods, the abandoning parents—and makes it art by scaling it down to the personal. We see that the boy will probably grow up with it—his family drama—inside, internalized. When he goes to the movies as an adult, he'll be fascinated with the limits of love and individuality—not the grandiose absolutes of abolishing war or accepting all differences, but the human limits.

When I was a child of four—my earliest memory—lost on Nantasket Beach, I was scared my mother had abandoned me. How could she leave this little prince with his sand bucket? Where could she find such a perfect, beautiful child, as she had convinced me I was? Well, my brother had come along just a few months earlier— and who knows who else might one day show up to displace me? In fact, my father had already turned up when I was two, back from the beaches of Normandy, though my mother reassured me that I was still number one with her. To persuade me that I was still number one, she took me on a week's vacation to relatives— just the two of us boarding the Pullman for the twenty-four-hour trip from Detroit.

But I was also hiding my own guilt. I knew within that in fact I was no prince. I had *wanted to escape,* I sensed on the beach, and had wandered off in some play fantasy, or perhaps even stole away to the forbidden water (as I would later steal into *The Boy with Green Hair*). However, in the great wide world of my first ocean beach I would need to trust someone—in fact, strangers. What was my name, they asked the crying, lost boy. And what was my *last* name?

◪

3 WOMEN

4 WOMEN

AMY HEMPEL

was looking for a house to rent on the East End of Long Island when a friend told me that Jean Stafford's house—the house she had lived in at the time of her death in 1979—was available. I wanted it even without knowing where it was, how big it was, or how much it would cost. Then my friend told me something I found unsettling. He said that Stafford's cleaning lady, to whom the writer had left the house, had left it exactly as it was. My friend told me that Jean Stafford's monogrammed stationery was still in a drawer of her desk. I heard that, and although it had been nearly ten years since I had last seen Robert Altman's *3 Women*, I thought immediately of Pinky Rose (Sissy Spacek) picking up the diary of her roommate Millie Lammoreaux (Shelley Duvall) and making an entry in it—as if she, Pinky, were Millie.

The first time I saw *3 Women* was when it came out, capping the seventies, my personal Lost Years, later reassessed as Research, a time that might have occasioned Blanche McCrary Boyd's consoling words, "Don't worry. It'll go away. It's only the present, and it's almost over."

Before it was over, I had—in a spectacular confusion of activity with action—moved twenty-six times in four years, this without ever leaving San Francisco (number twenty-six was a large Victorian flat that I shared with a woman doing her psychiatric residency, a woman who once asked me, in reference to our downstairs neighbors, "But what do lesbians do in the daytime?").

From San Francisco I went to Los Angeles, where I lived for a short time in an apartment complex I called Rancho Libido that was not unlike the apartment complex to which Millie Lammoreaux repaired after a day of work at the geriatric spa, the kind of place Frederick Barthelme has since made familiar in his fiction.

There I had two blind dates. The first was with a movie actor known for his brilliant, convincing portraits of psychopaths (he has since been allowed to branch out, and remains brilliant and convincing). The second was with an ophthalmologist I agreed to go out with strictly so that I could say I had had a blind date with an eye doctor.

Men were not the point; the seventies were, for me, about women. In the seventies, my mother killed herself, her sister killed herself, and I nearly killed myself and my best friend in a car crash. (On my car's bumper was a sticker of my own design: I BRAKE JUST LIKE A LITTLE GIRL.) My friend would climb into my hospital bed to watch television and nap off our pain meds; we would be awakened by a nonplussed nurse bringing two lunch trays without comment. We would put aside Esther Harding's *The Way of All Women* to read a section of Doris Lessing's *The Four-Gated City*. We found cartoons in the press: "It's a baby woman!" above the head of a newborn, and a little girl crying, "Help, I'm being held prisoner in a blue dotted-Swiss!" A woman who had been hired to be humor editor of *Ms.* wrote about her brief employment—she said a friend had asked if that wasn't like being divorce editor of *Seventeen.*

In the seventies, I became familiar with crisis, as well as with women's literature. I volunteered as a counselor at the Women's Center in San Francisco. I joined a counseling and referral group called Women Against Rape, largely because I wanted to be more like the group's leader. When we were introduced, this Texan named Jo had said, "Let's hope a Meg and a Beth join—we'll be Little Women Against Rape."

San Francisco was a good place to be lost. Good in that it was beautiful and tolerant, and people never asked where you had gone to school. On the other hand, what went on there in those years included the assassinations of Mayor George Moscone and Supervisor Harvey Milk; the Rev. Jim Jones's flight from the People's Temple to Guyana and the resulting mass suicides in Jonestown; the random insanity of the Zebra and Zodiac killers; the locals who regularly flung themselves off that "McDonald's of suicide," the Golden Gate bridge (in a counterphobic move, I subscribed to the "nooseletter" of the Suicide Club, a group of pranksters who held their annual banquet on the Golden Gate bridge).

I am suggestible. I begin to drawl in the company of friends from the South; I work harder in New York City than anywhere else; I keep a mental list of the ways in which I am like, and unlike, my mother, making sure that the latter column always exceeds the former (Nancy Friday, in her book *My Mother, Myself,* wrote of how a woman will insist, "My mother lives in a house, and I live in an apartment—we're *nothing* alike!").

If you believe that transition is dangerous, then—with the exception of dying—what could be more dangerous than merging? I was the target audience for *3 Women,* a film in which women move beyond the sphere of one another's influence to, in effect, *become* one another.

I first saw *3 Women* in my neighborhood "art film" theater (though what theater in San Francisco was *not* my neighborhood theater?). I was partial to this theater because I had once found an emerald-eyed serpent stickpin on the arm of the seat I had chosen. I went to a matinee by myself, the matinee possible because I never, in those days, had a *job* job, by myself because it precluded a trance-breaking comment when the film was over.

I watched *3 Women,* with its *female* existential heroes, and then I walked a few blocks through the fog to a club and ordered a Coke. I noticed that the band appearing there that night, one of the Bay Area's success stories, featured the singer who had phoned the hot line on a night I was on. She had called after her first set at a nightclub in the city; she had told me that the man who had raped her the week before was sitting in the audience.

◪

The first movies I liked as a child were horror films, in particular a trilogy called *Black Sabbath.* A babysitter took me to a 3-D shrieker; I kept taking the glasses off, the babysitter would force them back on. At some point I switched from horror to Hayley Mills (a favorite joke puts the question: What is Pollyanna's epitaph?—"I'm *glad* I'm dead!").

Perhaps the oddest and most satisfying movie moment came several years after my high school graduation when the boarding school I had attended turned up on screen as the Thorne family estate—the home of the young antichrist in *Damien—Omen II.*

I will close a book at the first infelicitous sentence, but will watch just about anything, neither art nor entertainment, on-screen.

3 Women is not my favorite movie—my favorite movie is probably *Rebecca,* from the Daphne du Maurier novel. *3 Women* is not the movie I have seen the most times; again, that is *Rebecca,* or possibly *The Women* (a friend of mine in Hollywood had seen

Dirty Dancing thirty-six times when a reporter from one of those entertainment news shows picked her out when she was standing in line to see it again. Embarrassed, my friend would only admit to having seen the movie twenty-six times).

3 Women is not a guaranteed weeper like *To Kill a Mockingbird* or *The Miracle Worker* or any film with an animal in it. It is not a movie that contributed to an erotic education, the way even *The Franz Liszt Story* figured in the life of an artist friend who recalls cutting school at age twelve to see this biography. "I didn't know what all that piano music was about," he said, "but Liszt's mistress had the biggest cleavage I had ever seen."

3 Women does not contain any of my favorite lines in films, such as the exchange between Carroll Baker and Eli Wallach in Tennessee Williams's *Baby Doll*, when Wallach/Mr. Vaccaro offers Baker/Baby Doll a pecan. (In fake Mississippi accents):

Baby Doll: "Excuse me, Mr. Vaccaro, but I wouldn't dream of eating a nut which a man had cracked in his mouth."

Mr. Vaccaro: "You got many refinements."

Did *3 Women* change my life? It did *define* a kind of life, not so unlike mine at the time I first saw it, in my mid-twenties; it accorded value to lives I did not think of as having value, as having interest. I would not have thought of these people, including myself, as having stories anyone else would want to know. The literary equivalent was reading Mary Robison's first collection of stories, *Days*, which was published at about the same time. From there, it was a short leap to the realization that what I knew, but didn't think of as being valuable, was. That realization was entitlement, and that enabled me to begin to write. And *that* changed my life. That is, it *gave* me one.

Odd that it was a *man's* vision. More specifically, a man's dream. Robert Altman has said that *3 Women* is a film that he dreamed. On-screen, there is water everywhere, pools and pools of it, in the Southern California desert. Water as archetypal symbol

for woman?—they work in it, in fact. Millie Lammoreaux (Duvall) **133**
and Pinky Rose (Spacek) are attendants in a spa for the aged. The
young female bodies lead the old bodies, some of them towel-draped
like sheeted ghosts, into hydrotherapy in the film's dreamy opening. Millie shows Pinky, the new girl, the job. Self-enchantress
that she is, Millie makes it known that she is going to enter the
contest to find a new Breck girl. Pinky is so eager for Millie's
friendship that when she overhears Millie tell another girl that she,
Millie, hates tomatoes, Pinky—at the first opportunity—assures
Millie, "I *hate* tomatoes." It is a little like the observation about
women who want to be friends, that one will tell the other, "I like
your shoes."

Millie wears "outfits." She is what we used to call a "grinder."
That is, someone it makes you grind your teeth to watch, but you
can't *not* watch; televangelists are in this category. She natters on,
supplying the answers to questions no one has asked, inviting
couldn't-care-less interns in the nearby hospital cafeteria to her
apartment for "Penthouse Chicken." Her self-delusion is comic
and excruciating. She is a woman with gifts that nobody wants.
Except for Pinky, who is in thrall to her, who tells Millie that she
is the most perfect person she, Pinky, has ever known.

◤

Soon Pinky is sharing Millie's apartment. There is water at
home, too—the swimming pool, the social center of the apartment
complex. The sides and floor of this pool are painted with murals
of figures described by various reviewers as "scaly fiends—cannibal
gods," "reptilean preterhuman beings," "etiolated humanoids in
mating gymnastics," and "grotesque humanoid figures in which a
fierce, priapic male terrorizes three females, one of whom is
pregnant."

Willie (Janice Rule) is the third woman. She painted the murals, and she is pregnant. She and her lecherous, boozing husband,

Edgar, own the apartments and they own Dodge City, the hangout Millie frequents to try to meet men (the off-duty cops alternate between the firing range and dirt bikes). Edgar used to be on the Wyatt Earp show on television. "He knows Hugh O'Brian," Millie says to impress Pinky. Willie never speaks, but can be found in their empty swimming pool with her paints and swollen stomach and straw hat.

Millie prepares the menu for one of her "famous dinner parties"—pigs-in-a-blanket, chocolate-pudding tarts, and Tickled Pink wine. She dresses in a backless hostess gown and wrist corsage, and is stood up by the entire guest list. When Pinky sees Millie leading Edgar to her bedroom later that night, Millie hisses, "Not one word. What do you know about anything?" Told to leave, Pinky throws herself off the balcony into the pool, her billowing nightgown seeming to suspend her over Willie's watery figures.

When Pinky comes out of the fall-induced coma, she is Millie, just about. The transpositioning is complete when Millie delivers Willie's stillborn child. In the final scene, the "old" Pinky is minding the bar at Dodge City, Edgar having expired in some sort of shooting "accident." Millie, wearing Willie's hat, gives the orders and is actually obeyed by Pinky, who calls her "Ma." Willie speaks for the first time on the porch swing outside what is now their communal home . . .

That is the "story," although I don't read for the story, or watch movies for the story. I like the practice of an artist I know, a Swiss woman, who will only enter a theater halfway through the feature. This protects her from knowing at the beginning what will happen at the end, and engages her in the process of making sense of what she is seeing, to the extent that she wants sense made of it.

◢

I have heard a successful screenwriter explain that *sex, lies and videotape* is really *Shane*, so it takes nothing away from *3*

Women for me when critics point out that it owes more than a little to Bergman's *Persona*. I watched both films again for this essay. And for all the cries of "masterpiece" directed at *Persona* and the mixed reviews for the flawed *3 Women* (the reviewer for *The Nation* called it "brain damage, wrapped in hocus pocus"; Cynthia Ozick brilliantly took it apart in *Ms.*; every woman I know who saw it saw it three or more times), it is still *3 Women*— *Persona in the Desert? Persona Plus One?*—that calls up a flawed decade for me.

3 Women is not available on videotape. To see it again, I had to borrow Robert Altman's own master copy (an assistant lent it to me; Mr. Altman was in Europe finishing *Vincent and Theo*).

I watched it in my house on the East End of Long Island that did not used to belong to Jean Stafford. I tried to watch as carefully as Edward Albee, who has said that on his nth viewing of *All About Eve*, he noticed in the opening scene—where Bette Davis/Margo Channing lights up a cigarette as Anne Baxter/Eve accepts the Sarah Siddons Award—Albee noticed that the lighter she pulls out bears the initials "B.D." Anyway, I watched *3 Women* again, and what came back to me were not details from the film but details from my own life in Southern California, even an old journal entry after a series of earth tremors: "I long for land that stands still."

Was it Joan Didion who wrote that it is wise to keep on nodding terms with the people we used to be, else they come knocking at the mind's door of a bad 4 a.m. and demand to know who deserted them? I was, as before, taken with, and shaken by, Millie Lammoreaux's need to be known, to make herself known to people who had not the least interest in her. This is part of what motivates a writer. In the past she made me wince; this time I felt a kind of fond forgiveness that was, in fact, *self*-forgiveness, I expect.

This made me return to the prologue of Anne Lamott's novel *All New People* (the title itself a perfect antidote to torturing oneself with one's past; a family member points out, "In a hundred years— All New People!").

The prologue is an account of a visualization exercise done with the help of a hypnotist. "I want you to go backwards in time," he tells Nanny Goodman, the narrator, "and ferret out the memories of pain: of despair, rejection, terror, shame. . . ." He instructs the adult Nanny to step into each scene and give the young Nanny a hand. The narrator's response: "Even in the trance I am filled with derision. This is precisely the sort of thing that gives California a bad name." But she swallows her reservations and gives a most moving account of a guided fantasy of forgiveness.

Watching Millie and Pinky trade places, I thought of my best friend, of climbing into—not *her* hospital bed, but the extra bed she had a nurse wheel into the room where my friend was dying. On her last trip out of the hospital, my friend drove me to give blood. On a form, I designated which hospital my blood was to go to, which patient. Then my friend took me to lunch and refused to tip the waitress for no reason at all, and then drove fast and badly, swearing at everyone on the road back to the hospital. After she died, *I* did all of those things.

I am writing this on the day that makes it nineteen years ago that my mother took her life, and I am now the age that she was then, and she has been dead now the same amount of time she was alive for me, and I cannot wear my hair the way my husband likes it best because it makes me look so much like her.

Watching the eerie twins who also work at the geriatric spa, Pinky asks Millie, "Do you think they know which ones they are?"

◪

For years I had long hair. Just before I saw *3 Women* this last time, I had my hair cut to a length of one inch. Then I found out that my cat, my companion for seventeen years, was dying of an untreatable cancer.

Who would I be without my hair? Who would I be without my cat?

I watched 3 *Women,* the film that came to Altman in a dream, **137** and *I* had a dream. In the dream, I went to pick up the personalized stationery I had ordered for myself in waking life. But in the dream, there was a different name at the top of each sheet.

I did not have to puzzle over what this meant. Those people whose names were on my stationery? It seems to me that I am every one of them.

◪

OUR VINES HAVE TENDER GRAPES

OUR BRAINS HAVE TENDER BUTTONS

JUDITH ROSSNER

 ears ago I had a friend who would tell me, "I know all your buttons," when something he said made me angry. If the notion of being predictable is at once comforting and irritating, I've long been aware that in art as well as in life, we all have our buttons. I've never wanted to read or see *The Visit* or any of a host of other plays or movies in which events move inexorably toward a given end. Inexorability presses one of my buttons. In my own stories, It-Doesn't-Have-to-Happen-if-Only-(S)he [my hero or heroine]-Can-Do-This-or-That-or [gulp]-Change.

I hadn't seen *Our Vines Have Tender Grapes* since 1945, in the Bronx (the RKO movies played at the Pelham, on White Plains Road, but MGMs were at Westchester Square), yet its name came immediately to mind when I was approached about this collection.

Its name, its brightest star (Margaret O'Brien, the dark-haired, terribly smart, and pretty little girl whom I adored to the exclusion of anyone less visibly precocious, more blond, and/or cutesy), and the scene I'd remembered more than once over the years, in which Margaret and a little boy I didn't remember as well are out alone in a rowboat on a country stream. What is clear to me, seeing the movie again for the first time after all these years, is that aside from being a lovely, well-made film, *Our Vines Have Tender Grapes* touched many of my most sensitive buttons.

Dalton Trumbo wrote (after a novel, *For Our Vines Have Tender Grapes*, by George Victor Martin) the somewhat idyllic account of the lives of two cousins (Margaret and that incredibly adorable Dennis-the-Menace antecedent, Butch Jenkins) in a Norwegian farming community in Wisconsin. Margaret's parents are Edward G. Robinson and Agnes Moorehead, both hard-working, loving, as benign as they would have to be to justify Margaret's perfection. Trumbo's populist and pacifist sympathies served well and were well served by the story, which opens as Margaret and Butch walk along a country road, discussing the war that was in its final stages as the movie was being made.

Butch says he will enter the army when he's old enough; Margaret says she'll be a Wac. Butch says he'll shoot lots of enemy soldiers; Margaret says she will, too. Butch tells her girls can't shoot and she says she'll shoot more than he does because she's older. He tells her Wacs don't even have guns. In frustration, she picks up a rock and throws it at a red squirrel; to her own astonishment and horror, she hits and kills it.

"You sure killed him, Sarah," Butch says. "Killed him dead."

She is terribly upset, says she hadn't meant to kill a little squirrel. Butch tells her the red ones are bad (They eat the crops) but she can't be consoled, pointing out that it hadn't been doing anything bad when she picked up the rock.

We follow Margaret's unsuccessful attempts to believe that

what she did was all right because red squirrels are predators. When even her adoring father fails to reassure her, he gives her a present—the calf to which their cow has just given birth, and which she names Elizabeth. One of the few moments in the movie that goes beyond the point where the corn can be relished occurs when she asks her father if the cow might have calved at the moment when the squirrel died, the squirrel's soul then presumably having entered the newborn calf.

One has to wonder if this is the fictional impulse at work, or the political Trumbo trying to teach us about the origins of religion in twenty-five words or less. In either event, the very first scene has shown us the difference between death's, and war's, easy rhetoric and difficult realities.

◥

The movie follows the adored only child, Margaret (Sarah is her movie name, but Margaret comes more readily to me); her father calls her *Yenti Mi* (Norwegian for "girl mine"; I'm not sure of the spelling), through a series of adventures with cousin Butch and her father, the former thoroughly mischievous, the latter utterly benign. (Mama Agnes is usually in the kitchen, preparing pancakes and other good things. She leaves her tasks only long enough to counsel Papa when he fails to discipline Margaret though she seems to have behaved badly, or when he's about to make an investment that will involve adding too much to his already heavy workload.)

Pa and Margaret visit a neighbor's (Morris Carnovsky) beautiful new barn, which Pa admires and envies.

"Do you want a new barn, Pa?" Margaret asks.

"Any man does," Pa tells her.

When she promises to pray for one, Pa tells her it will take considerable praying.

"What's one more barn to God?" Margaret asks, in one of

those many wonderful lines we feel Trumbo putting into his characters' mouths with some glee; here is a writer who can revel in
his irony and have us eat it, too.

Margaret gets a pair of roller skates for her birthday. She's
willing to let Butch try them, later, but he's not willing to wait.
Butch says she's a big old pig and she eats slop, then complains to
her parents about not getting his turn. When she tells them he's
been calling her names, Butch denies it, crossing his heart and
hoping to die if he's telling the lie he's telling. Ma tells Pa he's
too soft on the child, she should be punished—spanked—for refusing to share and lying to them on top of it. Pa says he can't
spank her, his hand's too big, he'd hurt her, but he then tells
Margaret to give Butch the skates or go to bed without dinner. She
takes off the skates and tries to go up, ready to sacrifice dinner
rather than allow Butch to benefit from his lies. Angry for the first
time, Pa not only sends her to bed but takes away the skates and
gives them to Butch! (Much later in the film, Butch's father makes
him give them back.)

I will not describe the heart-rending scene in which Pa, having
determined to be stern, is miserable, and Margaret, in bed in her
room over the grate in the living-room ceiling, cries herself to sleep
because he won't kiss her good-night. But at some point Ma tells
him that a circus will pass through town at four in the morning.
Relieved to have a chance at making the child happy without giving
in on a crucial point, he awakens her. Together they drive to town
and, as the caravan pauses to water the animals, he bribes a driver
to let the baby elephant come down the ramp to perform for his
daughter. Finally, seduced by Margaret as thoroughly as we have
been, the driver has the animal give her a brief ride wrapped in its
trunk. All is well again.

The adult romance in *Our Vines Have Tender Grapes* is provided by James Craig as the handsome, wise, charming, and te-
naciously honest editor of the local paper (his name is Nels

Halverson, but Margaret and Butch address him only as Editor) and Frances Gifford as the lovely new schoolteacher who has been assigned to the town for the year (she's getting a Ph.D. in education) because she speaks Norwegian. James has attempted to enlist in the army and been turned down for some reason that does not affect his desirability. Frances comes from Minneapolis and likes James but can't stand small-town life, although she is sympathetic to each and every inhabitant and makes a serious attempt to help Ingeborg, the lovely, "not-quite-right" young woman whose abusive father has never let her attend school. (Ingeborg is a beautiful Scandinavian blonde whom we've met quite early in the film, when she sees Margaret crying over the squirrel. She tries to comfort the young girl and is called back to work by her stern-to-the-point-of-evil father. This appears to be Hollywood's 1945 version of integration—that is, of including the less fortunate.)

In a later scene in the schoolhouse, Margaret is laughed at by the older kids for having said it was nice that Ingeborg could marry and have a baby on the same day. Schoolteacher Frances thinks that's perfectly lovely of Margaret and informs the others that Ingeborg suffers enough without being laughed at by those who should be her friends. (The Production Code dictating that even virtuous characters be punished for their sins is the only apparent cause of Ingeborg's off-screen death sometime thereafter.)

Then there is the scene—a screen memory, if you will—that I remembered—or, I should say, the idyllic part of which I remembered—for all these years.

Spring comes. The floodwaters are rising and Margaret and Butch can't play outdoors. Then Butch gets an idea. (Margaret says it won't work but she's wrong, a rare instance of such.) They take Pa's metal bathtub down from the barn wall (Mama Agnes envies running water more than she does new barns) to use as a boat, the rowboat I thought I remembered. Then they find pieces of wood that will serve as oars, and they push themselves through the shallow water in the yard into the deep stream created by the floodwaters just beyond the farm. Fortunately, a neighbor sees them, so that when they can't be found a short while later, it's understood immediately that the floodwaters have carried them out of control and toward the dangerous waterfalls outside the town.

Every able-bodied male rushes to the bridge over the falls. Pa sloshes through mud and water with great difficulty and in desperate haste. (Perhaps it's a part of the movie's charm that Ma and Pa are more like grandparents than parents.) When the tub finally comes into view there is dreadful anxiety because the children are nowhere to be seen. It rushes downstream toward the bridge and we are relieved to see Butch and Margaret lying down inside it. They will be safe if only Editor succeeds in climbing down the bridge supports and arresting it before it goes over the falls. Need I tell you more?

Editor's new attempt to enlist in the army is successful. Margaret wants to know why he has to go fight and be in danger when he's so good.

"Just because milk's good, doesn't mean we get it for free," Pa says. "Peace on earth, good will toward men. . . . If someone tries to take 'em away, you've got to fight to keep 'em."

"Does understanding mean you've gotta be glad about it?" Margaret asks.

He assures her it does not.

"Then I guess I understand," she tells him.

(It's this attempt to deal on a popular level with some of the more complicated issues of patriotism that seems to me to be one of the film's distinguishing aspects.)

There is a terrible thunderstorm. The phone rings. Morris Carnovsky's new barn has been hit by lightning and has gone up in flames. Everyone rushes to help but most of the animals are destroyed along with the barn, as is, of course, his livelihood.

In church, Editor makes a plea for money to help the family.

144   But when he and Frances (they are very much in love but her cooler head has prevailed and she's still intending to return to Minneapolis at the end of the school year) count the money, only a few dollars have been contributed (a couple of them by Pa).

Margaret raises her hand to ask whether donations are limited to money. Upon being told they're not, she donates her precious, now nine-month-old calf, Elizabeth. Her generosity shames the town's adults into making substantial offerings of animals, hay, silage, and so on. Her parents are unspeakably proud.

Frances can no longer imagine leaving this town and its wonderful people. She will marry Editor, whom she realizes now she's always loved, not just liked, and run the newspaper while he's in the army. Pa gives up his plan to finance a new barn, saying—when Agnes asks how he can bear to do this when he wanted it so much—"Maybe it's a good thing for a man to want something he ain't never gonna get." He will be consoled by the love of his family, most particularly of his daughter.

I will not deal here with the ironies attendant upon the blacklisting of the author of this glorification of everything America holds—or used to hold—dear. That's been done. And I think I've made clear my simpler affections for a solid, well-written, and beautifully acted movie. What I'm interested in doing now is linking—sewing onto the movie's fabric, if you will—my buttons.

◪

I was a dark-haired, homely, precocious little girl, an only child until my pretty, fair-haired baby sister was born in 1944 (the year before I saw *Our Vines Have Tender Grapes*). I was almost nine (I believe Margaret was eight when she made the movie; she and Jackie are supposed to be seven and five, respectively). If I'd never tried to hit a red squirrel and killed it instead, I was an aggressive, obstreperous kid who was constantly making my father and others (not my mother) angry—often in what could pass, to those not psychoanalytically inclined, for innocence. That is to say, I was frequently astonished and dismayed by the effect of actions committed by me without thought, much less with any thought of committing offense.

My mother was a pretty elementary-school teacher who was deeply attached to my father but deeply dissatisfied with life in the small town of their marriage. She retained throughout her adult life an active sense of having been displaced too early by a younger sister who was adorable and chubby (considered desirable in those years by their immigrant Jewish family, while she herself was thin, allergic to milk, and difficult in even less explicable ways), born when she herself was two. My father had been an only child in name only, feeling his life dominated by an uncle just four years older than he. They had intended to have only one child, preferably a girl, and it seemed clear to me that if I had been happier or prettier—had offered, that is, substantial proof of how much nicer life could be for an only child—they never would have arranged for another.

My father was the greater believer in the notion of children's need for discipline. He was also the one with the visible temper, possibly more violent than it would have been if my mother hadn't interfered with his simple, reactive attempts at discipline. There was in her something that wanted me to be a bad girl, a terribly aggressive one, someone who could resist the rules *for* her, since she had lost the will to resist them herself.

Perhaps there was a girl in me who wanted the order reversed, who wanted a father like Edward G., who couldn't bear to discipline me, and a mother like Agnes, who insisted it had to be done. It would certainly be fair to say that I'd happily have endured punishment for the sake of being awakened by him late at night and bundled off to town to ride a circus elephant or do anything else he might want to do.

Then there is the relationship between Margaret and Butch,

who is younger than she and jealous that he can't yet go to school—where he would doubtless be in constant trouble when he was old enough to attend. (I realize, having checked her age again, that through my first two videotape viewings, I still thought of her as my own age, as I did when I saw the movie. I was ten.)

I was two days older than Peter, the tall, dark, and terribly handsome neighbor's son on whom I had a crush and who wanted nothing to do with me. When we were in first grade, the teacher was so irritated by my behavior that at the end of the term, she recommended that Peter, but not I, the more visibly (or perhaps I should say audibly) precocious one of the two of us, be skipped a grade. Our parents were close and both families moved to a new neighborhood at this time. Peter and I remained in the same class. But I didn't forget the unfairness of it all—that Peter, with all his other superiorities and male advantages, should also have been scheduled to skip.

I loved to read and write no matter whose class I was in but tended to be well behaved with the disciplinarians, less so with anyone conflicted, along my mother's lines, about the purposes and results of discipline. My reasonably high I.Q. test results were apparently the highest in the small school, and I was treated as some sort of local treasure, getting away with all kinds of nonsense, particularly with bucking our difficult third-grade teacher, an unappetizing and unpleasant old (I'm not so sure of the old part anymore) woman who spat on the children in the first two rows as she spoke, and who had—of at least equal negative significance at Public School 108—leftist sympathies. (Only as I write do I see myself as something of a pawn in the battle between the Irish Catholic right-wing Democrat who was the principal during most of my time there and the left-wing commie Jew she detested for complicated reasons and whom the students loathed for simpler ones. My own parents were much closer to the teacher's positions than to the principal's, but their progressive, socialist sympathies seem not to have been linked to hers in my mind or anyone else's.)

I suppose that from art—even sometimes from craft—we learn that we are both more and less than we thought ourselves. We give up the pride in uniqueness for the pleasure of companionship. Our wild fantasies become less forbidden, our difficult realities more bearable because they are shared. I don't remember having fantasies about being Margaret O'Brien—although it must have occurred to me that if I could look like her, it would be easy to be well behaved and then my father would adore me as Edward G. adored her . . . as, for that matter, my father appeared to adore my tiny, blond, well-behaved (helpless) sister. And as my mother adored everything I wrote without any longer adoring me.

My sleep-time fantasies, like so many kids' in those days before Hollywood had fully emerged as the American kingdom, a place where one could dream of being royal without altering one's bloodline and history, were of being a princess and being adored. In the daytime, when I wasn't reading fiction, I was thinking about things to *do* that might draw attention, elicit the admiration I craved. I have only now, since I began writing this essay, connected something I did that was a high point of my time at Public School 108 to *Our Vines Have Tender Grapes.*

I went through the years of World War II, like many American kids, eating my spinach so I wouldn't have to hear any more about the starving children in Europe. (The very thought of the starving children in Europe was enough to send me to the pantry for cookies.) At some point, following a discussion—in school or at home, I know not where, or perhaps it was even something I read—of those starving children in Europe, I felt the need to *do* something. I conceived a plan, which I presented to the principal of my school, who gave me permission to execute it.

I wrote, cast, and acted the lead in a play that was presented in the school auditorium for an audience of students and their parents. The invitations specified an admission price of two cans of food per person. The large number of cans we received were packed and sent to the starving children in Europe—perhaps via the Red Cross. I've long since forgotten many of the details, but the school year was 1945–46.

Our Vines opened at Radio City Music Hall on September 7, 1945.

I've always sneered at the notion that a troubled person hovering at the edge of violence couldn't be sent over the brink to commit it by scenes in a movie or on television. But it has only occurred to me in the writing of this essay that Margaret's standing in church to offer her beloved calf when all the adults around her were doing little or nothing was the inspiration for my plot to relieve the agony of the starving children of Europe.

"We're all proud of her, Mrs. Jacobsen," the pastor says to Margaret's mother as the two watch Pa and his girl walk off, not into the sunset but into the parklike setting outside the church where little girls might wander off with their fathers. "Just as proud as you are."

My father, when I was very young and still very much his good little girl, had taken me for walks in the park near our home. Now life had changed for me for the worse, or so I felt. He still wanted me to be a good, obedient girl who did the things good little girls did and was contented with whatever she received in the way of love and attention. For one reason—or perhaps it was another—this was not possible for me. I had to seek those pleasures in the outside world in grander ways, sometimes doing good things for others in the process.

◪

CLASSICS

THE FATAL GLASS
OF BEER

W. C. FIELDS AS MASTER OF
THE AESTHETICS OF
BEING OUTRAGED

HAROLD BLOOM

 first saw *The Fatal Glass of Beer* (1933) some-
time during the autumn of 1959, in the old Lincoln cinema (now,
alas, gone) in New Haven. It was the short running before the
main feature, which I cannot remember, and never saw anyway,
since *The Fatal Glass of Beer* disabled me. Shocked into literally
painful laughter, I was helped out of the Lincoln by caring friends,
and carried off to recuperate in a State Street bar. Many subsequent
viewings have not altered my judgment that this two-reeler is the
sublime of cinematic art, beyond even Keaton's *The General,* let
alone *Duck Soup* or *Intolerance.* But my critical understanding of
The Fatal Glass of Beer developed only thirty years later. Last year,
sleepless in New Haven, I found myself watching a British TV film
on the last days of Hitler, with Alec Guinness improbably cast as
Hitler. Yet Guinness held me, so much so that after half an hour

152 I was compelled to remind myself that, after all, this was meant to be Hitler. Perpetually outraged by fate, Russians, craven generals, traitors, and incompetents, the furious Guinness-Hitler became irresistible, dragging some aspect of me into sympathy.

I had been victimized by what I have learned to call the aesthetics of being outraged, and Guinness's artistry suddenly reminded me of W. C. Fields, and of *The Fatal Glass of Beer* in particular. It is very difficult successfully to represent the state of being outraged. Fields was one modern master of such representation, and Nathanael West was another, as was Faulkner before him (Joe Christmas of *Light in August*). Philip Roth of *The Anatomy Lesson* and *The Prague Orgy* is our contemporary master, who consoled me once, at a bad moment, by solemnly assuring me: "Harold, we are here to be insulted!" In this, as in all else, Shakespeare remains supreme. His Macbeth, himself the bloodiest of outrages, still retains our imaginative sympathy precisely because he grows increasingly outraged as he experiences the equivocation of the fiend that lies like truth. Murdering onward, Macbeth prolongs himself in time, and yet is provoked only to perpetual refreshments of the sense of being outraged, as all his expectations become yet more confounded. Macbeth moves us, despite his naive murderousness, because we cannot resist a strong representation of a human being in the state of being outraged.

W. C. Fields, sublimely outraged by so many particulars—children, women, Philadelphia—is neither a Macbeth nor a Guinness-Hitler, but I think of him sometimes when I reread Nathanael West, whose Shrike is a Satanic version of the outraged outrager. After more than thirty years, I cannot recover altogether the shock first instilled in me by Fields's brief masterpiece, but repeated recent viewings strengthen my awareness of its sublime vileness. The Fields persona, here the dreadful Snavely, who has just devoured (with mustard) his favorite dog from his dog-sled team, is matched for once, both by his bleakly Arctic wife and by their hideous son, Chester, drinker of the fatal glass of beer.

To the endless chorus of Snavely's " 'Taint a fit night out for man nor beast," the drama unfolds of poor, dishonest people in search of gold nuggets, stolen bank-bonds, or the next fix of elk milk. No repast of Charles Chaplin's equals the Snavely family dinner, with Fields dipping a yard-long chunk of bread in his soup while guarding it from the tears of the weeping Chester, just back from three years in the state penitentiary. Clyde Bruckman, the director of this madness, builds to a catastrophe worthy of Aristophanes, as first Snavely, and then his frozen wife, alternate in breaking jugs upon the head of the wretched prodigal son Chester, who has made the mistake of coming home without either the stolen bonds or the cash thereof. Flung out into the night not fit for men nor beasts, Chester's exit is the worthy conclusion to fifteen minutes of sustained outrage.

Nothing could be more stunningly squalid than every element in *The Fatal Glass of Beer*: characters, setting, plot, pacing. Our laughter is not joyous as we watch; humorous outrage remains outrage. Fields, perfectionist of excess, practices the art of extravagance, of Binswanger's *Verstiegenheit*: wandering beyond limits, clambering out on the precipice beyond which, unaided, you cannot get back. The comedy of *The Fatal Glass of Beer* defies the Freudian definition: superego is not indulging poor ego before thwacking him unmercifully again. Even the traces of parody dissolve when we approach them: the evils of drink and of the city, the return of the strayed child, the ritualized lament for the lost sung to the dulcimer. Nothing is funny in itself here, not even the handful of snow thrown into Fields's face each time he intones the unfitness of the night for all creatures. It is the totality of outrageousness that matters, more even than the audacity of flinging all this at us.

The ultimate outrage is the necessity of dying, the final form of our outrage at being outraged. Genius could not go further than that grand title: the *fatal* glass of beer. When the wretched Chester is flung forth into the snow by Paw and Maw, he is most definitely a corpse, hardly having required the coup de grace of the maternal jug-breaking after the paternal smash. The college boy and the high-kicking Salvation Army lass are no more nor less culpable than the Snavelys, or horrible Chester himself. Fields's alienation effect is absolute, surpassing Brechtian imitations. "A thing so complete has a beauty in itself"—Sherwood Anderson's observation on a woman frozen to death in the snow, her corpse still feeding life in the wolves, is the humorless version of the ghastly sublimity at the fade-out of *The Fatal Glass of Beer.*

◪

I begin again with my movie goer's shock thirty years back, in order to break through to the kernel of the aesthetics of outrage. Shakespeare began just there, with *Titus Andronicus,* which today is as outrageous as ever. A director trying to stage it as a horror show needs extraordinary control in order to prevent the audience from explosions of defensive laughter, outbursts destructive of tragic illusion. *Gravity's Rainbow* falls from outrage to outrage, punctuated very rarely by epiphanies of unwilled pathos, the most memorable being the story of Byron the Light Bulb. But *Titus Andronicus* and *Gravity's Rainbow* are feasts of excess, overthrows or hyperboles, rather in the mode of Fields's second-greatest two-reeler, the obscene *The Dentist. The Fatal Glass of Beer,* though it piles on the snow and the grubbiness of deprivation, is simply a vision of things as they are, or daily life and death in the frozen North with the Snavelys, whose very name suggests slavery, bondage to wintry poverty. With Fields, as with Zero Mostel in Mel Brooks's *The Producers,* I like to turn the sound off and concentrate exclusively upon facial expression. Mostel was the sublime of mugging; Fields, of course, is hidden and crafty, neither as stony-faced as Keaton nor as overexpressive as Chaplin. We watch not so much for the Fieldsian glint or smirk or smile, as for the bafflement of being outraged, of knowing that even the barest expectation must be mortified.

The countenance of W. C. Fields, never more than in *The*

Fatal Glass of Beer, is like one of those landscapes upon which Emily Dickinson found the look of death. Everything, every detail, is fatal in this outrageous, frozen cosmos, where the high kick of the ex-chorus-girl Salvation Army lass inflicts upon the brotherless Chester the inevitable mark of Cain. The crime of breaking the tambourine is the equivalent of brother murder, and suddenly we see another of Fields's sly outrages: the Snavelys are Adam and Eve, transposed to a frozen postlapsarian Arctic, a hideous cosmological emptiness. Fields-Snavely, croaking his ghastly dirge to the uncertain sound of his dulcimer, is a parodic version of the Bard of Sensibility, a figure out of the primitivism of Thomas Gray or William Blake. The triumph of Fields is to have found snowy fields that match his wintry countenance, the face of a Gnostic fallen Adam, brutish and cunning, at once lord and victim of a Hobbesian state of nature.

If this begins to sound more grandiose than grand, I hasten to remind all of us how fatal it would be to condescend to the wily and malevolent Fields, a wonderfully bad and wonderfully intelligent man, who could stand up to the equally formidable Mae West in the superb *My Little Chickadee*. Fields's words show how deeply he had pondered the aesthetics of outrage: of being outraged, and of being outrageous. Consider one of the sublimely hurtful details in *The Fatal Glass of Beer*. Chester, chastened prodigal, is going to bed, tearfully vowing never to leave Paw and Maw (apt names!) again. He and Paw Snavely exchange broken admonitions of tender concern, each urging the other to open their windows a little, for the sake presumably of that fresh night outside, fit neither for men nor beasts. This touching concern for fresh air refigures the governing conceit of the song incanted to the dulcimer by Mr. Snavely, with its ancient contrast of country boy to the wicked town, center of the evils of drink. In that perspective, the goodnight tendernesses take on their savage overtones, intimating the murder of poor Chester by his egregious parents.

"Outrage, outrage—always give them outrage," might be

construed as Fields's aesthetic motto. What is his unique contribution to the aesthetics of outrage? In Shakespeare, the culmination of this mode is in the tragic farce of *Timon of Athens,* perhaps the only Shakespearean play that is still undervalued, in proportion to its enormous merits. The Timon of the final acts would feel quite at home in the closing moments of *The Fatal Glass of Beer.* Outrage at ingratitude and injustice has crazed Timon, but what has outraged Snavely, which is to ask: what, truly, outraged W. C. Fields? The question itself is aesthetic, rather than personal. Fields, one of the very greatest of comic geniuses, was outraged by the limitations of nature itself. There is an outrageous Gnostic aphorism in a Kabbalistic story by Borges, the early "Death and the Compass." It sums up the stance of Fields: "Mirrors and fatherhood alike are abominable, in that each increases the number of men." *The Fatal Glass of Beer* is one of the most American of short movies, and the ultimate outrage is a father's murder of his only child, a son insufficiently self-reliant and savage to survive in his barbaric father's state of nature. This dreadfully comic parable is a grotesque version of the biblical parable of the Prodigal Son. Fields, unwilling or unable to spare us any outrage, parodies in the manner of West's Shrike. As viewers, we are Miss Lonelyhearts in relation to Fields, who is Shrike. Fields is the butcher-bird who impales us upon thorns. Us he devours. But we expire laughing, as I did that evening in the Lincoln cinema. Only the greatest of artists can do what Fields does, which is to connect his outrageousness to what most outrages him, and us, the necessity of dying.

THE WOMEN
THE BITCHES

E. M. BRONER

wondered, fifty years after MGM produced *The Women*, if the MGM lion would appear to be yawning rather than roaring, and if the wit would have gone stale.

Out of hazy memory or nostalgia, or nostalgia once removed, I chose for this essay Clare Boothe's *The Women*, billed as a Hollywood "women's film" with all the women stars then current. My mother loved that film. She spoke of the wit, the humor, the good acting, the happy ending. How could I not choose it in her honor?

Besides, there was the suggestion, among my father's college friends, that Mother actually *looked* something like Norma Shearer! They often referred to one another as movie stars. The lead actor of the group was Maxwell Baker, a dapper, slender fellow with a thin mustache, compared to William Powell. A slender teacher was teased as looking like ZaSu Pitts; a perky woman was Janet Gaynor. The proud, broad-shouldered, tall woman in the group could have been Joan Crawford. The men were often shorter than their wives, less animated than Norma Shearer, not as perky as Janet Gaynor, or slender as ZaSu Pitts, or formidable as Joan Crawford.

These women were connected to the men who mostly had been my father's classmates at the University of Michigan in the early 1920s. The men went on to become professionals—dentists, schoolteachers, probation officers, lawyers, insurance men. Some of the women were dedicated teachers, and others were dedicated to manners and dress. Since *The Women* was a movie of manners and dress, this group must have felt at home with it.

In 1939 Norma Shearer was very much on view. She had just starred with Clark Gable in Robert Sherwood's *Idiot's Delight*. This, unlike *The Women*, which was a comedy of manners, had a different subtext. Where *The Women* kept to the drawing room, the powder room, the beauty parlor, the exercise room, and the dude ranch, the characters of *Idiot's Delight*, unemployed hoofers and acrobats, "fools," really, as in "a ship of fools," were to be found in sleazy vaudeville houses in the Midwest and a European hotel in a nameless country, on the eve of world war. The villains of *The Women* were other women. The villains of *Idiot's Delight* were the munitions manufacturers. But the main point is that Norma Shearer was announced by the Metro-Goldwyn-Mayer lion twice in that year, and my mother was in the audience.

◪

Somewhere along the way, my parents declared their lives historical and collaborated on their memoirs for their fiftieth wedding anniversary. *All Our Years*, they called it, although they outlived the memoir by more than a decade. *All Our Years* was not published, but it is the reference book, the text, in the family.

My father remembers the decade which ended with *The* **159**
Women.

In Detroit
40% of the people were out of work. . . . The automobile
industry, upon which Detroit depended, had collapsed. . . .
There was a general air of hopelessness. . . . People offered
to work for nothing on the chance that they would be hired
later on. . . . The libraries were filled with idle men, listless,
shabby, purposeless.

Father and his group of friends in the thirties would sing this
song:

> *I sing in praise of college,*
> *of M.A.'s and Ph.D.'s.*
> *But in pursuit of knowledge,*
> *we are starving by degrees.*

His life, then, was friendship:

The bad times were alleviated by the presence of our
friends, notably Max and Doris Baker. . . . Max was our
dearest and closest friend. I had met him in Ann Arbor
(while attending the University of Michigan). We were in
the same classes in Play Writing, Novel Writing and Short
Story Writing. He was an aesthete, interested in literature,
music, drama and the arts, and a gourmet. Moreover, Max
had a talent for friendship. . . . Handsome, witty, though
sometimes biting, he was protected by his friends and idol-
ized by women, although he was not a womanizer.

Max would come to our house practically every day.
We would sit until midnight or later discussing current
affairs. Often he would bring friends. Two or three times

a week he would take us to parties, meetings, lectures, discussions, movies or museums or to his apartment.

My parents were young, the movies their joy. But all of their college-educated friends were either out of work or not earning enough to keep them going, including the dapper Max.

My dad wrote:

> The Depression was the greatest trauma our generation suffered. It scarred us, made us too cautious, avid for security, afraid to risk, to gamble.

There they were, this group of handsome, educated people. And there was my mother, self-conscious about not completing school, having left Russia at the age of fifteen. She worked in a laundry, educating herself in night school. Unlike the American women in the group, she had an accent. And she was a housewife, seldom out of a starched cotton house dress, which she protected with a starched apron.

"How was it for you, Mama?" I asked her near the end of her life, not so long ago. She was still in a house dress.

"I was the only one who could welcome all of them," she told me proudly. "If Max suggested to them, 'Let's meet at your place or your place,' they'd say, 'Oh, it's not convenient,' or 'The place is a mess,' and 'I'd have to rush to get food prepared and you know I hate to rush.' No sooner had Max said, 'Bea?' than, one, two, three, I'd make a tuna salad with hard-boiled eggs and sweet pickles. I'd mix together poppy-seed cookies, make the coffee, set the table, and we'd all sit around for hours and talk."

"You, too, Mama? You sat around and talked?"

"I'd sit around and listen."

"And what were the women like? Were they nice to you?"

"Sometimes." Mother turns her face away. "Yes; Rae, the

teacher, was wonderful to me. She always said, 'Sit down, Bea. Take a load off your feet.' ''

"And the others?"

"The men were polite and the women a little bit snobbish."

"Did they insult you?"

"Oh no!" said my mother.

The women, in their fine visiting clothes, with their hats, sometimes gloves—the insurance man's handsome wife always had a hat and gloves—would sit at my mother's table, eat her cookies, hold out their cups for a refill on the coffee, all the time being entertained by Max.

Max would play our piano by ear. He would make up pieces. He would make up languages. There was laughter in the living room. Did my mother laugh? She would smile, I'm sure. My mother would laugh around her kitchen table, telling family stories. She would seem not to get the joke when she was out in public.

The women would look at her hair pinned behind her ears, at her dress from some bargain basement. She never went to the beauty parlor. She never ate out in restaurants, for she kept kosher.

"You know," said one of them, smoking a cigarette, perhaps in a holder, "she looks something like Norma Shearer."

My mother must have felt pleasure at that remark, for she often repeated it to me. Was it her light eyes, wavy hair, sweet smile, broad face? I have long thought of Norma Shearer as my mother. *The Women* showed my mother, Norma Shearer, under great stress which she handled with grace, as Bea might have done if she had had a make-up artist, hair stylist, costume designer, and voice coach in 1939.

Perhaps by the end of the thirties one tired of thinking about the Hoovervilles, the bread lines. Maybe 1939 was tired. More, it was the time when the rich began, once again, to protect their turf. And part of that protection was putting women in their place. Enter Clare Boothe. Enter Clare Boothe's prejudices, omissions, ragings,

162 and preachings, all dressed by Adrian in Technicolor, and therefore quite acceptable.

The Women is about Mary Haines (Norma Shearer), who loves her husband to distraction, who is his archivist, tending to his old hunting jackets, keeping the photo albums up-to-date. She has a daughter, well-bred little Mary junior (Virginia Weidler). There is her cousin, Sylvia Fowler (Rosalind Russell), rhymes with prowler, a trouble-making gossip.

Joan Fontaine is a breathless newlywed, a spoiled rich girl. When her husband wants to live within his income, not hers, she leaves for Reno.

There is ruthless, handsome, glitteringly dressed Crystal Allen (Joan Crawford), a shopgirl on the prowl, on the make for Stephen Haines. The family—rather, the family of the upper classes—is about to be wrecked by that coarse, ambitious perfume saleswoman.

It turns out that all of the families are in danger, that if only certain advice is followed, disaster will be averted. The mother of Mary Haines (Lucile Watson) tells her to forget this adulterous adventure, as she herself had forgotten that of her own husband. "Say nothing," says the mother. "I said nothing. I had a wise mother, too."

Mary objects that this is not like her mother's time, when women were chattels. These are modern times. "Stephen and I are equals. I won't qualify that relationship. It's wrong."

Mary will be punished for her pride.

The mother has more advice. "Don't confide in your girl-friends. I know my sex." She later tells Mary, "Stay alone in your own ivory tower." Friends are the enemy.

They are not the only enemy. It's not men who should be blamed. Men are helpless. It's the lower classes advancing on us, that crude Crystal, and the babbling manicurist who gives away the news about the adulterous affair, of whom one must beware.

At the same time, it's the downstairs maids who tell what's happening upstairs. The cook in the Haines household says, "A man has only one escape from his old self but to see a new self in someone else's eyes," and, "You can't trust none of them husbands." The all-around handy woman at the dude ranch in Reno (Marjorie Main) says the women came complaining of having been beaten, "but most women need beating." She can tell the women what she thinks of them because, without class, you can speak your mind. The women's behavior alters in the atmosphere of the Western dude ranch: they pull each other's hair, kick each other in the ass, break dishes, and become hysterical—behavior that is disguised in the civilized East. The ex–chorus girl about to marry into the group gives advice to prideful Mary Haines: "Compromise! A woman's compromised since the day she was born."

It is in Reno, awaiting her divorce, that the bride, Joan Fontaine, finds out she is pregnant. She and her husband reconcile after she apologizes for her silliness. Another upper-crust family is saved.

Will loving, beautiful Mary learn to swallow her pride? Will she take the advice of the Jewish chorus girl (Paulette Goddard), also trying to climb into the upper classes, to be sexier than Crystal? Will she stoop to the tactics used against her—the cattiness, the desperate gossip? And will she prevail if she becomes like the worst of her friends—disloyal, humiliating them, lying, painting her nails Jungle Red, putting on her evening gown and fighting on their turf? This paean to the Good Wife, the Good Mother, and her ultimate triumph must have been what endeared *The Women* to my mother.

How could she not have wanted to escape her world, at that time in the thirties, with fantasy? And she never understood, and she never got the punch line, that it was a dangerous fantasy.

This is how she remembered in her memoir a time of emergency in the mid-thirties:

> I woke up one night and I could hear Monte [the baby]
> breathing very heavily. He had an infection in both of his

ears. In the morning I called a pediatrician. I told him that
I have a very sick child, that he was running a high fever
and that I did not have the money right now but I swore
that at the very first job my husband got, I would send him
a check. He bawled me out, saying, how dare I ask him to
come without money? I called our friend Max Baker. He
knew the doctor. Max called us and said the doctor was
coming right over. The doctor lanced both ears and told us
that he'd be over again to see Monte the following day.
The first part-time job Paul got, I sent the check.

Mother did not have Monte resting in a canopied bed, with
a satin coverlet, where little Mary joins her mother. "The good
thing about divorce is that you get to sleep with your mother."

Instead, we were living in a cubicle behind her in-laws' grocery
store in the heart of poor, Black Detroit. We lived there while I
was recovering from scarlet fever. Then Mother moved in with her
family:

> Coming back to Mother's like moving into a palace.
> Mother was like the Rock of Gibraltar when it came to
> emergencies. [My brother] Charlie had been stricken with
> pneumonia. . . . Charlie did not work for about a year.
> [Neither did my husband.] Brother Abe was the only one
> working. . . . Two brothers, friends and neighbors of ours
> in Polonnoye [the Ukraine], came to Detroit . . . and Mother
> charged them $10 each for room and board. Mother rented
> them one of the bedrooms. This gave Mother a chance to
> keep the house running. Paul and I slept in a little room
> off the porch which was originally a hall. . . . In the summer,
> Mother slept on the porch but when it got cold she put up
> a cot in the kitchen. It was rough but everyone got along
> and there were no arguments or quarrels.

The Women feeds on arguments and quarrels, insults, com-
petitiveness. The women are not really quite human, in feeling,

dress, speech. In fact, in the opening credit, each woman is introduced by two things: her married name if she has one—that is, her husband's name—and the animal she most resembles. Mary Haines is a doe, as is her daughter. Crystal, the marriage wrecker, is a leopard. Mary's cousin, Sylvia, is a cat. Other characters are a monkey (Mary Boland), a fox (Paulette Goddard), an owl (Lucile Watson), a cow (a woman who keeps birthing, alas, daughters), a horse (Marjorie Main) and a lamb (Joan Fontaine).

In the opening sequences, rather than comprehensible conversation there is a cacophony, a barnyard of cackling, crowing, laughing, shrieking, quarreling women—the speech fast and not decipherable. These are, for the most part, the idle rich and those who would be.

But what is Mary? "She's contented to be what she is," says the one independent person in the group, a writer. The writer characterizes herself as an old maid, with "frozen assets." "What is she?" a friend asks the writer about Mary. "A woman." "And what are we?" "Females." A woman loves her man, child, home. A female is restless, discontent.

George Cukor directed everyone to distraction. Each character is so broadly drawn, she's a caricature—the prowling, malevolent cousin Sylvia; the loud-mouthed, Bronx-accented manicurist; the rich, foolish Countess (Mary Boland). There is no one of depth—except Mary, who manages to invest her role with a certain serenity, dignity, and, when necessary, pain.

My mother touched her hair, still thick and wavy, though white.

"I had hair like Norma Shearer," she said. "I also parted it in the middle like she wore it in *The Women*. Mine was dark and curly, too. And my eyes"—she had the grace to hesitate—"were hazel like hers. I never had her figure, but I never had the time to have a figure."

My father was out of work. Mother remembers in her memoir:

Paul got a few part-time jobs now and then. It was very painful to see him leave every morning, make the rounds and come back despondent. One day he got a call . . . telling him there was a job open as a janitor in the County Building. [They] asked him if he wanted to take it. In the meantime [they said] the first job that's available, we'll get you a transfer. Paul said, "I'll take it! I'll take it!" I had mixed feelings. I felt like he was degraded.

Paul would go to the judge's chambers, dust their offices, and they would say to him, "Never mind the dusting," and would sit and discuss politics for hours. He stayed there for six months and was transferred to the Photostat Department.

When Mother told me about the dusty job my father had, she burst into tears. Mother cried, in my memory, only once or twice, then and when my father died. She twisted the ring on her finger, though it had dug in deeply.

"There, there, Bea," said my father, patting my mother's arm. "The judges were so intelligent and we had such interesting discussions."

Then and later, in the thirties, Dad wrote about his attempts at free-lancing in Detroit:

Early in 1933 I got together with a photographer who had been laid off by the tabloid paper. I wrote feature stories— . . . about the Penny Pantries, restaurants where you could get coffee and a doughnut for 3 cents, a sandwich and coffee for 5 cents, a lunch for 8 cents; covered trade conventions for the trade papers, and sold everything we wrote.

When Roosevelt ran a campaign against Alf Landon and Frank Knox, Max and I made up a slogan which we tried to persuade the Democratic party to adopt—"On the rocks with Landon and Knox." . . . Max was writing ads for a new beer, which he named Regal Beer . . . I became editor of *The Michigan Democrat,* a monthly, and helped to gain civil service for county employees. . . . Max and I also put out an issue of *Beer and Bar* after Prohibition was repealed.

"Did you mind?" I asked Mother, "that Max was there all the time?"

"How could I mind?" said Mother. "Your father loved him."

The group talked about politics, art, literature. They talked of the misfortune that befell members of the group.

Max had a Phi Beta Kappa key. He bought it in a pawn shop.

"What does it say on it?" I asked.

"Don't tell the child," said my mother.

Max had had engraved on the Phi Beta Kappa key a good student once pawned and Max redeemed for himself, "I am one son-of-a-bitch."

"I'd been kept out of the Phi Beta Kappa Society," said Max, "by anti-Semites in the English department at the University of Michigan. I decided to let myself in."

Another member of the group, more of an intellectual than Max and less of an entertainer, was teaching in an intermediate school. The principal entered during one of his class periods, observed, took notes, and left. The principal accused the teacher of making inflammatory, unpatriotic statements. My father's friend was fired and never again taught. He would sit silently, seldom contributing to the conversation. I heard about him over the years, that he was a bookkeeper for the construction company that built the Alaskan highway. When I saw him later his face had weathered in Canada.

Another member had been admitted to the Detroit College of Medicine

and had put in one year. He used to peddle fruit during the summer vacation to earn the tuition, but times were so bad in the summer of 1931 that he couldn't earn a cent. His parents were old and penniless, his brothers couldn't help him. He felt the pressure mounting until it was unbearable. There seemed to be no way open. So one day, he walked into a police station and had himself committed to a mental institution, where he spent some years.

Clare Boothe was ahead of her time in her impatience to recover the past, the past of the twenties, not the thirties. According to my father's chapters on the thirties in my parents' memoir, the unions were organizing in plants, shops, department stores, restaurants. The war in Spain was going on. The favorite films then, like today, were the gangster movies with James Cagney (*Public Enemy*) or James Cagney and Paul Muni (*Angels with Dirty Faces*).

The thirties was the period of the refugee—a line of beat-up cars and trucks leaving the Dust Bowl, citizens evicted from their homes and their household goods piled on the sidewalk, the flight of the Jew and the intellectual from Germany.

My father's chapters had historical perspective; my mother's were the personal ones. The decade began with defiance: Gandhi's Salt March, to remove salt from the sea instead of buying it from the British Crown. About the same time, the Nazis became the second largest party in Germany, going from 12 to 107 seats in the Reichstag. Stalin, in 1931, became visible, taking over control of food distribution in the USSR.

In more than one way, it was a monstrous time, with Bela Lugosi in *Dracula*; with the Scottsboro boys, young black men on trial in Alabama, accused of raping white women; and with the Harlan County, Kentucky, miners' strike. The body of Charles Lindbergh's baby was found, badly beaten and decomposed. And the first concentration camp opened in Germany.

In these early thirties, La Guardia became the mayor of New York, Prohibition came to an end, and Claude Rains appeared, or disappeared, in the film *Invisible Man*. By 1934 Austria was under martial law, the socialist mayor of Vienna had been arrested, and, soon after, Chancellor Dollfuss was killed by the Nazis. That same year Mao Tse-tung marched north to save the army, while Fred and Ginger danced in *The Gay Divorcee*.

The Women bears a resemblance to *The Gay Divorcee*, except that there's divorce without gaiety. Norma Shearer suffers; her daughter suffers. Foolish or wicked, the deceived wives are shamed and they suffer, from the elegant, worthy Norma Shearer to the snake-tongued Rosalind Russell to the bovine Mary Boland. But, as in *The Gay Divorcee*, there is no evidence of poverty; there is no reality.

Within Clare Boothe's world there is only the landscape of competition, of working for male approval, of clawing one's way to success through marriage. This was, indeed, her own path—for she would marry Henry Luce, publisher of *Time*, one of the progenitors of cold-war myths, news stretched and shaped like trees espaliered against a trellis, data twisted beyond recognition.

Perhaps at the end of each decade we shake it off. Clare Boothe shook off Mussolini invading Ethiopia in 1935, Franco starting the civil war in Spain in 1936. She shook off Charlie Chaplin's *Modern Times*, the satire on Hitler and Mussolini (also with Paulette Goddard, this time as a gamine, not the social-climbing chorus girl of *The Women*). She shook off the O'Neill plays, the 1937 sit-down strikes, the bombing of Guernica and killing of its civilian population by German warplanes. She shook off the organizing of the Screen Actors Guild in Hollywood, with four hundred members, including that "villainess" Joan Crawford.

Boothe is more in the tradition of Walt Disney's 1938 *Snow White and the Seven Dwarfs*, with the princess/upper-class woman being deprived of her throne/marriage and entering a limbo, poisoned by the apple of jealousy/pride, until her prince/ex-husband comes to her rescue. The seven dwarfs in the Disney film are less

caricatured than the group of friends—who number about seven—
in *The Women*.

In Walt Disney's fairy-tale land, nature is malevolent, the
trees of the forest attack the wayfarer, and one's rescuers are non-
sexual dwarfs. In the fairy tale of *The Women*, reality is sexual.
Who offers the best sex? What is her titillating costume? How can
one emulate those creatures of the lower classes and reclaim the
kingdom?

When the play of *The Women* was on Broadway, Kristallnacht
occurred in Germany, with the random killing of Jews, the dese-
cration of synagogues, the destruction of Jewish-owned businesses,
the turning to shards of a population.

And what does Clare Boothe, in the guise of the upper-class
mother of the wronged heroine, say about the advent of the Nazis,
the establishment of the fourth concentration camp?

Mary is stretched out on her bed, grieving her newly single
state, and her mother, like Clare Boothe, knowing dimly that there
is a new, chic symbol in the world, comments dryly that being
single has its advantages: "Heaven knows, it's marvelous to be
able to spread out in bed like a swastika."

The swastika was in style. Reclaiming one's acquired or he-
reditary social status was in style. My parents were out of style.

My father wrote, of the end of the thirties:

> Nazi propaganda flourished and grew. [Father]
> Coughlin [the radio priest] gave a Nazi salute at a rally in
> the Bronx and shouted: "When we get through with the
> Jews in America, they'll think the treatment they received
> in Germany was nothing." . . . The activities of the Citizens
> Protective League, the Christian Front and above all, the
> German-American Bund, were at their height. Fritz Kuhn,
> the Bund founder and leader, worked at Ford's for eight
> years. William D. Pelley organized the Silver Shirts . . .
> proposed the elimination of the Jews. . . . The Black Legion,

an offshoot of the Klan, infested Detroit. . . . This was the
climate of the country and of Detroit before the outbreak
of World War II.

And what happened to such unemployed, educated men as
my father, and the energies of such women as my mother, when
war broke out? Max Baker had moved to California, taking a tearful
farewell from my father. He made a home movie in which I, bow
in hair, front teeth missing, am tap dancing in the jerky movements
of the early home-movie cameras.

"I want to remember you," says Max.

I was forever in his memory with pumpkin grin, flopping
bow, and shiny tap shoes. To my father, Max's departure was the
end of the idealism of their college years.

"But why didn't you follow Max out there?" I asked my
parents.

"He was afraid to just pick up and go," said Mother.

As my father had written, the cautiousness, the fear of risk
("The Depression . . . made us . . . avid for security"), was what
kept him and Max apart for twenty-five years. Each year my father
dreamed that he had joined Max in Los Angeles, where he would
be audience to his witticisms, part of another clever and adoring
crowd.

In the meantime, Maxwell Baker, *The Thin Man*, *My Man
Godfrey*, that sophisticated, dapper William Powell, faded. Their
collaborations—from political slogans to the post-Prohibition magazine *Beer and Bar* to an historical work, *The Jews Come to America*—were ended, but until his death, my father would look out of
the window and say, "There's no one like him. No one was ever
like him."

"And Max?" I asked. "How did he feel?"

"He never found anyone like your father," said my mother.
"It was David and Jonathan."

My parents, in Detroit, went on with their less glamorous lives.

Mother wrote about her journalist-trained husband finally being hired in his field:

> After the war broke out, newspapers starting hiring newspapermen. Paul . . . got a job at *The Detroit Times.* . . . When he first started working . . . he worked nights.
>
> I went to work at the Federal Building for the Social Security Office. I worked for two years. Although the OPA kept prices down, we needed more money as the children grew and we needed major repairs on our house. . . . Our boss was a retired fireman who walked around making things miserable for the girls. He knew nothing but criticism—the typed margins were not wide enough, the filing . . . not to his liking. For weeks he would talk about a folder that was crooked or slightly unalphabetically arranged. He went after each one of the girls, accusing, accusing. . . . There had been no pride in doing that type of job. Maybe one has a sense of pride helping someone or satisfying yourself—but this was neither.

Despite newly regained economic security, my mother was fearful:

> After living through the First World War, there was the dreadful feeling when the Second World War began: Darkness is falling on us once more.

There is never darkness in *The Women*. There is the sun on the meadow as the little daughter gallops on her horse toward her mother, who is recording this moment on the new home-movie camera (as Max photographed me). There is the artificial light of the nightclubs.

That is the world that we, in the nineties, have inherited from Clare Boothe, and it is not one of social concern. In Norma Shearer's other film of 1939, *Idiot's Delight*, she tells her paramour, the munitions manufacturer, of the effects of war, of the death of young men, the smear of blood all that is left of their lives. In the movie, Burgess Meredith, as the peace activist, warns the guests in the hotel (including Norma Shearer and Clark Gable) that munitions manufacturing and jingoism are the true enemies of the world. The young idealist, about to be dragged off to face a firing squad, tells them to beware of "things that make us blind, ignorant, and dirty."

He might have said the same about *The Women*. Or perhaps it is *The Women* that might more aptly have been called *Idiot's Delight*.

Although I attack *The Women*, in all fairness I cannot speak for my mother, who found herself in it validated as a wife and mother, even if in the disguise of high society.

But, then, people said that I looked like Ava Gardner, not Norma Shearer.

◪

The bringing of the African to America sowed the first seed of dis-Union.

—D. W. Griffith

THE BIRTH OF A NATION

DAVID BRADLEY

was dining in the freshman commons when the president of the Animal House invited me to a toga party. I almost choked on my Salisbury steak.

This was in the fall of 1968, in Philadelphia, at the University of Pennsylvania. Like many elite educational institutions, the university had been under pressure to alter its ethnic character. The code word for the pressure was "affirmative action," that benign decree of the Equal Employment Opportunity Commission that was supposed to make employers of suspiciously homogeneous work forces alter the situation. The university's work force was racially balanced, but only if you counted the janitors in with the professors. They—meaning the university's decision-making hierarchy—tried that. But somebody got a brilliant idea: instead of hiring a lot of black faculty members they could hire a lot of black students. And so was launched a recruitment drive intended to make the undergraduate student body look less like vanilla and more like chocolate chip. I was a chip.

Unfortunately, nobody wanted to admit that the place had a tradition of prejudice against "blacks and tawneys" dating back to its beloved founder, Benjamin Franklin. All anybody wanted to say about Ben was that he'd fathered a score of bastards. So the stated goal of the recruitment drive was not integration but "cultural diversity," an imprecise euphemism that became the crux of many problems, because almost nobody seemed to appreciate the difference between race and culture—in particular, that culture has a content, while race is just a fact. Some didn't think black students would *have* any culture and expected that after experiencing a few "adjustment problems" they would be indistinguishable from any undergraduate who'd spent his spring break tanning in the Lauderdale sun. Most assumed there was no difference; that black students would possess Black Culture as an unavoidable by-product of the Black Experience (whatever *that* was) and would culturally diversify the campus simply by dispersing into its nooks and crannies. Both sorts of simple-mindedness caused a decree to go out from the Dean of Men that all the university should be diversified— including the fraternities.

The fraternities objected, of course. To them the decree was a thrust at the heart of the Greek system, the right to pledge fealty to men with whom you share values, culture, experiences, education; the right to choose with whom you will and will not share that degree of brotherhood. But such objections—which they rarely articulated so clearly—were widely attributed to simple racism. Many of the fraternities were racist in theory, but in fact the university's own policies had denied them an equal opportunity to develop a tradition of racial discrimination. And in practice, the fraternities didn't have a hope in hell of culturally diversifying, because few (if any) of us chips had any intention of pledging allegiance to a bunch of honkies. Any chip interested in going Greek was angry that the university rebuffed approaches from black fraternities, but most of us didn't care about fraternities—we had our own notions of brotherhood. Also, the Society of African and Afro-American Students insisted that every black student was a member, whether or not he or she paid dues; the problem wasn't getting into SAAS, it was getting out of it. I was never in—not because SAAS frowned on fraternities but because it frowned on fraternization between blacks and whites. Which was a big part of what I'd come to the university for.

◢

I was born and raised in Bedford, a hamlet in rural western Pennsylvania. Not a bad place—though I hated it—but not . . . culturally diverse. There were only about fifty blacks, and a couple of Semitic families, who attended the Christian churches—people said they "used to be Jewish." There were a lot of Christian churches—in that sense the place was diverse as hell.

My personal culture was diverse. Religion and history were big parts of it. My church was the African Methodist Episcopal Zion, the first black denomination in the world, and my connection went beyond attending Sunday services; my great-grandfather had become an AME Zion preacher sometime before 1815, while he was still a slave; my grandfather and granduncle had followed in his footsteps, as had my father, who by the time I was born was a "general officer"—next door to a bishop. Before I began grade school my father started taking me on trips he made to run church-sponsored summer workshops in "leadership education." By the time I went to high school I'd been a frequent visitor to rural Virginia and North Carolina, and had fallen in love with Southern land, Southern language, the Southern black folk. My father was also a historian; he held a B.A. from a black college, Livingstone, in North Carolina, an M.A. from the University of Pittsburgh, had done all the course work for his Ph.D. at New York University. By the time I went to college, he had completed a two-volume history of the church and given me a solid, if informal, grounding in the methods of history.

Music also was a part of it: my father couldn't carry a tune in a feedsack, but my mother was an accomplished singer of German lieder and Negro spirituals. She hailed not from Bedford, but from Redbank, in Monmouth County, New Jersey, but her talents were much appreciated in the hinterland of Pennsylvania, where she often was invited to sing spirituals and explain their form and origins to congregations of angular-bodied brethren and round-faced Mennonites.

And so, when I became a freshman—a chip—my cultural identity was a mélange of white hillbilly, rural Southern black, black Methodism tinged by half a dozen other Christian sects, anecdotal and formal history, Beethoven and spirituals. It was not exactly what people at the university called a black identity. Nor did I think of it that way. I didn't think about it at all. I didn't have to; it was mine.

But I did think about other people's cultural identities—I was fascinated by them. I decided to attend the university in part because my visits to the campus had given me glimpses of the odd traditions of the university's major tribes, upper-class White Anglo-Saxon Protestants and Jews. It was of no moment that these tribes were white—I'd grown up with whites—but I'd never known anybody who'd "prepped" at Choate and "summered" in Bar Harbor, or who'd gone to Hebrew school and been bar mitzvahed in Brooklyn. I went to Philadelphia determined to learn about these alien folk.

I soon discovered that they were at their most tribal when gathered in fraternities, which did have a tradition of religious discrimination. There were Christian houses and there were Jewish houses, or "goy" houses and "kike" houses, depending on whom you were talking to (the goyim said a kike was a Jew who'd left

178   the room, the kikes said a goy was an Anglo-Saxon putz who was still in the room but didn't know any Yiddish). There were even separate-but-equal jock houses. And so I risked the wrath of my SAAS brothers by accepting a number of invitations from the Greek brothers.

The invitations derived from the fact that rushing at Penn began with a semester-long courtship, or "informal rush," during which the brothers tried to turn freshmen into pledges by feeding them and getting them drunk. Formal rush and pledging came in the spring semester; I had no intention of sticking around that long. I felt no guilt about that; I'd figured out that the Greek brothers needed to rush black freshmen to get the Dean of Men off their cases, and I was about the only black freshman male who would even *talk* to them. And they, like the university itself, had figured out that affirmative action didn't really require that you *do* anything; you had to interview people you didn't want, but you could still select those you did. The only difference between fraternity rushing and faculty hiring was that the latter had to show a "good-faith effort" to the Equal Opportunity Employment Commission, the former to the Dean of Men. And so there developed between me and several houses a kind of gentleman's agreement: as evidence of their good-faith effort I would eat, drink, and make merry through the fall—and disappear come spring. But I had never eaten, drunk, or made merry at the Animal House.

The Animal House was, well, *different.* The university had no real Fraternity Row, but most fraternities were situated near Locust Street, part of which the university had bricked over to make a pedestrian thoroughfare called Locust Walk. But the Animal House squatted on the dark periphery of the campus, in the odoriferous environs of the Veterinary School—some said the stench came from the Animal House, not from the kennels. Some fraternities were known for drinking, some for drugs, some for sex. The Animal House wasn't *known* for anything, but rumor had it that the Animal House could not be bothered with kegs of beer or tubs of grain punch—at Animal House parties scotch, bourbon, gin, and vodka were poured from the bottle, with tequila as a hangover cure. Also that alcohol was the only inebriant at the Animal House, it being the sentiment of the brotherhood that drugs were a decadence foisted upon decent men by Commie-Jew-faggot preverts. Not that there was no preversion at the Animal House; resident advisors told coeds they should not visit in groups of less than six—and so did the brothers of the Animal House.

That was about all they told anybody. Other frat men talked of fraternity happenings and bragged that their initiation "hell night" was more hellish than anybody else's (an argument usually won by the brothers of—well, never mind—who all had brands on their behinds) but the brothers of the Animal House barely even acknowledged each other in public. It was said they identified themselves by secret sign, and responded to even innocuous inquiries with the rote line: "Those who say don't know, and those that know don't say." Which of course made a lot of people say a lot of things. Like: Animal House initiation was indistinguishable in form and content from that of the Ku Klux Klan. And: all Animal House brothers joined ROTC to train for the Second Coming of the Confederacy.

I'd heard the rumors. That was why, when the president of the fraternity invited me to the toga party, I almost choked. But I didn't believe the rumors. That was why I went.

◪

The door of the Animal House—massive, medieval, studded with black wrought iron—was opened by a doorkeeper with a head like a bulldog. Before he could bite me, the president appeared. He showed me where to hang my clothes, draped me with a sheet, placed a plastic garland on my head, and ushered me into the main hall, where a sheeted senate of semi-inebriated brothers and a legion of female guests gyrated to Motown melodies cranked out by an all-white band. He poured me a bourbon on the rocks—one rumor confirmed—and introduced me to an attractive blonde who was dateless and only half bombed. She and I proceeded to culturally diversify the dickens out of the Animal House dance floor. I was enjoying her company, and was pretty sure she was enjoying mine, but the music was too loud for conversation; I didn't think I was getting to know her all that well. So I was surprised when, an hour later, she led me to "The Den."

There's a Den of some name at every fraternity party: a dark, comfortably furnished room where couples go to "be alone"—to engage in foreplay without the commitment to copulation implied by adjournment to an upstairs room. The Animal House Den was furnished in a way that made such adjournment unnecessary— wall-to-wall mattresses—but a whirring film projector cast inhibiting illumination on couples petting on the floor along with bright images of Woody Woodpecker on the wall. I can't claim I watched the film, but I was dimly aware, sometime later, that Looney Tunes Technicolor had changed to a washed-out pinkish-white. But it was a long time later before I was in position to focus on a projected image: a black man, his eyes wide, white, rolling, surrounded by figures wearing white robes and weird headdresses. He was pleading—and I knew atavistically for what, and why.

And I had a vision of my past, present, future: first, dancing with this female in full view of the inebriated and togaed brothers— only now their costumes did not allude to the *Senatus Populusque Romanus*; now, here, in this not-stygian-enough darkness, engaged in . . . what I was engaged in, while the brothers gathered at the door, waiting only for the climax of this film or of this female before falling upon me; then, beaten bloody, hanging helpless in some basement where no one with sense would think to look for my body because no one with my body and any sense would have been there in the first place. On the wall, the sheeted figures dragged

the man away. And I went crabbing, across the mattress, scuttling
for the door.

◢

The next night found me in the Van Pelt Library, because
the next day the president of Animal House came by my room to
return my clothes and find out what prompted my impromptu
exit—the brothers had a bet. I boasted of inebriation, and then,
trying to learn what atrocity had been on the Animal House agenda,
added that I was sorry I'd missed the end of the film—the latest
in-thing in porno, I supposed. The president was shocked. "Porno?
That was *The Birth of a Nation*. Hollywood classic. Come by some
night, we'll show you the rest." He left me holding my pants.

I was furious, because I'd run home at 2:00 a.m. wearing
nothing but Jockey shorts and a Cannon sheet, with visions of
excruciation, emasculation, and excoriation dancing in my head,
and because even now, and even knowing that those visions were
inspired by nothing more than shadows made for mass consump-
tion, I remained afraid. I'd not been terrified; I'd been terrorized.
And, if the president was to be believed, by something I should
have recognized. I'd been terrorized by my own ignorance, far
beyond the Animal House's power to add to or detract. The only
thing I knew that would free me was to know the truth. So I'd
hied myself to the library.

The truth will make you free. It might also make you unhappy. The first thing I learned about *The Birth of a Nation* was
that the Klan won. I couldn't believe it; once I'd realized it was a
Hollywood film, I'd assumed I'd seen the scene that frightened me
out of context—in the next reel the cavalry would come to the
rescue. It hadn't happened like that in history: the 1870s edition
of the Klan had in fact waged a successful guerrilla campaign against
Reconstruction before being investigated by Congress and officially
disbanded. But accuracy never bothered Hollywood; the good guys

always won. Which meant that in 1915 Hollywood, the Klan was the good guys.

The second thing I learned made me more unhappy: the film had started as a book, *The Clansman: An Historical Romance of the Ku Klux Klan,* by Thomas Dixon, published in 1905. Worse, the book was part of a trilogy, which began with *The Leopard's Spots* and continued with *The Traitor.* And worst of all, the trilogy was part of a tradition, the "moonlight and magnolia school," which had begun in 1884 with a bunch of sentimental short stories by one Thomas Nelson Page and a novel, *Thorns in the Flesh: A Romance of the War and Ku-Klux Periods,* by somebody named N. J. Floyd, flourished in the mid-1890s with Thomas Jefferson Jerome's *Ku Klux Klan No. 40* and Page's novel *Red Rock,* and continued into this century with Dixon's novels and one by Joel Chandler Harris, that wonderful fellow who gave us Uncle Remus. In all, the Klan was a constant: one encountered night riders gamboling in the moonlight 'neath the magnolias as frequently as fainting virgins.

I didn't need that. Because I'd been unhappy through most of my teens, in large part because I felt sinfully inadequate. In my family, my tradition—my culture, if you will—at least one male in every generation was called to the ministry, and I was the only male in my generation. Yet I knew I could never be a minister of the Gospel, for I was a Christian by culture only, not by faith. I'd long awaited the flash of light that would lead me to the necessary belief; it had never come. But in my first months at the university I'd received what I interpreted as a call—not to the pulpit, but to the pen. It happened while I was reading William Faulkner—*Absalom, Absalom!* to be precise—who I knew was a racist pig. But the book wasn't. The book was beautiful. The book was true. Which to me meant that through the act of writing, through a sincere effort to write well, one might transcend personal and philosophical failings and give utterance to a truth that was beyond the limits of one's faith. Thus, I'd settled on my vocation. But now this racist literary tradition threatened my newfound faith.

These were obscure texts, I reminded myself; nobody had nominated Dixon for the Nobel Prize or *The Clansman* for a Pulitzer. And they had failed the test of time: all these books may have once been read by many, but only scholars read them now. And even the many may not have actually read *The Clansman*; Dixon had adapted it for the stage. It was perhaps made popular by the illiterati. Such rationalizations were comforting to me, for I firmly believed that education cured bigotry. My own mother had thus assured me, following my initial encounter with violent racism—a pair of first-grade bullies chanting "dirty black nigger" to a rhythm beat on my legs with sticks. People who even *thought* such things, she'd said, were uncultured oafs—poor white trash, to be precise. If from such had come the clamor for *The Clansman*, fine.

Only it wasn't fine. Because the biography of Dixon revealed him to have been an educated man. He'd distinguished himself at Wake Forest and then, along with a young Virginian named Woodrow Wilson, had gone to Johns Hopkins, part of the first phalanx of American graduate students. He'd never completed graduate study, but—and this, as far as I was concerned, was worse—he did enter the ministry. Which made him worse than an educated bigot; he was a *Christian* bigot. Which explained why his novel depicted something others did not: the Klan rallying round a flaming cross.

Other explanations of that symbolism were put forth, some by Dixon himself. One claim was that the cross harked back to the clans of olde Scotland. Another was that the cross was, indeed, a symbol of the 1870s Klan. Maybe it had been—but there was little evidence of it; certainly it had not been a universal sign. It was this Dixon, this *Reverend*, who had decided that the Cross of Jesus was a proper emblem for the murder of men.

It was with a numb feeling that I read on: how this Reverend

Dixon—at least he was a Baptist—tried to turn his play into a film, failed for lack of funding, but made contact with a director named David Wark Griffith; how Griffith salted Dixon's scenario with material from Dixon's other novels and other sources, thus giving syrupy variations on themes from Shakespeare an epic context; and how Dixon, seeing what Griffith had wrought, decried *The Clansman* as too tame a title; this, he said, was the birth of a nation.

My numbness did not fade until I saw a reference to the film in the writings of a man I'd come to see as my ghostly griot, partly because he'd had his own misadventures at the university, but mostly because he wrote as elegantly as I one day hoped to: W. E. B. Du Bois. Du Bois compared *The Birth of a Nation* to the invasion of Haiti.

◪

What brought me out of numbness was an allusion to attempts to suppress the film.

Those attempts were the first thrust of activism by the National Association for the Advancement of Colored People, which needed to show some strength to counter charges that it was impotent because of the prominence in it of whites—Du Bois was the only black director. They were at first successful; there was resistance to the film's distribution in every city in the North. The Massachusetts legislature nearly banned it, and criminal proceedings were instituted against Griffith himself.

But Dixon called on his old school chum Woodrow Wilson, whose scholarship was quoted in the film, and whose performance as President proved he still understood the imperatives of the Southern way of life: early in his administration he'd segregated the federal service. Wilson and his cabinet took their heels off the head of Haiti long enough to attend a private showing. "It is like writing history with lightning," the President said afterward, adding that his only regret was that "it is all so terribly true." And a member of the cabinet, Secretary of the Navy Josephus Daniels, arranged an audience with U.S. Chief Justice Edward White, at which Dixon offered the Supreme Court a private showing. "You tell the true story of the Klan. . . . You've told the true story of that uprising of outraged manhood?" demanded White. Dixon said they'd tried. "I was a member of the Klan, sir," White told him. "Through many a dark night I walked my sentinel's beat through the ugliest streets of New Orleans with a rifle on my shoulder."

So ended efforts to suppress the film. "We did what we could to stop its showing," Du Bois lamented, "and thereby probably succeeded in advertising it even beyond its admittedly noble merits." There were scattered protests when the film opened—it was egged in New York City, and there was a riot in Boston—but it played to packed houses everywhere, although the price of admission was two dollars, and it ended up grossing $18 million.

A disturbing story, and I was disturbed. But what I next learned was worse. That in those days there had been a man in Georgia, one William Joseph Simmons, who called himself a colonel because he'd been a private, and who was a defrocked minister— a Methodist, unfortunately. In 1915 he was calling himself a "fraternalist"; he was a leader of Masons in several flavors, Knights Templar, Woodmen of the World, and made his money selling burial insurance to his fraternal brothers. Simmons claimed that his daddy had been a Klansman and that his dear old black mammy had lulled him to sleep with tales of triumphant white terrorism and that while in a hospital in 1911 he'd had a vision: a reincarnated Klan.

Others said he stole the notion, but be that as it may, when *The Birth of a Nation* was announced, Simmons seized the opportunity. A week before the film's Atlanta opening he ferried a dozen ill-met fellows to the foot of Stone Mountain. They climbed to the summit, where they built a cross of pine, soaked it with kerosene,

186   and set it ablaze, a symbol intended, as the ex-Reverend Simmons put it, to "summon the Invisible Empire" from its "slumber of half a century" to "take up a new task and fulfill a new mission for humanity's good and to call back to mortal habitation the good angel of practical fraternity among men."

And it did—with the help of paid announcements for "The World's Greatest, Secret, Social, Fraternal, Beneficiary Order." The first appeared in an Atlanta newspaper next to an advertisement for *The Birth of a Nation*. And behind the organization was a classic pyramidal sales structure in which recruiting officers called Kleagles split a ten-dollar initiation fee—a Klectoken—with district managers called King Kleages and district sales managers called Grand Goblins and of course with ex-Reverend Simmons, the owner of the incorporated Klan. In 1921 Simmons's profit was $170,000, augmented by another $25,000 in back pay and a $33,000 house, which he called Klan Krest. By 1925, when thousands of robed Klansmen paraded in Washington, D.C., down Pennsylvania Avenue, membership was five million—not just from the South, but from Kansas and California, Oregon and Ohio, Indiana and New York, New Jersey and Pennsylvania. The Klan licensed one company to manufacture Klan regalia, another to print and purvey Klan publications—like the official *Kloran*—a third to manage real estate; it owned a small Atlanta college grandly labeled Lanier University, where Simmons taught a course.

And it owned politicians. Among its first ninety members was one Robert Ramspect, later a congressman. William D. Upshaw was another Klansman congressman. In 1923 Earl B. Mayfield of Texas became the first acknowledged Klansman in the U.S. Senate. Chief Justice White had belonged to the old Klan, but Associate Justice Hugo Black, appointed in 1937, had been a member of the new one. And even at that, the Klan was primarily a local power; it nested in jailhouses and courthouses, where the sheriffs were Klansmen and the judges were Klansmen and it was Law that wore the blindfold while Justice watched, and winked.

There was an awful lot to wink at. In 1916, a year after Stone
Mountain, fifty Negroes were reported lynched. In 1917, when
many Klansmen went to war and those on the home front were
distracted by the business of putting down shipyard strikes,
hunting down draft dodgers, and marching in patriotic parades, the
number dropped to thirty-six. But in 1918 it resurged to sixty,
topped in 1919 by seventy-eight. And that was only what was
reported.

Little wonder that 1916 was the beginning of the great mi-
gration. By 1918, 500,000 black men had braved the discourage-
ment of the Southern landowners and the Klan and made the
journey north. In the classic immigrant pattern, they found work,
saved money, sent for their kin—first brothers, cousins, uncles,
then mothers, wives, children. But their success made the refugees
from Southern violence the targets of Northern violence. Whites,
many of them immigrants who had somehow—perhaps via the
vehicle of projected images—learned to see blacks as their enemies
without actually seeing any black people, fell upon them like mag-
gots on easy meat. In 1917 East St. Louis, Illinois, erupted twice
in riots. Only one black died in the first uprising—a young man
who had drifted to the wrong side of a segregated swimming area—
but after the one that preceded the Fourth of July a congressional
investigating committee was "unable to give accurately the number
of the dead." The lowest estimate was thirty-nine Negroes "killed
outright," while hundreds were wounded and maimed. Six thousand more were driven from their homes. In 1918 relatively minor
riots in Philadelphia and in Chester, Pennsylvania, a few miles to
the south, were notable not so much because of the combined death
toll (four blacks, five whites) as because those cities would soon
boast a dozen Klan Klaverns. In 1919, Chicago erupted for thirteen
days; twenty-three blacks and fifteen whites died, and more than
five hundred were injured. Seven died in Knoxville and in Millen,
Georgia, six in Washington, D.C. Troops were called to Norfolk
and to Omaha. A posse comitatus in Phillips County, Arkansas,

killed an uncertain number of blacks—a minimum of twenty-five; some sources said fifty; others one hundred twenty—to destroy a sharecropper union. All in all, there were some twenty-six riots between April and October; the poet James Weldon Johnson called it the "Red Summer."

I was no virgin; I knew that there had been such violence, although until this night I had not realized the magnitude of the numbers. And I had not realized how close it came to home—that while my mother was reaching puberty in Red Bank, the Klan was frolicking in her own recreation park a few miles away, or that while my father was reaching manhood in the town of Bedford, some fine fraternal fellows in the town of Everett, eight scant miles away, were discussing castrating a black man.

And I had not realized, as I now discovered, that after 1915 racial violence had taken on a peculiar sadism. The Omaha incident, for example, had started out as a lynching of classic cause and form. The victim, a black man charged with raping a white woman, was dragged from his jail cell by the usual suspects, who hanged him. But they shot him first and burned him afterward—it was not a lynching but a massacre.

And then there was the incident in Valdosta, Georgia, in 1918, the account of which liberated me from terrorism by obliterating the vision of my own imagined lynching with one more terrible: white men surround a black woman. She hangs, suspended by rope tied to her wrists, from a tree. She does not kick or cry as the men douse her with gasoline, smear her with darker substances—motor oil and God knows what else. When they are done, she twists slowly from residual impetus. Then a man—not one of her previous tormenters, another man—steps forward. He takes out his pocketknife, unfolds the blade. He slits her belly open. A fetus falls to the red Georgia earth. It gives two feeble cries before another man crushes its head with his heel. And then they set the woman— Mary Turner was her name—afire.

◪

I might never have seen *The Birth of a Nation* had I not been trained from puberty to abhor prejudice. But I had, and when I learned that the movie was being shown on campus as part of a film festival, it struck me that, despite my research, I'd formed an opinion based only on printed hearsay and some shadows on a wall. So at the appointed hour I made my way to the designated hall.

I was happy to see that the audience, apart from being all white, was very different from the brotherhood of the Animal House. Not only were they sober; they were serious, notebook-toting, graduate-student and professor types. The film was preceded by an equally serious lecture delivered by an ancient-looking scholar in chambray, corduroy, and chukka boots who gave an outline of Griffith's biography, ending with a description of the director's view of life: idyllic, sentimental, naive, romantic, based on traditional values—family, fidelity, chastity, the Golden Rule, Christian charity. But mostly he spoke of Griffith's cinematic in-novations: the fade-in and the fade-out, the close-up, the montage, crosscutting, flashbacks, pre-shot rehearsals, masking, the use of a film stock called Peach Blossom, which gave the black-and-white an antiquated-looking tint. Griffith had not necessarily invented these techniques, the lecturer said, but he had brought them all together to their fullest advantage in *The Birth of a Nation*. Lis-tening, I began to look forward to a brilliant artistic expression. That anticipation didn't last beyond the first caption: "The bringing of the African to America sowed the first seed of dis-Union."

It got worse, of course. Absent the realization that the "blacks" were whites in blackface, I could not have watched it. By the end I understood how the images of these pseudo-blacks—slavering, slobbering *things* which would make even a merciful God avert His sight—could cause havoc in the cities. Take a bunch of ignorant immigrants, show them a black-faced beast chasing a girl—not a woman, but a child—until she leaps to her death; then show them the man being shot in the back and the bastard being strung up and then dumped on the lawn of a mulatto named Lynch; get 'em fired up with *Die Walküre* (an anticipation of Munich and Kristallnacht, *nicht wahr?*)—then have them salute a flag. How could the audience not think that nigger-bashing, not baseball, was the national pastime? How could they not riot?

But what almost made me riot, what surely made my stomach turn, was the scene in which the intrepid hero bathes the cross in the lynched man's blood—"the sweetest blood ever shed," he says—turning it into a veritable calvary for the Klan cavalry. It made me want to vomit. I didn't; I couldn't; I merely wished to —more, I wished that I could expel the images from my memory like bile from the belly.

The lights came up. The audience applauded. The lecturer invited questions. Someone inquired about Griffith's symbolism. The lecturer responded with a sophomoric discussion of kittens, cooing doves, and bedposts rampant with references to Freud. That was it. I couldn't believe my ears. Or my eyes; the rest of the audience seemed quite happy with the film.

And so I rose—trembling, for reasons I did not then understand—and asked the lecturer quite politely if he was an idiot, or merely blind? How could he speak of symbols and make no mention of the cross, or note that when the lynching starts the cross is a spindly, anemic thing, but once it's bathed with a black man's blood it becomes an engorged shaft, licked by flame brandished by a horseman? How could he ignore the Freudian symbolism of that?

And didn't he know—didn't any of them know—that it wasn't just empty symbolism? Didn't they know that *The Birth of a Nation* had been the birth of a symbol, that the flaming cross, never seen before that night on Stone Mountain, was surely seen again? And didn't they know that *The Birth of a Nation* had been the rebirth of the Klan, a "High Class Order for Men of Intelligence and

Character" with a taste for terrorism? Didn't they know how many black folk died at the Klan's fraternal hands, how many black women were raped by fraternal phalluses, how many families had fled in fear of a fraternal visitation? Didn't they understand what had been inspired by this misbegotten movie? Didn't they care?

The audience was silent, made uneasy by my outburst, unsure of what further form it might take. I'm sure they thought that I was angry. In fact, I was afraid to a degree beyond my simple togaed terror. Because until this night I'd felt safe in the Ivy League, no matter that it was so alien. Certainly I'd felt safer than I'd ever felt in Bedford, surrounded by poor white trash. I'd felt safe because I'd believed that at the university I would be surrounded by people who, though mostly white, were surely not poor, and probably not trash; people whose tradition of free inquiry elevated them above— if not bigotry, then prejudice; if not hatred, then violence. The Animal House, I'd thought, was the exception that proved the rule—it was called the Animal House because it was an unwelcome aberration from a cultured norm. I had been scared out of my toga while inside; I had felt safe as soon as I was outside. And I had felt safe tonight, entering a lecture hall to confront the very images that had inspired my prior terror, because I'd believed that this audience would not countenance racist drivel. But they *had* countenanced it. They'd *applauded* it. They'd pronounced it wonderful. They'd pronounced it art. And now I knew that I had not been safe, that I was not safe, that I would never be safe.

The lecturer was angry, too, although he seemed calm as he decried my objections as the very ones that had been used by those who'd tried to suppress Griffith's magnificent film. He recalled the restraint of Griffith's responses: a pamphlet on "freedom of the screen" and another great film, *Intolerance*, an examination of intellectual prejudice through the ages, symbolized in the end by the crucifixion of Christ. But, perhaps because I'd stayed standing, or because he saw some danger in my face, he added, "What you say happened, happened. But you have to get beyond history and deal with the aesthetics." I have hated men before and since, but I have never hated any man more.

◢

On a cold day in February, twenty years later, I gave a reading for a national organization of writing teachers which had come to Philadelphia for its annual convention. I decided to read from my first novel, *South Street*, a sort of Dickensian Western set in inner-city Philadelphia, to give the visitors a glimpse of life they would not see on the standard Independence Hall–Liberty Bell–Art Museum tour.

I had thought the reading went all right, until the next morning, at the business meeting, when a nervous, thin-faced white woman "responded" to my reading, which, she said, had been so offensive in its brutal treatment of women that it had made her tearful and nauseated; she'd had to leave the room. The organization, she said, should not permit such things to be read.

When she was finished, a feminist friend of mine rose and said that while she could see the woman's point, she knew I would neither write nor read with hurtful intent, and . . . I interrupted; point of personal privilege.

I thanked my friend for her faith, I said, and hoped it was not misplaced. But I believed a writer, an artist, had the right, indeed the responsibility, to create or publish—or, in this case, perform—material that reflected his—or her—vision. If I could not exercise that right before an organization of writers, if I even had to explain it, I was misplaced. Then I went to the bar, ordered several shots of bourbon, and had a silent, solitary fit. I will not recount my rantings; suffice it to say that had that nervous liberal-Nazi bitch been present she would have again been moved to tears and nausea. But it came to me that there wasn't much difference between what that nervous liberal-Nazi bitch had said about *South*

Street and what I had once said about *The Birth of a Nation*. Or,
to put it a better way, somehow my work had made her feel the
same way Griffith's work had made me feel.

The thought did not move me to retract the names I'd called
her, but it forced me to apply them to myself. And—and this was
hard—to Du Bois. Not that he'd ever been happy with his position;
he'd called it a "miserable dilemma." But Du Bois, no fool, knew
what evil lurked in the hearts and minds of Americans; that was
why he'd hated and feared the film. Just as I had hated and feared
it. Just as that poor nervous woman had hated and feared a depiction
of violence done to women.

◪

I had to view *The Birth of a Nation* because I'd agreed, for
reasons I had not yet understood, to write about it. I found I didn't
know what to say. And I frankly couldn't face the thought of
watching that drivel again. Then one morning came a letter from
an old classmate, a fellow chip, who is now director of Alumni
Relations. It was addressed "Dear Alumni Leader"—which I'm not,
so maybe I got it by mistake—and said that the president of the
university had formed a Committee to Diversify Locust Walk and
was requesting "opinions and advice for consideration" so that the
university could "communicate symbolically and more accurately
to ourselves and to our visitors the wonderfully varied texture of
this human community."

Oh hell, I thought, this is where I came in. If you're "diversified," who needs the symbols? And if you're not, aren't your
symbols lies? It made me mad enough to do what I should have
been doing: fire up the VCR and watch *The Birth of a Nation*.

You know, it wasn't all that good. It struck me, watching it,
that a lot of the hoopla about the film is because it was innovative,
not good; Griffith was the first to do a lot of things—sort of like
Ed Brooke, the first black to get elected senator since Reconstruc-

194 tion. (Also, please note, the last.) That long-ago lecturer should have listened to himself; get beyond history, deal with the aesthetics. The results would have been different. I mean, Naismith invented basketball, but that don't make him Michael Jordan.

To tell the truth, I thought the film was kind of funny. Especially the part where the white liberal congratulates the mulatto on wanting to marry a white woman, and then goes crazy when he finds out it's *his* daughter. And I think those puppies pissed on Ben Cameron's shoe.

But to tell more truth, finding out I could laugh at something that used to make my gorge rise if I only *thought* about it made me feel giddy as a geetchie on the first of August. But then came the scene, that cross engorged, and I had another thought: symbolism matters. Just not as much as people think. Enough to cause suffering; not enough to end it, forever and for all. And so, while it is wrong to make war on shadows, it is just as wrong to forget that sometimes shadows lead to acts.

So hear me now, my Klans and terrors: rest easy in your dens. Drink your bourbon and play "Dixie" on your comb kazoos, get weepy over the Stars and Bars, and, yes, sit back and watch *The Birth of a Nation.* And afterward, if you need some air, put on your bedsheets and slouch up a mountain like rough beasts bound for Bethlehem. And if it makes you feel like men, go ahead, burn a cross. But as you gambol in its fiery light, know that that symbol, your symbol, is my symbol, too. And if you should come snaking down with mischief on your scaly mind, this Christian soldier will be waiting with hobnailed heels.

◤

FOREIGN FILMS

Z
THE MOVIE THAT CHANGED MY LIFE

LOUISE ERDRICH

ext to writing full-time, the best job I ever had combined two passions—popcorn and narrative. At fourteen, I was hired as a concessioner at the Gilles Theater in Wahpeton, North Dakota. Behind a counter of black marbleized glass, I sold Dots, Red Hot Tamales, Jujubes, Orange Crush, and, of course, hot buttered popcorn. My little stand was surrounded by art deco mirrors, and my post, next to the machine itself, was bathed in an aura of salt and butter. All of my sophomore year, I exuded a light nutty fragrance that turned, on my coats and dresses, to the stale odor of mouse nests. The best thing about that job was that, once I had wiped the counters, dismantled the machines, washed the stainless steel parts, totaled up the take and refilled the syrup cannisters and wiped off the soft drink machine, I could watch the show, free.

I saw everything that came to Wahpeton in 1969—watched every movie seven times, in fact, since each one played a full week. I saw Zeffirelli's *Romeo and Juliet*, and did not weep. I sighed over Charlton Heston in *Planet of the Apes*, and ground my teeth at the irony of the ending shot. But the one that really got to me was Costa-Gavras's *Z*.

Nobody in Wahpeton walked into the Gilles knowing that the film was about the assassination in Greece of a leftist peace leader by a secret right-wing organization and the subsequent investigation that ended in a bloody coup. The ad in the paper said only "Love Thriller" and listed Yves Montand and Irene Papas as the stars.

"Dear Diary," I wrote the morning after I'd seen *Z* for the first time. "The hypocrites are exposed. He is alive! Just saw the best movie of my life. Must remember to dye my bra and underwear to match my cheerleading outfit."

I forgot to rinse out the extra color, so during the week that *Z* was playing, I had purple breasts. The school color of my schizophrenic adolescence. My parents strictly opposed my career as a wrestling cheerleader, on the grounds that it would change me into someone they wouldn't recognize. Now, they were right, though of course I never let anyone know my secret.

I had changed in other ways, too. Until I was fourteen, my dad and I would go hunting on weekends or skating in the winter. Now I practiced screaming S-U-C-C-E-S-S and K-I-L-L for hours, and then, of course, had to run to work during the matinee. Not that I was utterly socialized. Over my cheerleading outfit I wore Dad's army jacket, and on my ankle, a bracelet made of twisted blasting-wire given to me by a guitar-playing Teen Corps volunteer, Kurt, who hailed from The Valley of the Jolly Green Giant, a real town in eastern Minnesota.

No, I was not yet completely subsumed into small-town femalehood. I knew there was more to life than the stag leap, or the flying T, but it wasn't until I saw Z that I learned language for what that "more" was.

After the third viewing, phrases began to whirl in my head. "The forces of greed and hatred cannot tolerate us"; "There are not enough hospitals, not enough doctors, yet one half of the budget goes to the military"; "Peace at all costs"; and, of course, the final words, "He is alive!" But there was more to it than the language. It was the first *real* movie I had ever seen—one with a cynical, unromantic, deflating ending.

At the fourth viewing of the movie, I had a terrible argument with Vincent, the Gilles's pale, sad ticket taker, who was also responsible for changing the wooden letters on the marquee. At the beginning of the week, he had been pleased. He had looked forward to this title for a month. Just one letter. It was he who thought of the ad copy, "Love Thriller." By the middle of the run, he was unhappy, for he sided with the generals, just as he sided with our boss.

Vincent always wore a suit and stood erect. He was officious, a tiger with gatecrashers and tough with those who had misplaced their stubs while going to the bathroom. I, on the other hand, waved people in free when I was left in charge, and regarded our boss with absolute and burning hatred, for he was a piddling authority, a man who enjoyed setting meaningless tasks. I hated being made to rewash the butter dispenser. Vincent liked being scolded for not tearing the tickets exactly in half. Ours was an argument of more than foreign ideologies.

Vincent insisted that the boss was a fair man who made lots of money. I maintained that we were exploited. Vincent said the film was lies, while I insisted it was based on fact. Neither of us checked for the truth in the library. Neither of us knew the first thing about modern Greece, yet I began comparing the generals to our boss. Their pompous egotism, the way they bumbled and puffed when they were accused of duplicity, their self-righteous hatred of "long-haired hippies and dope addicts of indefinite sex."

When I talked behind the boss's back, Vincent was worse than horrified; he was incensed.

"Put what's-his-name in a uniform and he'd be the head of the security police," I told Vincent, who looked like he wanted to pound my head.

But I knew what I knew. I had my reasons. Afraid that I might eat him out of Junior Mints, the boss kept a running tab of how many boxes of each type of candy reposed in the bright glass case. Every day, I had to count the boxes and officially request more to fill the spaces. I couldn't be off by so much as a nickel at closing.

One night, made bold by Z, I opened each candy box and ate one Jujube, one Jordan Almond, one Black Crow, and so on, out of each box, just to accomplish something subversive. When I bragged, Vincent cruelly pointed out that I had just cheated all my proletarian customers. I allowed that he was right, and stuck to popcorn after that, eating handfuls directly out of the machine. I had to count the boxes, and the buckets, too, and empty out the ones unsold and fold them flat again and mark them. There was an awful lot of paperwork involved in being a concessioner.

As I watched Z again and again, the generals took on aspects of other authorities. I memorized the beginning, where the military officers, in a secret meeting, speak of the left as "political mildew" and deplored "the dry rot of subversive ideologies." It sounded just like the morning farm report on our local radio, with all the dire warnings of cow brucellosis and exhortations to mobilize against the invasion of wild oats. I knew nothing about metaphor, nothing, in fact, of communism or what a dictatorship was, but the language grabbed me and would not let go. Without consciously intending it, I had taken sides.

Then, halfway into Christmas vacation, Vincent told on me.

The boss took me down into his neat little office in the basement **201** and confronted me with the denouncement that I had eaten one piece of candy from every box in the glass case. I denied it.

"Vincent does it all the time," I lied with a clear conscience.

So there we were, a nest of informers and counterinformers, each waiting to betray the other over a Red Hot Tamale. It was sad. I accused Vincent of snitching; he accused me of the same. We no longer had any pretense of solidarity. He didn't help me when I had a line of customers, and I didn't give him free pop.

Before watching Z again the other night, I took a straw poll of people I knew to have been conscientious in 1969, asking them what they remembered about the movie. It was almost unanimous. People running, darkness, a little blue truck, and Irene Papas. Michael and I sat down and put the rented tape of Z into the video recorder. Between us we shared a bowl of air-popped corn. No salt. No butter anymore. Back in 1969, Michael had purchased the soundtrack to the movie and reviewed it for his school newspaper. It had obviously had an effect on both of us, and yet we recalled no more about it than the viewers in our poll. My memories were more intense because of the argument that almost got me fired from my first indoor job, but all was very blurred except for Irene Papas. As the credits rolled I looked forward to seeing the star. Moment after moment went by, and she did not appear. The leftist organizer went to the airport to pick up the peace leader, and somehow I expected Irene to get off the plane and stun everyone with her tragic, moral gaze.

Of course, Yves was the big star, the peace leader. We watched. I waited for Irene, and then, when it became clear she was only a prop for Yves, I began to watch for *any* woman with a speaking role.

The first one who appeared spoke into a phone. The second

woman was a maid, the third a secretary, then a stewardess, then finally, briefly, Irene, looking grim, and then a woman in a pink suit handing out leaflets. Finally, a woman appeared in a demonstration, only to get kicked in the rear end.

Not only that, the man who kicked her was gay, and much was made of his seduction of a pinball-playing boy, his evil fey grin, his monstrosity. To the Costa-Gavras of 1969, at least, the lone gay man was a vicious goon, immoral and perverted.

Once Yves was killed, Irene was called in to mourn, on cue. Her main contribution to the rest of the movie was to stare inscrutably, to weep uncontrollably, and to smell her deceased husband's after-shave. How had I gotten the movie so wrong?

By the end, I knew I hadn't gotten it so wrong after all. In spite of all that is lacking from the perspective of twenty years, Z is still a good political film. It still holds evil to the light and makes hypocrisy transparent. The witnesses who come forward to expose the assassination are bravely credible, and their loss at the end is terrible and stunning. Z remains a moral tale, a story of justice done and vengeance sought. It deals with stupidity and avarice, with hidden motives and the impact that one human being can have on others' lives. I still got a thrill when the last line was spoken, telling us that Z, in the language of the ancient Greeks, means "He is alive." I remember feeling that the first time I saw the movie, and now I recalled one other thing. The second evening the movie showed, I watched Vincent, who hadn't even waited for the end, unhook the red velvet rope from its silver post.

Our argument was just starting in earnest. Normally, after everyone was gone and the outside lights were doused, he spent an hour, maybe two if a Disney had played, cleaning up after the crowd. He took his time. After eleven o'clock, the place was his. He had the keys and the boss was gone. Those nights, Vincent walked down each aisle with a bag, a mop, and a bucket filled with the same pink soapy solution I used on the butter machine. He went after the spilled Coke, the mashed chocolate, the Jujubes pressed flat. He scraped the gum off the chairs before it hardened. And there were things people left, things so inconsequential that the movie goers rarely bothered to claim them—handkerchiefs, lipsticks, buttons, pens, and small change. One of the things I knew Vincent liked best about his job was that he always got to keep what he found.

There was nothing to find that night, however, not a chewed pencil or a hairpin. No one had come. We'd have only a few stragglers the next few nights, then the boss canceled the film. Vincent and I locked the theater and stood for a moment beneath the dark marquee, arguing. Dumb as it was, it was the first time I'd disagreed with anyone over anything but hurt feelings and boyfriends. It was intoxicating. It seemed like we were the only people in the town.

There have been many revolutions, but never one that so thoroughly changed the way women are perceived and depicted as the movement of the last twenty years. In Costa-Gavras's *Missing*, *Betrayed*, and *Music Box*, strong women are the protagonists, the jugglers of complicated moral dilemmas. These are not women who dye their underwear to lead cheers, and neither am I anymore, metaphorically I mean, but it is hard to escape from expectations. The impulse never stops. Watching Z in an empty North Dakota theater was one of those small, incremental experiences that fed into personal doubt, the necessary seed of any change or growth. The country in Z seemed terribly foreign, exotic, a large and threatened place—deceptive, dangerous, passionate. As it turned out, it was my first view of the world.

◤

It is the flattest and dullest parts that have in the end the most life.

—*Robert Bresson*

DIARY OF A COUNTRY PRIEST

FILMS AS SPIRITUAL LIFE

PHILLIP LOPATE

he earliest film I remember seeing was *The Spanish Main*, made shortly after World War II had ended. I must have been all of three or four—which is to say, too young to offer the auteurist apology I would now, that the wonderful romantic director Frank Borzage was simply misused in a swashbuckler. I remember a good deal of blushing orange-pink, the color of so many movies by the time a print got to our local theater. But what irritated me were the love scenes, especially the long clinch at the end, when the hero held Maureen O'Hara in his puffy sleeves. "Cut out the mushy stuff!" I yelled.

What children want from movies is very simple: a chair smashed over the gunman's head, a battle with a giant scorpion. They get restless through the early development scenes that give background information, the tender glances, the landscapes. But

then a knife is hurled through the air and they are back into it.
The kinetic at its most basic captivates them.

This was the initial charm and promise of the medium, as a somewhat astonished Georg Lukacs reflected in 1913 after a visit to the motion-picture emporium:

> The pieces of furniture keep moving in the room of a drunkard, his bed flies out of his room with him lying in it and they fly over the town. Balls some people wanted to use playing skittles revolt against their "users" and pursue them uphill and downhill. . . . The "movie" can become fantastic in a purely mechanical manner . . . the characters only have movements but no soul of their own, and what happens to them is simply an event that has nothing to do with fate. . . . Man has lost his soul, but he has won his body in exchange; his magnitude and poetry lie in the way he overcomes physical obstacles with his strength or skill, while the comedy lies in his losing to them.

What Lukacs could not have predicted was that side-by-side with this fantastic cinema of movement would develop a cinema of interiority, slowness, contemplation. Certain directors of the so-called transcendental style, like Dreyer, Bresson, Ozu, Mizoguchi, Rossellini, Antonioni, Hou Hsiao Hsien, would not be content until they had revealed the fateful motions of their characters' souls on film.

I remember the first time I saw such a movie, in college: Robert Bresson's *Diary of a Country Priest*. The picture follows the misfortunes of a young priest, alienated from his worldly and cynical parishioners, who undermines his health in a quest for divine communion by eating nothing but bread soaked in wine. At the end he dies, attaining grace on his deathbed. Bresson frustrates conventional expectations of entertainment by denying the audience melodrama, spectacle, or comic diversion, offering instead an

206   alternation of tense theological discussions and scenes of the priest alone, trapped by landscape or interiors in psychic solitary confinement. No doubt I identified, in my seventeen-year-old self-pity, with the hero's poetic heartache. But what affected me so strongly at the time was something else.

There was a solitary chapel scene, ending in one of those strange, short dolly shots that Bresson was so fond of, a movement of almost clumsy longing toward the priest at the altar, as though the camera itself were taking communion. Suddenly I had the impression that the film had stopped, or, rather, that time had stopped. All forward motion was arrested, and I was staring into "eternity." Now, I am not the kind of person readily given to mystical experiences, but at that moment I had a sensation of delicious temporal freedom. What I "saw" was not a presence, exactly, but a prolongation, a dilation, as though I might step into the image and walk around it at my leisure.

I'm sure most people have at one time or another experienced such a moment of stasis. If you stay up working all night and then go for a walk in the deserted streets at dawn and look at, say, a traffic light, you may fixate with wonderment on the everyday object, in an illumination half caused by giddy exhaustion. Recently, while watching *Diary of a Country Priest* on videotape, I confess I kept dozing off, which made me wonder whether that first celluloid experience of eternity was nothing more than the catnap of a tired student faced with a slow, demanding movie. But no, this is taking demystification too far. Bresson's austere technique had more likely slowed down all my bodily and mental processes, so that I was ready to receive a whiff of the transcendent.

In Paul Schrader's *Transcendental Style in Film*, he accounts for this phenomenon by arguing from the bare, sparse means of Bresson's direction, which eschews drama and audience empathy:

> Stasis, of course, is the final example of sparse means.
> The image simply stops. . . . When the image stops, the

viewer keeps going, moving deeper and deeper, one might say, *into* the image. This is the "miracle" of sacred art.

All I know is that I was fascinated with the still, hushed, lugubrious, unadrenalated world of *Diary*. I kept noticing how the characters gravitated toward windows: could not their transparency be a metaphor for the border between substance and immateriality? "Your film's beauty," wrote Bresson to himself in *Notes on Cinematography*, "will not be in the images (postcardism) but in the ineffable that they will emanate." Perversely, it seemed, he was struggling to express the invisible, the ineffable, through the most visually concrete and literal of media. Yet perhaps this is less of a paradox than it might at first appear; perhaps there is something in the very nature of film, whose images live or die by projected beams of light, that courts the invisible, the otherworldly. The climax of Murnau's *Nosferatu*, where the vampire, standing before the window, is "dissolved" by the rays of morning light, must derive some of its iconic power from self-reflexive commentary on the medium itself.

I noticed at the time that Bresson was also very fond of doors— in much the same way that Cocteau used mirrors in *Orpheus*, as conductors from one world to another. *Pickpocket*, Bresson's greatest film, has a multitude of scenes of a door opening, followed by a brief, tense dialogue between well-meaning visitor and protagonist (the pickpocket), and ending with the frustrated visitor's exit through the same door. This closed-door motif suggests both the pickpocket's stubbornness, his refusal of grace, and the doors of spiritual perception, which (Bresson seems to be saying) are always close by, inviting us to embrace salvation. Bresson's world tends to be claustrophobic, encompassing a space from the door to the window and back, as though telling us how little maneuvering room there is between grace and damnation. Curious how such a chilly idea, which would be appalling to me as a precept to follow in daily life, could prove so attractive when expressed in cinematic form.

But part of its attraction was precisely that it seemed an intensification, a self-conscious foregrounding of problems of cinematic form.

A director must make a decision about how to slice up space, where to put the camera. Jean Renoir generously composes the frame so that it spills toward the sides, suggesting an interesting, fecund world awaiting us just beyond the screen, coterminous with the action, if momentarily off-camera; a Bresson composition draws inward, implodes, abstractly denies truck with daily life, cuts off all exits. In many scenes of *Diary*, the priest, let into a parishioner's house, encounters almost immediately a painful interview in which his own values are attacked, ridiculed, tempted. There is no room for small talk; every conversation leads directly to the heart of the matter: sin, suicide, perversity, redemption, grace.

I wonder why this forbidding Jansenist work so deeply moved me. I think it had something to do with the movie's offer of silence ("Build your film on white, on silence and on stillness," wrote Bresson) and, with it, an implicit offer of greater mental freedom. A film like *Diary of a Country Priest* was not constantly dinning reaction-cues into me. With the surrounding darkness acting as a relaxant, its stream of composed images induced a harmony that cleansed and calmed my brain; the plot may have been ultimately tragic, but it brought me into a quieter space of serene resignation through the measured unfurling of a story of human suffering.

I could say a good deal more about Bresson's *Diary*, but, first of all, the film has already been picked clean by scholars and academics, and, second of all, rather than fall into the prolixities of scene-by-scene analysis, I want to concentrate on the challenge at hand: to explain how this one movie changed my life. It did so by putting me in contact with a habit of mind that I may as well call spiritual, and a mental process suspiciously like meditation.

The monks in Fra Angelico's order were each assigned a cell with a painting on which to meditate. It may sound far-fetched to speak of watching a movie as a meditative discipline, given the passivity of the spectator compared with the rigors of Zen or monastic sitting; but parallels do exist. There is a familiar type of meditation called one-pointedness, which focuses the meditator's attention through the repetition of a single sound or mental image. Yet another meditation practice encourages the sitter to let thoughts fall freely and disorientedly, without anchoring them to any one point. The films of Mizoguchi, say, seem to me a fusion of these two methods: by their even, level presentation of one sort of trouble after another, they focus the viewer's mind on a single point of truth, the Buddhist doctrine of suffering; and by their extreme cinematographic fluidity they arouse a state akin to free fall.

At first I used to resist my mind's wandering during such films, thinking I was wasting the price of admission. But just as in Buddhist meditation one is instructed not to brush aside the petty or silly thoughts that rise up, since these "distractions" are precisely the material of the meditation, so I began to allow my mind to yield more freely in movies to daily preoccupations, cares, memories that arose from some image association. Sometimes I might be lost to a memory for minutes before returning with full attention to the events on-screen; but when I did come back, it was with a refreshed consciousness, a deeper level of feeling. What *Diary of a Country Priest* taught me was that certain kinds of movies—those with austere aesthetic means; an unhurried, deliberate pace; tonal consistency; a penchant for long shots as opposed to close-ups; an attention to backgrounds and milieu; a mature acceptance of suffering as a sort of fate—allowed me more room for meditation. And I began to seek out other examples.

◥

In various films by Ozu, Mizoguchi, Naruse, there will be a scene early on where the main characters are fiddling around in the house and someone comes by, a neighbor or the postman (the traditional Japanese domestic architecture, with its sliding shoji, is particularly good at capturing this interpenetration of inside and outside); a kimono-clad figure moves sluggishly through the darkened interior to answer; some sort of polite conversation follows; and throughout this business, one is not unpleasantly aware of an odd aural hollowness, like the mechanical thud-thud of the camera that used to characterize all films just after sound came in; and it isn't clear what the point of the scene is, except maybe to establish the ground of dailiness; and at such junctures I often start to daydream, to fantasize about a movie without any plot, just these shufflings and patient, quiet moments that I like so much. Ah, yes, the lure of pure quotidian plotlessness, for a writer like myself, who has trouble making up plots. But then I always remember that what gives these scenes their poignant edge is our knowledge that some plot is about to take hold, so that their very lack of tension engenders suspense: when will all this daily flux coalesce into a single dramatic conflict? Without the catastrophe to come, we probably would not experience so refreshingly these narrative backwaters; just as without the established, calm, spiritual ground of dailiness, we would not feel so keenly the ensuing betrayals, suicide pacts, and sublimely orchestrated disenchantments.

I tried to take from these calm cinematic moments—to convince myself I believed in—a sense of the sacredness of everyday life. I even piously titled my second poetry collection *The Daily Round*. I wanted the security, the solace of a constant, enduring order underneath things—without having to pay the price through ecstasy or transcendence. My desire had something to do with finding an inner harmony in the arrangement of backgrounds and foregrounds as I came across them in real life; an effort, part spiritual, part aesthetic, to graft an order I had learned through movies onto reality. How it originally came about was this way: watching a film, I would sometimes find myself transfixed by the objects in the background. I remember a scene in Max Ophuls's

Letter from an Unknown Woman, when the heroine is ironing in the kitchen, and suddenly I became invaded by the skillets and homely kitchenware behind her. For several moments I began to dream about the life of these objects, which had become inexplicably more important to me than Joan Fontaine.

Certain directors convey a respect for rooms and landscapes at rest, for the world which surrounds the drama of the characters and will survive it long after these struggles are over. Ozu frequently used static cutaway shots of hallways, beaded curtains in restaurants—passageways made for routine human traffic, which are momentarily devoid of people. Bresson wrote: "One single mystery of persons and objects." And: "Make the objects look as if they want to be there. . . . The persons and objects in your film *must walk at the same pace, as companions.*" Antonioni also engaged in a tactful spying on objects, keeping his camera running long after the characters had quit the frame. Why these motionless transitions, I thought, if not as a way of asserting some constant and eternal order under the messy flux of accident, transience, unhappiness?

I tried, as I said, to apply this way of seeing to my own daily life outside movie theaters. I waited on objects to catch what Bresson calls their "phosphorescence." In general, these exercises left me feeling pretty pretentious. Just as there are people whom dogs and children don't seem to trust, so objects did not open up to me, beyond a polite, stiff acquaintance. They kept their dignified distance; I kept mine.

◪

Once, I took Kay, a woman I had been dating for several years while steadfastly refusing to marry, to see Dreyer's *Ordet.* It has been as hard for me to surrender spiritually as conjugally; I have long since become the kind of skeptic who gets embarrassed for someone when he or she starts talking about astrology, out-of-body experiences, past lives, or karma. I don't say I'm right, just that I'm rendered uncomfortable by such terms. And if the exotic vocabulary of Eastern religions makes me uneasy, the closer-to-home terminology of Christ the King and Christianity makes me doubly so—perhaps for no reason other than that I'm an American Jew. In any case, there we were at the Carnegie Hall Cinema, Kay (who is Presbyterian) and I; we had just seen the magnificent final sequence, in which Dreyer "photographs" a resurrection: the mentally disturbed Johannes, invoking Jesus Christ, raises Inger from the dead—not by any optical trick, mind you, but simply by filming the event head-on, unadorned. One moment the woman is lying in her bed; the next moment she sits up and kisses her husband. I don't know which moved me more, Dreyer's own seeming faith in miracles, his cinematic restraint, or the audacity of his challenge to the audience to believe or disbelieve as we saw fit. The lights went up, and just as I was wiping away a tear, Kay punched me. "You see, you can take it in films, but you can't take it in life!" she said.

◪

Sometimes I think I am especially inclined to the spiritual, and that is why I resist it so. At other times this seems nothing but a conceit on my part. You cannot claim credit for possessing a trait you have run away from all your life. This does not prevent me from secretly hoping that spirituality has somehow sneaked in the back door when I wasn't looking, or was miraculously earned, like coupons, through my "solitary struggles" as a writer. (It would not be the first time that making poetry or art was confused with spiritual discipline.)

Every once in a blue moon I go to religious services or read the Bible—hoping that this time it will have a deeper effect on me than merely satisfying some anthropological curiosity. I do not, by and large, perform good works; I do not pray, except in des-

peration. I have never pursued a regular meditative practice, or
even meditated under a learned person's guidance (though I have
many friends and relatives who described the experience for me).
No, the truth is I probably have a very weak (though refusing to
die) spiritual drive, which I exercise for the most part in movie
theaters.

It is, I suppose, a truism that the cinema is the secular temple
of modern life. A movie house is like a chapel, where one is alone
with one's soul. Film intrinsically avows an afterlife, by creating
immortals, stars. In its fixing of transient moments with perma-
nence, it bestows on even the silliest comic farce an air of fatalism
and eternity. All well and good. What I want to know is: Did I
purposely seek out the spiritual in movies, in order to create a
cordon sanitaire, to keep it from spilling into the other facets of
my life?

Films have been a way for me to aspire to a spiritual vocation,
without taking it altogether seriously. *Diary of a Country Priest*
may have helped shape my sense of beauty, but I notice that as a
writer I have never striven for Bressonian purity. I am too gabby;
such austerity is beyond me. In fact, when I encounter Bresson on
the page, in interviews and in his writings, he sometimes seems to
me insufferable. Even some of his films, especially the later ones
like *The Devil, Probably* and *Lancelot du Lac*, have passages that
now strike me as moronically solemn. And, as I am not the first
to observe, there is often something mechanical in the plots of
Bresson, along with other modern Catholic storytellers—Graham
Greene, Mauriac, Bernanos (who supplied the novel on which *Diary
of a Country Priest* is based)—that stacks the deck in favor of sin,
perverse willfulness, and despair, the better to draw grace out of
the pile later on. I think even as a college student I suspected this,
but the very air of contrivance, which alluded to theological prin-
ciples I ill understood, filled me with uncertainty and awe.

Another reason why I did not build more on the glimpses of

214   spiritual illumination I received in movies occurs to me belatedly:
All the films I was attracted to were either Christian* or Buddhist.
I could not travel very far along this path without becoming disloyal
to Judaism. Though I haven't been a particularly observant Jew, I
retain an attachment to that identity; put bluntly, it would horrify
me to convert to another faith. What, then, of Jewish models? Was
there no Jewish transcendental cinema? I think not, partly because
modern American Judaism doesn't appear very big on transcendence. There may be transcendental currents in the Old Testament,
the Kabbalah or Kafka, but Judaism doesn't seem to me to put
forward a particular ideology of transcendence. Catholicism asserts
that death can bring redemption and an afterlife, but it is unclear
whether Judaism even believes in an afterlife. In my experience of
Judaism there is only morality, guilt, expiation, and satisfaction in
this life. Catholicism insists on the centrality of a mystery. Bresson
quotes Pascal: "They want to find the solution where all is enigma
only." And in Bresson's own words: "Accustom the public to
divining the whole of which they are only given a part. Make
people diviners." This language of divination and mystery seems
to me very far from the analytical, Talmudic, potentially skeptical
methods of Jewish study; as it happens, it is with the latter that I
have come to identify.

One of the most beautiful passages in motion pictures is the
ending of Mizoguchi's *Ugetsu,* when the errant potter returns to
his cottage after long travels and a 180-degree pan finds his old
wife sitting there, preparing him a meal. He falls asleep happy,
only to wake up the next morning and learn from neighbors that
his wife is dead: the woman who had tended him the night before
was a ghost. The 180-degree movement had inscribed the loss all
the more deeply through its play on absence and presence, invis-

---

* Even Buñuel, another early favorite whom I took to be antireligious by his parodies of
the transcendent, seems, in films like *Nazarín, Viridiana, Simon of the Desert,* heavily
shaped by a Catholic world view. To turn something inside out is still to be quite dependent
on it.

ibility and appearance. Such a noble presentation of the spirit life, common in Buddhist art, would be extremely rare in Jewish narratives, where ghosts are not often met.

If you were to think of a "Jewish cinema," names like the Marx Brothers, Woody Allen, Ernst Lubitsch, Jerry Lewis, Mel Brooks spring to mind—all skeptical mockers, ironists, wonderful clowns, and secular sentimentalists. Yiddish films like *Green Fields* and *The Light Ahead* do have scenes of religious piety and custom, but even these celebrate the warmth and sorrows of a people, rather than the spiritual quest of a lonely soul straining toward God. Whatever the virtues of Yiddish movies—humanity and humor in abundance—they are not aesthetically rigorous: indeed, it is the very muzziness of communal life which seems to constitute the core of their triumphant religious feeling.

As I look back, I realize that I needed to find something different, something I did not know how to locate in my watered-down Jewish background. I took to the "transcendental style" immediately; it was obviously the missing link in my aesthetic education. Movies forced me out on a limb by introducing me to a constellation of ritual and spiritual emotion that I could willingly embrace so long as it was presented to me in the guise of cinematic expression, but not otherwise. At that point these appeals, these seductions, came into conflict with a competing spiritual claim, indefinitely put off but never quite abandoned: to become a good Jew, sometime before I die.

◪

BEAUTY AND THE BEAST

THE DREAM AND I

GRACE SCHULMAN

first saw Jean Cocteau's *Beauty and the Beast* some years after World War II, at the Thalia, a drafty foreign-film cinema with a tiny screen on New York's Upper West Side. When Miss Rosenfeld, my high school teacher, announced that she was taking the Advanced French class to the film, I was not keen on the plan. To be sure, I liked the source, Madame Leprince de Beaumont's eighteenth-century fairy tale in the shiny pink-and-gold cloth-covered children's book our teacher had brought to class. Like the folk ballads I knew, it had exact details: Beauty had two sisters, three brothers, and a merchant father. Also like those songs, it had, despite sharp outlines, a mystery at the heart of the narrative.

Nevertheless, I craved films that had a more direct bearing on actual events. Next to *Grand Illusion* and *The Rules of the Game*, which were shown in revival occasionally at the Thalia, *Beauty and the Beast* seemed stagy. One of the stills in the glass cases was of an elegant Josette Day as Beauty mounting a flying white horse. Another was of Christian Bérard's set of the Beast's castle, in whose great hall Beauty glided under wall fixtures of living human arms that held lighted candles. Still another showed a mirror with an ornate frame in which Mila Parély, as Adélaïde, one of Beauty's sisters, sees a monkey wearing a bonnet that resembles her own. Looking at those photographs, I failed to connect Cocteau's magic with truth, his use of fantasy to invent the real.

Besides, then as now, I considered movie images to be less consequential than words. At the time I retained few movie scenes but held clearly in my mind Dante's description of souls in hell's dim light, squinting at visitors, who "sharpened their vision like an old tailor peering at the eye of a needle." Of an illustrated edition of Milton's *Paradise Lost*, I have forgotten the engravings, but I do recall—and will until I die—the lines that tell of Raphael as he flew from Heaven to Paradise to warn Adam and Eve of their approaching enemy. I knew at once how "prone in flight / He speeds, and through the vast ethereal sky / Sails between worlds and worlds. . . ." The language caught the emotions. Raphael soared. And although I did not believe in angels, I gave credence to what I saw, heard, felt.

On the other hand, I was drawn to films less for the intrinsic power of their images than for their social content. I liked documentaries that were craggy, unpolished, harsh. *Man of Aran*, by Robert J. Flaherty, which I saw several times at the Museum of Modern Art, depicted impoverished fishermen struggling to survive on an island in Galway Bay. More than any single image, I remember feeling empathy for those islanders who were no longer remote, standing mute in their slickers by sheer cliffs.

Of course, there were factors that kept me from enjoying films. There was the war, and the peace that would be protected, I thought, only by learning. Often alone after school, I read at the

GRACE SCHULMAN

St. Agnes Branch of the New York Public Library, a narrow stone building on Amsterdam Avenue near Eighty-third Street. "I'll be at St. Agnes," I would say to Susan, one of my few friends. I pronounced the saint's name like an amulet, confident my disapproving classmates would not understand.

At the small progressive private school I attended, liberal values were taught but not easily accepted by children of a new prosperity. In that atmosphere, I felt that the best way to convey social protest was to suffer reproach. My fellow students called me one of the grouches, as distinct from the sweeties. I seldom smiled. I played "Sixteen Tons" on the guitar. In league with other grouches, I wrote to congressmen of my opposition to an act that would register aliens, a forerunner of the McCarran Act. At the other extreme were Sandra Flemming's dozen, who met in her family's duplex penthouse on Central Park West, where a butler in striped pants served Cokes in crystal goblets on a heavy silver tray. Once when I visited Sandra, she showed us the black dress she would wear, with nylons and suede pumps, when she went tea dancing at the Plaza. The girls, who were indifferent readers, borrowed class notes from me and greeted me with mixed courtesy and disdain. Ambivalent as they, I wanted to be included, but grew bored when I was. Secretly, though, I cultivated their mockery, enjoying the superior status I derived from guarding my own kind of treasures.

Like the St. Agnes branch library, Miss Rosenfeld's Advanced French class was a refuge for me. Among many attractions, the study of French called attention to the present perfect tense. I have been graduated from . . . I have left . . . I have gone . . . I have done . . . I have been. . . . Perhaps, under the cloak of a present perfect tense, there lay concealed a luminous conditional: When I have gone, I will be. When I have left this neighborhood, with its cardboard executives-in-training, I will find out it's all right to be different.

French gave me exotic names for trees and flowers. Many of them were spelled as they were in English—*violet, columbine*—but to a child of a West Side bricks neighborhood, they sounded as woodsy as the foliage itself. I learned some unusual flower names—*muguet, balsamine*—and identified them in Central Park and at the Brooklyn Botanic Garden.

Miss Rosenfeld was a beacon in dark waters. She stood for moral beauty in an intellectually repressive neighborhood where children emulated parents who measured worth in terms of shiny new cars they dared not drive on city streets. In class we read a volume of Rolland's *Jean-Christophe,* and she stressed individuality. She suggested I read Stendhal's *The Red and the Black* in English, and together we praised the character who could not fulfill conventional expectations.

A French-Jewish refugee who held an M.A. from Columbia, Miss Rosenfeld told me of books that I rushed to read at St. Agnes. Although I see now that I missed the depth, and a good deal of the text, of Balzac's *The Human Comedy*, I enjoyed passages for their meaning to her. Once my teacher showed me a copy of *Les Temps Moderne,* a magazine that contained an article by Simone de Beauvoir. I tried to read the French but soon felt that I was drowning in cascades of new vocabulary and content.

"She believes in—oh, something like the pursuit of an expanded existence as the only absolute, as opposed to the fixed goal of beauty or knowledge or happiness," Miss Rosenfeld said. Then, seeing my blank stare, she added: "Look. It has to do with what you are. Your being. Nothing else is ultimate, not a new dress, not even St. Agnes."

It was one of the few times she tried to provide at least a partial explanation to a puzzling idea. More often, she would send me in search of clarity. In the course of researching my own queries, I realized that answers shifted under the inquiry. My teacher had won me over to investigation as a way of life. A few other students followed her teaching, but many were indifferent, and some were hostile. "My mother says de Beauvoir has marks in her," Sandra said, waving her hand dismissively.

"Can she mean Marx?" my mother interpreted. "If so, there's not *much* Marx there, but there are worse things wrong with de Beauvoir." Her reply bothered me only until I remembered seeing de Beauvoir's book, *Le Sang des autres*, on my parents' shelves. On the whole, they did not discourage my attachment to Miss Rosenfeld, embarrassed by the neighborhood shallowness and concerned about my strange inwardness. Often they said she was attractive, even if I insisted on wearing white sneakers to school, just as she did.

I wore them every day, though. I adored her. She was long-limbed and delicate, and had a silvery laugh that was genuine. Her voice was low. What I admired most was her freedom, her lack of concern about what others thought of her convictions. She swung her arms when she walked. Her very name conjured up roses. Miss Rosenfeld: the garden in *Le Roman de la rose*. The beloved flower in *Le Petit Prince*. Mr. Gordon, our history teacher, called her Estella. Estella Rosenfeld. Star in a field of roses.

Stars fell, though, and hers did when, on the day before the class trip, I heard her say to Mr. Gordon: "This movie is sure to be popular with the girls in the class. Love-love-love is all they think about."

I caught a glimpse of her then. She was smiling, but her voice was shrill. She looked harried, and her gait was slower than usual, her arms down at her sides as though tied there.

I was quieter than usual at dinner that night, and I volunteered for extra kitchen duties to avoid conversation. I had questioned her choice of movie but never imagined it was a deliberate condescension. My cheeks flushed as I thought of her as a pander to my classmates, gleefully watching them swoon to Josette Day's ro-

mance with Jean Marais. When the class met at the theater I was
heavy-hearted, and I said not a word to Miss Rosenfeld.

◪

In that time and place, and under clouds of disillusionment,
I watched *Beauty and the Beast* and felt restored. My memory of
it begins with the small Thalia, crowded for a weekday afternoon,
its bare interior in stark contrast to the mosquelike movie palaces
in my neighborhood, in whose dark, smoke-filled balconies I secretly tried my first cigarettes. The projector flashed its beam, the
picture wiggled until it adjusted into focus, and the stark black-
and-white titles came on. It was a more intense, active experience
than seeing, at Loews or at the RKO, Daffy Duck in Technicolor,
Robert Benchley shorts in black-and-white, and previews of coming
attractions. When those still photographs in glass cases of Josette
Day and the horse, and of Mila Parély and the monkey, were set
in motion, they flooded the picture-frame screen. Their strangeness
heightened the illusion of the fairy tale in such a way as to present
the truth of human feeling.

When the theater's lights faded, all I saw of my classmates
were their silhouettes. Familiar outlines gone, I anchored my sense
of reality on the film's world. By and large, the scenes followed
the tale. For dramatic reasons, though, the movie began at that
point when Beauty's father, the ruined merchant whose cargoes
had been lost at sea, settled his family in a grand but not opulent
country house. Two daughters, Félicie and Adélaïde, had subjugated
a third, Beauty, who bore their insults as she cleaned, cooked, and
tended her weak but well-meaning father.

The two major sets, the merchant's manor house and the
monster's castle, revealed the theme's opposite poles. In the merchant's house, an angular wooden staircase with a balustrade was
the background for family bickering; in the castle, a stone staircase
was the setting for silence. There, standing motionless, were

breathing, blinking plaster statues; the head of an actual man, exhaling smoke, supported the top of a stone column; human arms draped in chain mail lifted curtains at the entrance to a corridor. At the head of the stairs, Beauty's room was furnished with a carpet made of planted grass and a boat-shaped bed covered in gauze. Brambles crept over the walls.

Josette Day as Beauty had a fragile appearance and a strong character. Seeing her in an apron and peasant shoes, I faulted her for catering to her spineless father and for not rebelling against her servitude. At the time I accepted her conduct as an active moral stance: opposing the others, provoking her sisters to mockery, she repudiated the family's materialism and held fast to standards.

I saw her world's evil in mine. When the merchant left to claim a ship that was reported found, the bad sisters asked him to return home bringing them dresses and jewels. I beheld my class-mates, Sandra and Joan, superimposed on Félicie and Adélaïde, demanding Tiffany wrist watches. I followed the camera as it moved in for a shot of Marcel André, as the merchant, on his horse, asking Beauty what she would like, and hearing her reply: "Bring me a rose, Father, for none grow here."

Beauty's characteristics emerged with her wardrobe. In the apron, she was stoical; in a hooded cape, she was adventurous, setting out for the Beast's castle on his flying horse, Magnifique, bent on sacrificing herself for her father. Suddenly imperious, she exclaimed: "*Va où je vais, Magnifique. Va. Va. Va.*"

In the castle, Beauty was glamorous. She wore yards of silk, her hair was loose, her bosom décolleté, the unwanted jewels draped now in her hair and around her neck. She was Beauty the princess on the stone staircase, or in the Beast's park, holding out hands filled with spring water for him to drink.

Then as now, the film's powerful duality was figured forth by Jean Marais, who played the Beast as well as Avenant, Beauty's suitor. As the Beast, his acting intensified the illusion. He had a lion's head with elongated fangs and was dressed in a seventeenth-century nobleman's doublet. Brutish though he was, the Beast had dignity and was more compelling than the human Avenant. Before Beast's first appearance, the wind blew dead leaves and wafted the merchant's hat to the ground. The Beast roared, then came into sight. Coldly, he condemned the merchant to death for stealing a rose from his garden for Beauty, and said he might send one of his daughters to die instead.

With a hauteur that matched Beauty's, he told the merchant: "I am not called My Lord, but the Beast. I don't like compliments."

Pitying the Beast, I was moved by his dilemma. He desired Beauty but never tried to make love to her. When Beauty fainted at the sight of him, he carried her to her room, restraining his lust. Divided within himself, alien to her, he did not cross the boundary between their two worlds. I was struck, too, by his kindness. He sent Beauty to her sick father, trusting her with all of his magically endowed possessions: the horse Magnifique, the glove that would return her to him, the mirror in which she would see him dying of love for her.

As he spoke, bowed, pleaded, and cursed, the Beast gradually became beautiful. The effect was achieved not by a change in Jean Marais's make-up but by his dramatic impersonation of the frustrated Beast, trapped in his skin, struggling to be free and yet practicing a defiant civility.

The ending disappointed me. Transformed by Beauty's love, the Beast turned into the prince he had been and flew off with her to his castle. The moral: Love can change man into beast and beast into man. Before the metamorphosis, however, Cocteau had created an image of a despondent though glorious animal-man who resisted compromise, whether pressured by his nature or by convention. For their valor, Beauty and the Beast were my exemplars.

At the time, I praised *Beauty and the Beast* for its courageous moral stance. Today, as I watch the film on videocassette, I admire it still, but for different reasons and with more complex views of its morality. For one thing, rightness is given no dimension. True, it is an adaptation of a fairy tale, but even as such it resembles many realistic films of the period in that women are portrayed as being either utterly virtuous or, with a few transgressions, utterly sinful. In *Beauty and the Beast,* the vanity of the evil sisters is paramount; the vanity of the male characters, on the other hand, is less distressing. The self-absorbed merchant is one who needs and deserves Beauty's love; the silly brother, Ludovic, plays a minor role; the tale's two other brothers do not appear in the film.

More gravely, I have misgivings about the filmmaker's behavior. Most certainly my doubts pale when I think of Céline, whose novels I read despite my contempt for his fascism. Still, my knowledge of Cocteau's weaknesses would have thwarted me as a child, when I saw the film as an image of a free France, whose people dared to live by honorable choices. Francis Steegmuller, author of a full-length biography of Cocteau, wrote in an essay of the artist's laxity during the Nazi occupation of Paris:

> [Cocteau] most clearly revealed what will always be seen as his greatest weakness—frailty of moral principle. He was no gross collaborator, but the relish he expressed for the "excitement" of the Nazis' arrival, his speedy seeking of the German official license indispensable for the staging of his plays, his sponsoring of an exhibition by Hitler's official sculptor, Arno Breker, can cause little surprise to close observers of his previous career: certain kinds of fortitude were not to be expected of him, while a taste for ultimate novelty in however bizarre a form might be predicted.

In another essay, Dore Ashton points out that during the occupation, Cocteau was one of the artists who "maintained an uncomfortable, ambivalent existence, sometimes coming into direct social contact with their Nazi conquerors." In these and in other accounts of Cocteau's wartime laxity there is no suggestion of real collaboration. Still, the question remains of whether social connections helped him to survive and work.

The reports troubled me. I had read in Cocteau's journal *Beauty and the Beast: Diary of a Film* (1972) of how the crew shot the movie in 1945 postwar France, in the little village of Rochecorbon, where they had but minimal supplies to build sets, where they worked with cameras that jammed and with old, broken lenses. The account resembled Jacques Chabrier's recollection of the making of *Children of Paradise* in 1943, when members of the film crew left Paris for St. Paul de Vence to plan in safety. Over both accounts hangs the question of tolerance for the regime.

As to technical reservations, I feel today that Bérard's costumes are seemingly without plan: in the film's modern version of the eighteenth-century tale, characters wear seventeenth-century court dress. Moreover, in a tavern scene, men are grouped to resemble a seventeenth-century genre painting.

All that aside, though, *Beauty and the Beast* is magnificent. I believe that the film's imagery is its enduring strength and that it is most alive for the detailed precision of Bérard's sets. Unlike the costumes, his sets are thrilling. Cocteau described the backgrounds as "a merging of Vermeer and of Gustave Doré's illustrations of Perrault."

Among those background images are the bedsheets. Hung on bamboo poles, spread to dry, they become translucent screens for shadows. Ludovic, Beauty's miscreant brother, manipulates them like stage curtains, turning back corners to reveal the house, the benches, the family. In one scene the sheets surround Beauty, who has returned from the castle wearing silk and pearls. "Who has done my washing?" she asks, the contrast between riches and poverty reinforcing her ingenuity.

Because of its imagery, the film's passion comes through to

me now as it never did at the time I first saw it. I think of the Beast as one who is torn between animal behavior and manly bearing, lust and restraint. I see him yearning for Beauty while, involuntarily, his ears twitch at a leaping stag. I remember him watching Beauty cast sidelong glances at him as she moves sinuously in a flowing velvet gown with a deep squared-off neckline and a tight waist. I picture him carrying Beauty to her bed, tending her with self-denying care. At times I am impatient with the portrayal of Beauty as a woman who loves the creature the more for his mutilation, and the most when he is dying of love for her. The notion of love as self-debasement, regarded then as a woman's pleasure, annoys me now. It does not, however, alter my admiration.

Jean Cocteau once observed that life and death are, metaphorically, two sides of the same coin, and that in luminous moments the artist can see both sides at once. The comment is fundamental. Often he presents a balance of contraries, each of the opposites only tenuously supported and continuously at risk. In their juxtaposition, both sides are clearly seen: the Beast and the prince; the commonplace sheets endowed with spiritual life; the worlds of manor house and castle as they echo one another; the mirror's monkey and the mirror's pearls.

Beauty and the Beast awakened in me a simultaneous perception not only of life and death, but of how things are and of how—with some magical intervention or fortuitous heightening of the senses—they might become. The process is important in the poems I write now. From Cocteau I learned to explore the actual scene even as it becomes a metaphor, the object and the image coexisting in the mind, both subject to imminent loss. As a child I could affirm only object or image, just as I could countenance only a single view of human endeavor. Today I find his dual vision indispensable to my life and work.

THE EXTERMINATING ANGEL

GEOFFREY HARTMAN

lthough no movie ever changed my life, the first one I saw remains a distinct screen memory. It was not the film itself that got to me (I don't even recall whether it was *Mrs. Miniver* or some other sweet-sad production popular in England during World War II) but the curtain as it parted and went up in the darkened room. I sat with a group of teen-agers in a hall that usually hosted town meetings, bingo games, charity sales, or shows by local schools; this time we were in the presence of mystery. The slow lifting of that curtain stays, while the movie itself has long since faded. I'd like to see a short feature just about the curtain, perhaps also about the screen caressed into life by shadowy fingers of light. Many years later, when I had enough money to occasionally visit Radio City Music Hall, it was partly to experience again the uplift of that curtain, corruptly spectacular, and doubled because of the double show.

◪

Curtains have gone, replaced by flashy ads, stellar logos, and a foreplay of intricately designed credits. But even the last are often displaced to the end of the film, while a lead-in episode thrusts us into the middle of the action, forestalling the title and subverting what sense of distance is left between viewer and what is viewed. We are surrounded by the latest improvement in all-around sound; the screen hurtles toward us from the outset, as if every moment had to be a forceful and pristine repetition of archaic footage in the history of the cinema, such as a train speeding into the audience.

A wish to have the curtain rise again, to re-create a lost feeling of initiation (as if film removed a film from sight), keeps me a sporadic addict. I go to the movies to satisfy and purge my reality-hunger. I want to know what is behind the curtain, any curtain. Fredric Jameson has claimed that "the visual is *essentially* pornographic." Yet what is naked is never naked enough: we need to remove another veil and another, even the body itself. In horror movies (a type of pornography) every canon of visual beauty derived from the human form is violated. Sight is assailed, penetrated as if it were flesh. Buñuel's sequence, in *Un Chien andalou*, of an eyeball bisected with a razor is a limit-image. Does the movie maker wish to restore body to sight or to venture deeper than sight, to the surreal core of the real? "By horrible gropings we come to the central room" (Melville).

No film escapes that groping entirely, even when it is as decentered as Antonioni's *L'Avventura*. It would be like taking the bull's-eye out of the target. The most sophisticated movie is, in that sense, but a step away from the unhappy pornography of *The Devil in Miss Jones*, a morality play that places human desire between nothing (virginity) and nothing (gaping, unstuffable lust). The hell of having to watch, as in *A Clockwork Orange*, also comes to mind: not being allowed to shut things out by the "fringed

curtain" of the eyes. To make the visible a little harder to see, to
experience "the colors of our inner life," seems to require a gothic
episode followed by a grateful return to ordinary color, shape, and
light.

Movie going, as in John Hollander's poem on the theme, is
an entire way of life. In that sense one is changed, but only when
the recognition I have described—the internal parting and reclosing
of the curtain, not once but continually—doesn't degenerate into
technique. We realize that the cinematic imagination, not just when
it is fixed on "that obscure object of desire," as in Buñuel's film
of that name, uses images to go beyond images. The warmth and
vitality of the actors, the intelligence of the director, can outsmart
the pornographic drive, and temper or even exploit its defeat. There
must be, Wallace Stevens says, "a seeing and unseeing in the eye."
What better medium for that than the movies? The lust for knowledge—for exposing everything—is only as great as the lust to have
knowledge coincide with visibles. An impossible project, that, based
on an inexhaustible drive. It simply renews even as it routinizes
mystery.

I have introduced the child's, or rather adolescent's, point of
view. Yet the dreams that pass before us on the screen are not so
easily reduced to incubuslike residues of a past. The magic of movies
expresses the future as much as the past: it attempts to make us
believe they are realistic. No medium manipulates us more savvily
and shamelessly to that end. Though we are rebellious and skeptical
moderns, when the lights dim, and a greater light hypnotizes, we
turn into suckers who sit emptily in a void, waiting for the screen
to fill us up, to transform wasteful or superfluous experience (what
in German is called *Erfahrung*) into a just and decisive immediacy
(*Erlebnis*).

We know perfectly well what goes on while the film is being
made, the massive manipulation of the viewer, the simulation of
personalities or whole villages. But we also know (if not instinc-

230 tively, then through the gossip columns and well-placed confessions) that there are scenes behind the scenes, so that "Hollywood" is a world in which genuine and simulated emotions revolve so efficiently that we must allow ourselves to be fooled, to accept the actor within ourselves, too, that sort of (self) manipulation. The movie hour, like the psychoanalyst's, encourages a timed surrender without shame—indeed, with the hope that the consenting faculty will be strengthened rather than seduced. Bergman's *The Magician* suggests how deep that need for self-estrangement and surrender goes; all his films, of course, do something with the theme. So the moment of recognition in the movies, whether or not it has the power of changing us, maintains itself not only against a magical or meretricious plot but also against the moment of recognition itself. The latter should not become so didactic that it disrupts the charm with a sad and deadly "I know all this."

◪

It has been said that if the stars came out only once a year we would retain our sense of wonder. Every film aims to be a starry event like that. Its ambition is less increase of knowledge than a renewal of the sense of wonder, though the greatest films do both. Scientific advances have always, of course, produced wonder as well as knowledge: movies, in that respect, are simply mobile telescopes and microscopes. But sheerly as a medium, as a random eye, movies are now so powerful that panning anything, from stray people to a window to a close-up of a flower, is spellbinding as such. Our reality-hunger is far from being exhausted, despite a plethora of films that are merely voyeuristic or technique obsessed. Wonder, through the medium of film, can therefore become a wonder-effect, and block thoughtful knowledge. This wonder-effect is a dangerous additive, since it can be used to enhance causes that foster mystification.

To some extent, then, film has to work against the charm of

its medium, one that substitutes spectacle for narrative. Film con-   **231**
tinues to insist on story; it remains indebted to novel and drama.
Yet nonphotographic fiction, in turn, has to resist a hypnotic thrill
coming from within its own mode. We see this most clearly with
the rise of the mystery story toward the end of the eighteenth
century. Two contrary desires were to be satisfied: a growing sense
of realism, related to the Age of Reason, to advances in science that
inspired the hope of controlling nature, the economy, and eventually all human affairs; and a wish to modernize the legacy of
romance, or "fine fabling," rather than to abandon it to the scientific
mentality.

The formula of the gothic novel, from Walpole's *The Castle
of Otranto* to contemporary detective fiction, is that of the mysterious event (murder or its equivalent) being demystified. But
before you "solve the mystery"—which satisfies the scientific, rational part—you allow *other* sensations full scope. The story remains a thriller, aiming to renew marvelous feelings rather than
to reduce novelty to knowledge.

Buñuel's early link to the surrealist movement frees him to
introduce wondrous incidents. And the scheme whereby he controls
rather than resolves these incidents is indebted to the Gothic genre
of the *surnaturel expliqué,* which uses irrational or miraculous
episodes in the service of reason. His mastery of mystery comes
less, however, from plotting an ingenious story than from his
inventive translation of it into the medium of film. Consider *That
Obscure Object of Desire.* It begins with an extraordinary scene:
Mathieu, an elegant Spanish gent, dowses Conchita with a bucket
of water from the train's toilet as she attempts to board. (Often in
Buñuel the surprising incident has the appearance of a grotesque
or cruel joke.) As in the mystery story I have described, Mathieu's
narrative follows to "explain" his act. Yet cinematically the dou-
bling of Conchita in personality and physique (two actresses play
her part) creates a new mystery, while the emergence of a second

uncontrolled happening—terrorist explosions that move visibly nearer to Mathieu's life, until they merge fatally with it—constitutes a subplot unconnected to the basic narrative. The explosions have nothing to do with Mathieu. Their intrusion into his story, however, brings together the love obsession and the terrorism, and establishes Mathieu as a fortuitous target. We are made to sense a teleological momentum that is terrifying in itself. Quite irrationally, the blood of the deflowered virgin and the blood exacted by terrorism link up to evoke a superstitious, even sacrificial plot, cannily expressive of the Catholic imagination as it turns against itself and chooses Mathieu as the symbol of a social order that must be destroyed.

The inner drama in all of Buñuel's movies centers on Catholicism, specifically Spanish Catholicism. Yet it is as a powerful type of imagination rather than as an anticlerical and politically subversive polemic that his greatest films affect us in America. It is the same with Bergman, whose films might be said to show a love-hate relation toward a strict and repressive Protestant mentality. I can't sort out the ideological and the imaginative qualities in Buñuel, and perhaps the difficulty of reducing his films to either political protest or liberating feats of imagination increases their impact. The surrealist rebel and cinematic poet whose 1929 program listed "devastating images, smashed faces, fantastic painting, automatic writing, primary anticlericalism, exhibitionism, unpleasant pleasantries" is not overwhelmed by the embattled artist and social critic of 1961, who proclaims, with respect to *Viridiana:*

> I am against conventional morals, traditional phantasms, sentimentalism and all that moral uncleanliness that sentimentalism introduces into society. . . . Bourgeois morality is for me immoral, and to be fought. The morality founded

on our most unjust societal institutions, like religion, patriotism, the family, culture: in brief, what are called the
"pillars of society."

Though *Viridiana* and *Tristana* are greater in scope and in-
ventiveness, the movie that may be unparalleled in its economy of
means is *The Exterminating Angel.* What makes me single it out
is my tendency to be affected by films that remain realistic despite
the pressure of fantasy and the medium's capacity to blur the line
between realism and surrealism. I was truly taken in, for instance,
by the visionary sequence about the New York subway that opens
Adrian Lyne's *Jacob's Ladder,* scenes demystified though not dis-
enchanted by the Vietnam trauma gradually revealed. (There again,
though not very persuasively, we find the gothic pattern of the
surnaturel expliqué.) And despite the fact that there are many
Bergman films more ambitious and moving than *Through a Glass
Darkly,* that movie haunts me because it presses so starkly against
its realistic frame.

In *The Exterminating Angel,* wonder-devices are used spar-
ingly. There is, in fact, only one such device. Set in "Providence
Street," part of the film's strength is that it accepts its magical
frame without a trace of self-consciousness. While the sequences
are less surprising than in other Buñuel movies, the progress of
the theme is ultra-relentless, and conducted with a grim humor
that is visually rather than moralistically reinforced.

The Exterminating Angel is an apocalyptic fable. A group of
people belonging to the upper ranks of the bourgeoisie are trapped
without possibility of exit in the drawing room of a mansion, after
a dinner party punctuated by disturbing repetitions, strange
snatches of conversation, and some unexpected but not alarming
contretemps. Setting the group up this way concentrates the dramatic effect as in a Classical theater dominated by unities of place
and time. The sense of theater is certainly very strong; perhaps

234   liturgical drama, though in a profane setting, would be a more accurate description. That kind of drama, as if *it* were the disruptive force, pushes here against the larger and freer medium of film.

There are, of course, interiors to the interior of this stagelike room in Mr. Nobile's mansion. Some of these are cinematic allusions: the drawing room central to *L'Age d'or* comes to mind, with its overt reference to Sade's libertine castle in *The 120 Days*. For Buñuel, moreover, interior space is not homogeneous: there is a tricky relation of room to room which satirizes the bourgeois "sanctity of the home." (Think of Conchita in the Flamenco Bar, dancing respectably downstairs and exhibiting herself to the Japanese and their cameras upstairs.) Buñuel is out to *violate* Nobile's drawing room; and as he does so, other interiors open, such as the closets adorned with religious motifs which must be used as toilets or for the disposal of a corpse or for the lovers who sleep together and commit suicide. But these interiors are dead ends: Buñuel has created a powerful *huis clos*, a closet-drama which prepares the unsuspecting guests for the Last Judgment and an Angel of Death whose means are more refined (more bourgeoisified?) than trumpets, whips, earthquakes, fire from heaven.

The entire action of *The Exterminating Angel* unfolds between Nobile's house and the cathedral (the opera, from which the guests have come, is off-stage). We start outside the house, with its mistress firing a butler—other servants, too, feel a mysterious urge to leave, even though dinner preparations are in full swing. The servants are courteous, even humble, but refuse to yield. There is no direct challenge to the authority of mistress or master, just a feeling that must be heeded. They are responding at their own level to a destined moment. Only in the movie's penultimate glimpse of rioting and shooting does the thought of revolution enter.

The high-society guests who assemble to dine and talk are superficial and self-involved, yet Buñuel's satirical glance is light-hearted rather than savage: the foibles of this group are universal, not class-bound. He is after larger game. Having brought everyone together in a single room, he imprisons them by the marvelous device of an invisible barrier. The open threshold between drawing room and anteroom seems blocked. This discovery is not made all at once. As the evening wears on, and the guests prepare to go home, they gradually realize that they cannot leave the room. The hours become days; they are forced to go without food and drink, and life together becomes increasingly tense. Deeper fault-lines of character then appear. The veneer of sophistication (the "charm of the bourgeoisie") gives way to cruelties and superstitious practices. A woman produces chicken feet from her handbag; the freemasons sign to one another; the name of the Lord is invoked in Hebrew. Some blame their host, Nobile, and demand his death as a sacrifice that would release them. Several climaxes occur in quick succession. Nobile steps out from behind a curtain (disclosing another interior), willing to shoot himself with a small pistol. Blood flows from the suicidal lovers who have entombed themselves in one of the closets. After the camera pans momentarily to activity in front of the house—several attempts to encourage people to enter it fail—a small flock of sheep file toward the drawing room and a bear's prowling silhouette is seen. (The bear and sheep were glimpsed earlier on in the kitchen wing, possibly reserved as a practical joke.) The guests are saved from starvation. Then one of them realizes that everyone in the room is occupying the same position as they had at the beginning of their trial. This repetition strikes the guests as miraculous; it gives them the courage to cross the invisible barrier and escape.

It is remarkable that Buñuel can make *us* accept the wonder-effect of that spell. We become accomplices and understand that it does not matter whether the spell is or is not self-induced. It is made palpable through art. In suspending our disbelief, we approach a superstitious attitude parallel to that of the guests, and which lends credence to the screen-magic before us. If the guests in No-bile's house are in a hypnotic position behind a transparent screen, we are in a hypnotic position in front of that screen. Gazing at the spellbound people circulating in the room, we too find ourselves in a "profane" (before a sacred threshold) position, gazing at a rec-tangular stage, or "through" a screen from which the curtain has been removed. The curtain is displaced to farther inside and made into a stage effect when Nobile emerges from behind it to offer himself as a sacrificial lamb. The small repetitions, which at first indicate the inanities of social intercourse but then climax in a Return of the Same undoing the spell, may recall another magical premise of art: that it claims to be the imitation of an action and that this imitation is itself produced with a view to being repeated.

◤

The rituals of the social, especially the bourgeois, world begin to appear as if they were defenses against more primitive rituals, and as a repression whose price is too high. The artist himself does not escape this fatality. In the final act of the drama, located in the cathedral, where a *Te Deum* is solemnly celebrated as a thanksgiving mass, the redemptive power of repetition (mastery through re-enactment) is subverted. As the mass ends and worshipers and priests make for the doors, they find it impossible to leave the church, to step over a resistant threshold. I do not recall a more chilling moment in my experience of film. As we watch, in the final moments, soldiers shooting at the crowd in the square outside, and a flock of sheep, again, filing in the direction of the church, we know that all those dressed-up and dignified people in the draw-ing room of the cathedral are doomed. One thinks of the trapped master class as sheep milling about in an abattoir.

In *The Exterminating Angel* we see through the screen as well as with it. The invisible hand of the director creates a visibly in-visible barrier; and the final ambiguity, which questions the effec-

tiveness of the Church, though not enough to make supernatural **237**
agency a less chilling presence, is: Have we imprisoned ourselves?
Are we the victims of our own charm? Can we break out of the
"open mystery" of repetition?

The liaison between Church and upper class is not salvific but
destructive, even to the parties in this compact. The reversal
whereby it is hinted that the master class will be exterminated,
that they are bound to become not just servants but the sacrifice
itself (filing upstairs for the dinner party at the great house, the
guests already resemble the sheep)—this hint turns the religious
imagination against itself by literalizing its central tenet of sacrifice.
When we remember that the action of the film takes place between
opera and cathedral, we perceive even more clearly a conflation
that subverts both institutions and may not spare the cinema itself.
Buñuel's films continue to be indebted to ritual and repetition:
"The perished patterns murmur" (E. Dickinson). Yet Buñuel knows
that he must turn the wonder and magic of his medium against
similar but powerfully occulted qualities in religious politics.

◪

MUSICALS

The women was sobbin' sobbin' sobbin' fit to be tied
Every muscle was throbbin' throbbin' throbbin' from
that riotous ride . . .
They acted angry and annoyed
But secretly they was overjoyed . . .
                        —Johnny Mercer, "Sobbin' Women"

SEVEN BRIDES FOR SEVEN BROTHERS

FRANCINE PROSE

I was seven years old and for several years I had refused to get my hair cut. Waist length, it required daily braiding, unthinkably high maintenance. But my parents indulged me, because this was 1954, and the milder opinions of Sigmund Freud had filtered down through *McCall's* and *Good Housekeeping*. Parents had learned to their horror that a child could be *traumatized*, but though I lived in a state of perpetual existential trauma, no one seemed to notice. The point was that my haircut should and could be delayed until it would be less traumatic.

Freud might have assumed he knew one big thing about why I hung on to my hair, something about virginity or castration or some combination thereof. But I think that in fact there were many things: vanity, the sheer exercise of will, and also the options for androgyny that long hair seemed to provide. I was the oldest kid on our block; in braids I was a troublemaker, a witchy, almost feral after-school bully, and though the neighborhood boys were only slightly younger, they did what I said. But on special occasions I undid my pigtails and became the precocious, freakish Victorian angel out of a Lewis Carroll photo—the child Rainer Maria Rilke in his ringlets and dress.

Eventually it was decided for me that a haircut was in order, and, faced with implacable grown-up will, I pretended it was my idea. To minimize the trauma, my mother took me to the Best & Co. department store, to a special children's hair salon, more expensive and frivolous than any place she would ever have taken herself. After the haircut we planned to go out to lunch and to a movie. It was intended to be a rare ritual of mother-daughter closeness, compensation for how little time we spent together. My mother worked five, sometimes six days a week, often for ten-hour days—only one of the ways in which our lives failed to match the fifties' domestic ideal.

I loved the children's hair salon with its circus motif. I loved the attention, the light, the soap and warm water, the perfumy aromas, loved above all the intense *femaleness* of the entire enterprise. So it came as a shock when I looked in the mirror and saw the effect of my "Italian" short haircut. Until then I'd thought of myself as floating somewhere above gender, beyond gender, or, more accurately, as being able to change gender as I pleased. I could boss around the boys on my block and then get on the school bus and nurse my hopeless secret romantic crush on a sixth-grader named Anthony.

But in that exquisitely little-girl hair salon I'd been totally transformed—changed forever into a little girl, but not a very successful one, a little girl who looked like a little boy. I had become something else: a new creature with a new smell, a little androgyne who had dressed up as a girl and, as if under a spell, got stuck there with the wrong haircut.

Still in considerable shock, I went with my mother to see *Seven Brides for Seven Brothers;* perhaps it was playing at the Criterion, or the Roxy or Radio City Music Hall. Everything about it was, in those fifties words, *glorious* and *magic*: rugged outdoorsy pioneer life in glorious Technicolor, the magic of Cinemascope, glorious music, magical painted sets that made the Oregon frontier look like a Japanese print, the glorious Wild West. The dancing—who can forget that barn-raising scene?—was exuberant, Martha Graham filtered through Hollywood (not unlike Freud through *Good Housekeeping*), craggy handsome guys in beards twirling "purty" girls in pastel—a sea of swirling crinolines!

I sat beside my mother, completely lost in the movie. Two important, contradictory things had happened to me in one day. In the hair salon I had had an intimation that a whole set of options and choices would soon be closed off, and that many things about my life were about to get very complex. But the movie was reassuring me that the new world I was entering was actually cleaner and more clear-cut than the one I sensed I was leaving. Guys were guys and girls were girls—things could be very simple indeed.

I imagine my mother was happy I liked the movie, that our mother-daughter outing was working out so well. Together we sat in the elaborate darkness of that now-vanished movie palace and watched the film that from that day on would become the favorite movie of my childhood: a film about civilization and sex, about gender and socialization, about the civilizing mission of women—a buoyant, light-hearted, genial hymn to the joys and the social necessity of rape.

Bless your beautiful hide
Wherever it may be
We ain't met yet
But I'm a-willin' to bet
You're the gal for me.

Bless your beautiful hide
You're just as good as lost.
I don't know your name
But I'm a-stakin' my claim
Unless your eyes is crossed.

—Johnny Mercer,
"Bless Your Beautiful Hide"

Not to put too fine a point on it, *Seven Brides for Seven Brothers* is, it seems to me now, one of the most repulsive movies about men and women and sexual relations that has ever been made. Though film historians will correct me, it is still, as far as I know, the only extant musical about rape. (It is also, though again I may be wrong, the only musical that quotes Plutarch in its most famous song.) The script is based on a Stephen Vincent Benét story, "The Sobbin' Women," which—some will have already guessed— is in turn based on the story of the Roman rape of the Sabine women.

In the movie, seven lusty mountain men decide they're needin' wives and just go down to town and throw blankets over the girls and toss 'em over their shoulders and take 'em back home to the mountains. In some ways it is more disturbing than another movie I saw recently, a horror film, made around the same time, which devoted a rather large percentage of its footage to scenes of women being ritually dismembered in bathtubs. The horror film was, to say the least, honest about declaring its intentions, less covert and invidious—and in any case, my mother wouldn't have taken me to see *Feast of Blood*.

What's chilling about *Seven Brothers for Seven Brothers* is its innocence, its fifties naiveté, its unexamined goodheartedness: what an insidious, sinister piece of fluff it has come to seem over time. When I watch it, thirty-six years later, my mind keeps shifting inappropriately to that scene from *A Clockwork Orange*, that ballet of violence choreographed to "Singin' in the Rain."

If Freud's theories had sifted down through *Good House-keeping,* there were still, apparently, sheltered corners of Hollywood that his disturbing ideas about motivation and instinct had not yet reached. *Seven Brides for Seven Brothers* is campily pre-Freudian—that is, it comes from an era when the general assumption was (as it is becoming once again) that nice people weren't dirty-minded. The scene in which six unmarried brothers linger outside newlywed brother Howard Keel's bedroom on his wedding night just would not *wash* in these sniggering times, though I do recall a more recent movie, *Reds,* in which the sexual fade-to-black is avoided by cutting to the couple's exiled-from-the-bedroom dog.

There *is* sex in *Seven Brides*—healthy married sex. After that wedding night, Jane Powell (here with a startling resemblance to Dolly Parton and what looks like a twelve-inch waist) is so energized by one night with Howard Keel that she gets up and makes all seven brothers porridge, pancakes, muffins, bacon, coffee: breakfast extravaganza. It is sex like a swim, like a shower—it puts you in a good mood. There is also sex that can be withheld for power: after the six bachelor brothers kidnap wives, the women barricade themselves in the house until spring, when the men are suitably contrite and the snows have melted so that the preacher is able to come up the mountain from town and legalize the proceedings.

In fact, it is not uncommon for some of the favorite things of our childhood and youth to seem, in retrospect, immature, embarrassing, banal, sentimental, etc. (Adult Readers of Hermann Hesse is a fairly small constituency.) But it's less usual to come across old cultural loves that seem not only benighted but almost unimaginably vile. (It's uncommon but hardly rare: an obvious example might be *Gigi,* another colorful, much-loved musical which from the perspective of age appears to have been about the molestation of pre-adolescent girls.)

And yet I and many of my friends—in fact, most of the women

I know in their late thirties and early forties—remember *Seven Brides for Seven Brothers* as a movie we saw as little girls, a movie that we loved. What was it that we were responding to? What was it that we were seeing?

> *Tell ya 'bout them sobbin' women*
> *Who lived in the Roman days*
> *It seemed that they all went swimmin'*
> *While their men was off to graze.*
> *Well, the Roman troop was ridin' by*
> *And saw them in their me-oh-my*
> *So they took 'em all back home to dry*
> *At least that's what Plutarch says.*
>
> —Johnny Mercer,
> "Sobbin' Women"

Given what we have learned since 1954, how we've come to view the world in general and gender roles in specific, the plot of *Seven Brides for Seven Brothers* sounds less like a coherent narrative structure than like a succession of separate moments, each outdoing the previous moment for camp and sublime unselfconscious bad taste.

The film begins with the bouncy, ersatz-Copland melody that will become "Bless Your Beautiful Hide" playing in the background, while the buckskinned and bearded Adam (Howard Keel) drives into town; he's come to buy twenty-five pounds of chewing tobacco and, if possible, a wife—preferably a "widow woman" used to hard work. Without a woman's domestic touch, the cabin where Adam and his six brothers live is, by his own account, a "pigsty." Cruising the already "promised" marriageable girls (his bold up-and-down looks make them blush and giggle—oh, Lordy!) and issuing pronouncements like "a girl has no right to stay single," Adam bursts into song.

"Bless Your Beautiful Hide" is one of those generalized   **247**
musical-comedy hymns to the female sex, here at a more mature
(or possibly flayed and tanned) stage than the "little girls" for
whom Maurice Chevalier leeringly thanked heaven at the beginning
of *Gigi*. (When I watched the movie on videotape recently with
my husband and younger son, they both refused to believe that
the lyric was really "Bless your beautiful hide." My husband insisted that it was "heart," my son that it was "eyes.") In a kind
of musical bridge, an interlude in the song, Keel courts and marries
Jane Powell, who when she sees him nearly drops the ax with which
she'd been capably chopping wood and goes instantaneously gaga
in the face of the visible and undeniable full force of his manhood.
After a stop along the way for Powell to sing a long, dreamy song
to love, and dance by herself through the painted woods like the
heroine of a large-budget Bombay Hindi musical, the newlyweds
arrive at home—and to the reality of a "pigsty" teeming with
seven ill-mannered brawling brothers.

But after one night with her new husband, our heroine's up
and awake at dawn, not only doing serious breakfast for eight but
(like the popular current image of the female sports reporter) ignoring delicate male sensibilities, disregarding male modesty, and
tyrannizing the hapless male into surrendering some vital part of
himself, in this case the brothers' long winter underwear, which,
Powell has noticed (one shudders to imagine how) desperately needs
a-washin'. In almost no time, a Snow White regimen has evolved—
the difference being that this Snow White has rewarding monog-
amous sex with the eldest dwarf. Everyone lives together in harmony and with a remarkable absence of any sexual tension
whatsoever until the boys go down to town for the fateful barn-
raising dance.

Though one might observe that the mountain men seem less
turned on by the pretty girls than by their Big Number with the
girls' townie fiancés—one of those high-kicking dance rituals of

male rivalry and competition that would later reach an apotheosis with *West Side Story*'s Sharks and Jets—it's the girls to whom the brothers ultimately lose their hearts. Each girl represents a slightly different physical type (like the madam of a bordello, the casting director offers variety), but all of them are so uniformly squeaky clean and perky and good that the easiest way to tell them apart is by the colors of their dresses: each comes in a different pastel shade, like some unhealthful fifties candy.

The girls, however, are "promised"—and not to these overgrown yetis from up in the hills. Lots of lovesick moping and gloomy baritone moaning ensues ("I'm a lonesome polecat . . .") until at last one of the brothers threatens to abandon mountain life for the uxorious comforts of town. This threat to the status quo forces big brother Adam's hand and leads to the pivotal scene and the memorable song, that history of courtship mores à la Johnny Mercer, "Sobbin' Women."

Seconds into the song's introduction one begins cringing, as brother Adam explains and exhorts: "Do like the Romans did with the Sobbin, or Sabine women, or whatever they were called. The Romans were in the same fix you're in. They were opening up new territory and women were scarce, just like here. So what did the Romans do? They went down there and they carried 'em off. If you can't do as good as a bunch of old Romans—you're no brothers of mine."

The frisson of irritation, exhaustion, and faintly nauseating familiarity that the contemporary audience may have begun to feel intensifies with every verse until, charged up and inspired by this anthem to proper manly behavior, the boys saddle up the horses. In six separate episodes of what some feminist sorehead might mistake for forcible criminal abduction, we see the men luring the unsuspecting young women outside onto their porches or overtaking them in their bedrooms, wrapping quilts around them and lugging off their writhing, squealing human bundles. True to history, and to their credit, the girls do a good deal of shrieking, **249** especially when an avalanche seals them off from their pursuing menfolk—fiancés, brothers, and fathers.

Unsurprisingly, Jane Powell is horrified to realize that her clean-underwear regime has failed to change her brother-in-laws' basic primitive nature. She gives the traumatized kidnaped girls a crash course in sexual withholding (it's a kind of tribal thing, the exchange of sex for a wedding ring, what one hears about fifties courtship). Interestingly, this enforced period of abstinence is as difficult for the women as for the men. In one scene, a roomful of girls in revealing camisoles and ruffled pantaloons writhe on their beds and express their longing in song, a sort of frontier "I Feel Pretty." Where did Broadway and Hollywood pick up this idée fixe of a roomful of pretty girls singing and dancing around in their underwear?

Spring, the season of fake blossoms and real calves, brings mating, reconciliation, and a new baby for Powell and Keel, an infant daughter who even from the cradle is girl enough to complete the civilizing process. Keel, who has been stewing in exile higher up on the mountain, feeling wrongly underappreciated for his role in the girls' abduction, suddenly realizes how *he* would feel if someone were to abduct his daughter—an ethical deduction that owes less to Classical or biblical moral thinking than to the more sobering of Engels's theories on the origin of family as property. And so our story ends in a joyous sextuple wedding that may remind the jaded, jumpy, and by this point frankly appalled nineties' viewer of those creepy mass marriages staged by the Reverend Sun Myung Moon.

The VCR doesn't lie—or it doesn't lie very much. Even if we allow for the peculiar omissions—half the frame, for example— necessitated when Cinemascope is reduced for the TV screen, what we see now is more or less what we saw as children. But if that was what we saw—what was it that we loved?

Partly it was the pastels, the pretty dancers and frilly dresses, the peculiar mystical pull that all had and still seems to have for the young female psyche. It has become a cliché by now to speak of the feminist mothers (that is, ourselves and our friends) who vowed to raise their daughters surrounded by dolls *and* trucks, and were frustrated and mystified by their daughters' preference from birth for dolls—their inexplicable, apparently inborn attraction for nail polish, lace, and the color pink.

Partly it was movie romance, the promise of a mountain man of our own, a big brute who would naturally know how to learn what we would instinctively know how to teach him. Though Keel and Powell make a remarkably unsexy couple, there's something about their connection—the instantaneous attraction, the chemistry of male and female—that does hint at what we did and do find sexually compelling.

Partly it was history. We were the young products of our sociopolitical era, and we weren't too young to sense that Jane Powell was the perfected ideal of the fifties housewife—pert, tireless, sensible, uncomplaining, hardworking, sexually available, always cheerful and merry. And those of us who might have had doubts (the same doubts that I was having on that day after my haircut) about how we were meant to effect this personal transformation from the neighborhood punchball team captain into a pancake-making machine in an apron and gingham dress were so *relieved* to learn that love and the right man would make it not only possible but *easy*. One "riotous" ride in a blanket over the right mountain man's shoulder (and one night in his bed) would magically dispel any troubling uncertainties about what else we might possibly do with our lives. All of this floated around, inchoate, in our seven-year-old brains.

More inchoate still were the stirrings of female sexuality, with its cloudy gothic elements of submission and surrender. No one had to explain to me why the seven brothers were *cuter* than the girls' pallid fiancés from town. No one obliged me to think this, no one forced me to *love* this movie or to watch it again and again. There was something in the film that spoke to us, fascinated and attracted us. This does not—I repeat, does not—mean that women want to be raped.

It is more than a little confusing. My eight-year-old son (an ironic child, anyway) thinks the movie is boring, beneath contempt. He thinks it's ridiculous that Jane Powell would want to marry a geek like Howard Keel (with that embarrassing baritone vibrato!) just a few minutes after meeting him. But a friend who loved the movie as a child reports that her nine-year-old daughter loves it, too, and watches it again and again, on tape. It's one of her favorite films. When my friend asks her daughter what it is exactly she likes, the little girl cannot explain.

The contradictions seem endless. My mother was a doctor, I was the androgynous seven-year-old neighborhood tough, but we sat and watched this movie about wasp-waisted superhousewives as if it were the story of our lives and the key to our future. Basically it was thanks to Freud that I was in that theater in the first place, but the movie came to us from a world in which there was no Freud and no unconscious and everything (including rape) was what it seemed: good, clean, old-fashioned fun.

The life (and the vision of marriage) portrayed in that movie could hardly be further from anything I know, but I am married to a man (named Howard!) whom English-department secretaries have mistaken for a motorcycle gang member, and when I married him—after essentially falling in love at first sight—I left the city and went with him to live up in the mountains. As much as I loved it, the movie was hardly strong enough to imprint itself on my consciousness the way the face of the first creature they see is said to imprint itself on baby ducks. Yet how to explain the odd correspondences between that unreal vision of the world and my current life? And how to explain an atmosphere of such gross innocence and naiveté that no one then apparently realized what this movie was *about*?

The world has changed profoundly since that day when I got my hair cut and went with my mother to see *Seven Brides for Seven Brothers*—or changed just enough so that, all these years later, I am astonished and shocked to see that a beloved childhood film was a glorification of rape. But what's more shocking is how much of our culture has changed very little indeed. One could (tediously) list the major studio films, released every week, that endeavor to entertain by doing fairly frightful things to women, which make fifties musicals look like the harmless, or at least unconscious, confections that they were. One could write books (and books have been written) about the ways in which the brutal treatment of women is not taken seriously or viewed as a critical social problem.

As much as it amazes me that *Seven Brides for Seven Brothers* was ever made, it wouldn't surprise me a bit to hear that Hollywood is right at this minute planning a remake.

◼

THE WIZARD OF OZ

TERRY McMILLAN

grew up in a small industrial town in the thumb of Michigan: Port Huron. We had barely gotten used to the idea of color TV. I can guess how old I was when I first saw *The Wizard of Oz* on TV because I remember the house we lived in when I was still in elementary school. It was a huge, drafty house that had a fireplace we never once lit. We lived on two acres of land, and at the edge of the backyard was the woods, which I always thought of as a forest. We had weeping willow trees, plum and pear trees, and blackberry bushes. We could not see into our neighbors' homes. Railroad tracks were part of our front yard, and the house shook when a train passed—twice, sometimes three times a day. You couldn't hear the TV at all when it zoomed by, and I was often afraid that if it ever flew off the tracks, it would land on the sun porch, where we all watched TV. I often left the room during this time, but my younger sisters and brother thought I was just scared. I think I was in the third grade around this time.

It was a raggedy house which really should've been condemned, but we fixed it up and kept it clean. We had our German shepherd, Prince, who slept under the rickety steps to the side porch that were on the verge of collapsing but never did. I remember performing a ritual whenever *Oz* was coming on. I either baked cookies or cinnamon rolls or popped popcorn while all five of us waited for Dorothy to spin from black and white on that dreary farm in Kansas to the luminous land of color of Oz.

My house was chaotic, especially with four sisters and brothers and a mother who worked at a factory, and if I'm remembering correctly, my father was there for the first few years of the *Oz* (until he got tuberculosis and had to live in a sanitarium for a year). I do recall the noise and the fighting of my parents (not to mention my other relatives and neighbors). Violence was plentiful, and I wanted to go wherever Dorothy was going where she would not find trouble. To put it bluntly, I wanted to escape because I needed an escape.

I didn't know any happy people. Everyone I knew was either angry or not satisfied. The only time they seemed to laugh was when they were drunk, and even that was short-lived. Most of the grown-ups I was in contact with lived their lives as if it had all been a mistake, an accident, and they were paying dearly for it. It seemed as if they were always at someone else's mercy—women at the mercy of men (this prevailed in my hometown) and children at the mercy of frustrated parents. All I knew was that most of the grown-ups felt trapped, as if they were stuck in this town and no road would lead out. So many of them felt a sense of accomplishment just getting up in the morning and making it through another day. I overheard many a grown-up conversation, and they were never life-affirming: "Chile, if the Lord'll just give me the strength to make it through another week . . ."; "I just don't know how

I'ma handle this, I can't take no more. . . ." I rarely knew what
they were talking about, but even a fool could hear that it was
some kind of drudgery. When I was a child, it became apparent to
me that these grown-ups had no power over their lives, or, if they
did, they were always at a loss as to how to exercise it. I did not
want to grow up and have to depend on someone else for my
happiness or be miserable or have to settle for whatever I was
dished out—if I could help it. That much I knew already.

I remember being confused a lot. I could never understand
why no one had any energy to do anything that would make them
feel good, besides drinking. Being happy was a transient and very
temporary thing which was almost always offset by some kind of
bullshit. I would, of course, learn much later in my own adult life
that these things are called obstacles, barriers—or again, bullshit.
When I started writing, I began referring to them as "knots." But
life wasn't one long knot. It seemed to me it just required stamina
and common sense and the wherewithal to know when a knot was
before you and you had to dig deeper than you had in order to
figure out how to untie it. It could be hard, but it was simple.

◪

The initial thing I remember striking me about Oz was how
nasty Dorothy's Auntie Em talked to her and everybody on the
farm. I was used to that authoritative tone of voice because my
mother talked to us the same way. She never asked you to do
anything; she gave you a command and never said "please," and,
once you finished it, rarely said "thank you." The tone of her voice
was always hostile, and Auntie Em sounded just like my mother—
bossy and domineering. They both ran the show, it seemed, and I
think that because my mother was raising five children almost
single-handedly, I must have had some inkling that being a woman
didn't mean you had to be helpless. Auntie Em's husband was a
wimp, and for once the tables were turned: he took orders from

256   her! My mother and Auntie Em were proof to me that if you wanted to get things done you had to delegate authority and keep everyone apprised of the rules of the game as well as the consequences. In my house it was punishment—you were severely grounded. What little freedom we had was snatched away. As a child, I often felt helpless, powerless, because I had no control over my situation and couldn't tell my mother when I thought (or knew) she was wrong or being totally unfair, or when her behavior was inappropriate. I hated this feeling to no end, but what was worse was not being able to do anything about it except keep my mouth shut.

So I completely identified when no one had time to listen to Dorothy. That dog's safety was important to her, but no one seemed to think that what Dorothy was saying could possibly be as urgent as the situation at hand. The bottom line was, it was urgent to her. When I was younger, I rarely had the opportunity to finish a sentence before my mother would cut me off or complete it for me, or, worse, give me something to do. She used to piss me off, and nowadays I catch myself—stop myself—from doing the same thing to my seven-year-old. Back then, it was as if what I had to say wasn't important or didn't warrant her undivided attention. So when Dorothy's Auntie Em dismisses her and tells her to find somewhere where she'll stay out of trouble, and little Dorothy starts thinking about if there in fact is such a place—one that is trouble free—I was right there with her, because I wanted to know, too.

I also didn't know or care that Judy Garland was supposed to have been a child star, but when she sang "Somewhere Over the Rainbow," I *was* impressed. Impressed more by the song than by who was singing it. I mean, she wasn't exactly Aretha Franklin or the Marvelettes or the Supremes, which was the only vocal music I was used to. As kids, we often laughed at white people singing on TV because their songs were always so corny and they just didn't sound anything like the soulful music we had in our house. **257** Sometimes we would mimic people like Doris Day and Fred Astaire and laugh like crazy because they were always so damn happy while they sang and danced. We would also watch square-dancing when we wanted a real laugh and try to look under the women's dresses. What I hated more than anything was when in the middle of a movie the white people always had to start singing and dancing to get their point across. Later, I would hate it when black people would do the same thing—even though it was obvious to us that at least they had more rhythm and, most of the time, more range vocally.

We did skip through the house singing "We're off to see the Wizard," but other than that, most of the songs in this movie are a blank, probably because I blanked them out. Where I lived, when you had something to say to someone, you didn't sing it, you told them, so the cumulative effect of the songs wore thin.

I was afraid for Dorothy when she decided to run away, but at the same time I was glad. I couldn't much blame her—I mean, what kind of life did she have, from what I'd seen so far? She lived on an ugly farm out in the middle of nowhere with all these old people who did nothing but chores, chores, and more chores. Who did she have to play with besides that dog? And even though I lived in a house full of people, I knew how lonely Dorothy felt, or at least how isolated she must have felt. First of all, I was the oldest, and my sisters and brother were ignorant and silly creatures who often bored me because they couldn't hold a decent conversation. I couldn't ask them questions, like: Why are we living in this dump? When is Mama going to get some more money? Why can't we go on vacations like other people? Like white people? Why does our car always break down? Why are we poor? Why doesn't Mama ever laugh? Why do we have to live in Port Huron? Isn't there someplace better than this we can go live? I remember thinking this kind of stuff in kindergarten, to be honest, because times were hard, but I'd saved twenty-five cents in my piggy bank for hot-dog-and-chocolate-milk day at school, and on the morning I went to get it, my piggy bank was empty. My mother gave me some lame excuse as to why she had to spend it, but all I was thinking was that I would have to sit there (again) and watch the other children slurp their chocolate milk, and I could see the ketchup and mustard oozing out of the hot-dog bun that I wouldn't get to taste. I walked to school, and with the exception of walking to my father's funeral when I was sixteen, this was the longest walk of my entire life. My plaid dress was starched and my socks were white, my hair was braided and not a strand out of place; but I wanted to know why I had to feel this kind of humiliation when in fact I had saved the money for this very purpose. Why? By the time I got to school, I'd wiped my nose and dried my eyes and vowed not to let anyone know that I was even moved by this. It was no one's business why I couldn't eat my hot dog and chocolate milk, but the irony of it was that my teacher, Mrs. Johnson, must have sensed what had happened, and she bought my hot dog and chocolate milk for me that day. I can still remember feeling how unfair things can be, but how they somehow always turn out good. I guess seeing so much negativity had already started to turn me into an optimist.

I was a very busy child, because I was the oldest and had to see to it that my sisters and brother had their baths and did their homework; I combed my sisters' hair, and by fourth grade I had cooked my first Thanksgiving dinner. It was my responsibility to keep the house spotless so that when my mother came home from work it would pass her inspection, so I spent many an afternoon and Saturday morning mopping and waxing floors, cleaning ovens and refrigerators, grocery shopping, and by the time I was thirteen, I was paying bills for my mother and felt like an adult. I was also tired of it, sick of all the responsibility. So yes, I rooted for Dorothy when she and Toto were vamoosing, only I wanted to know: Where in the hell was she going? Where would I go if I were to run away? I had no idea because there was nowhere to go. What I did know was that one day I would go somewhere—which is why I think I watched so much TV. I was always on the lookout for Paradise, and I think I found it a few years later on "Adventures in Paradise," with Gardner McKay, and on "77 Sunset Strip." Palm trees and blue water and islands made quite an impression on a little girl from a flat, dull little depressing town in Michigan.

Professor Marvel really pissed me off, and I didn't believe for a minute that that crystal ball was real, even before he started asking Dorothy all those questions, but I knew this man was going to be important, I just couldn't figure out how. Dorothy was so gullible, I thought, and I knew this word because my mother used to always drill it in us that you should "never believe everything somebody tells you." So after Professor Marvel convinced Dorothy that her Auntie Em might be in trouble, and Dorothy scoops up Toto and runs back home, I was totally disappointed, because now I wasn't going to have an adventure. I was thinking I might actually learn how to escape drudgery by watching Dorothy do it successfully, but before she even gave herself the chance to discover for herself that she could make it, she was on her way back home. "Dummy!" we all yelled on the sun porch. "Dodo brain!"

The storm. The tornado. Of course, now the entire set of this film looks so phony it's ridiculous, but back then I knew the wind was a tornado because in Michigan we had the same kind of trapdoor underground shelter that Auntie Em had on the farm. I knew Dorothy was going to be locked out once Auntie Em and the workers locked the door, and I also knew she wasn't going to be heard when she knocked on it. This was drama at its best, even though I didn't know what drama was at the time.

In the house she goes, and I was frightened for her. I knew that house was going to blow away, so when little Dorothy gets banged in the head by a window that flew out of its casement, I remember all of us screaming. We watched everybody fly by the window, including the wicked neighbor who turns out to be the Wicked Witch of the West, and I'm sure I probably substituted my mother for Auntie Em and fantasized that all of my siblings would fly away, too. They all got on my nerves because I could never find a quiet place in my house—no such thing as peace—and I was always being disturbed.

It wasn't so much that I had so much I wanted to do by myself, but I already knew that silence was a rare commodity, and when I managed to snatch a few minutes of it, I could daydream, pretend to be someone else somewhere else—and this was fun. But I couldn't do it if someone was bugging me. On days when my mother was at work, I would often send the kids outside to play and lock them out, just so I could have the house to myself for at least fifteen minutes. I loved pretending that none of them existed for a while, although after I finished with my fantasy world, it was reassuring to see them all there. I think I was grounded.

When Dorothy's house began to spin and spin and spin, I was curious as to where it was going to land. And to be honest, I didn't know little Dorothy was actually dreaming until she woke up and opened the door and everything was in color! It looked like Paradise to me. The foliage was almost an iridescent green, the water bluer than I'd ever seen in any of the lakes in Michigan. Of course, once I realized she was in fact dreaming, it occurred to me that this very well might be the only way to escape. To dream up another world. Create your own.

I had no clue that Dorothy was going to find trouble, though, even in her dreams. Hell, if I had dreamed up something like another world, it would've been a perfect one. I wouldn't have put myself in such a precarious situation. I'd have been able to go straight to the Wizard, no strings attached. First of all, that she walked was stupid to me; I would've asked one of those Munchkins for a ride. And I never bought into the idea of those slippers, but

once I bought the whole idea, I accepted the fact that the girl was
definitely lost and just wanted to get home. Personally, all I kept
thinking was, if she could get rid of that Wicked Witch of the West,
the Land of Oz wasn't such a bad place to be stuck in. It beat the
farm in Kansas.

At the time, I truly wished I could spin away from my family
and home and land someplace as beautiful and surreal as Oz—if
only for a little while. All I wanted was to get a chance to see
another side of the world, to be able to make comparisons, and
then decide if it was worth coming back home.

What was really strange to me, after the Good Witch of the
North tells Dorothy to just stay on the Yellow Brick Road to get
to the Emerald City and find the Wizard so she can get home, was
when Dorothy meets the Scarecrow, the Tin Man, and the Lion—
all of whom were missing something I'd never even given any
thought to. A brain? What did having one really mean? What
would not having one mean? I had one, didn't I, because I did well
in school. But because the Scarecrow couldn't make up his mind,
thought of himself as a failure, it dawned on me that having a
brain meant you had choices, you could make decisions and, as a
result, make things happen. Yes, I thought, I had one, and I was
going to use it. One day. And the Tin Man, who didn't have a
heart. Not having one meant you were literally dead to me, and I
never once thought of it as being the house of emotions (didn't
know what emotions were), where feelings of jealousy, devotion,
and sentiment lived. I'd never thought of what else a heart was
good for except keeping you alive. But I did have feelings, because
they were often hurt, and I was envious of the white girls at my
school who wore mohair sweaters and box-pleat skirts, who went
skiing and tobogganing and yachting and spent summers in Quebec.
Why didn't white girls have to straighten their hair? Why didn't
their parents beat each other up? Why were they always so god-
damn happy?

And courage. Oh, that was a big one. What did having it and not having it mean? I found out that it meant having guts and being afraid but doing whatever it was you set out to do anyway. Without courage, you couldn't do much of anything. I liked courage and assumed I would acquire it somehow. As a matter of fact, one day my mother *told* me to get her a cup of coffee, and even though my heart was pounding and I was afraid, I said to her pointblank, "Could you please say please?" She looked up at me out of the corner of her eye and said, "What?" So I repeated myself, feeling more powerful because she hadn't slapped me across the room already, and then something came over her and she looked at me and said, "Please." I smiled all the way to the kitchen, and from that point forward, I managed to get away with this kind of behavior until I left home when I was seventeen. My sisters and brother—to this day—don't know how I stand up to my mother, but I know. I decided not to be afraid or intimidated by her, and I wanted her to treat me like a friend, like a human being, instead of her slave.

I do believe that *Oz* also taught me much about friendship. I mean, the Tin Man, the Lion, and the Scarecrow hung in there for Dorothy, stuck their "necks" out and made sure she was protected, even risked their own "lives" for her. They told each other the truth. They trusted each other. All four of them had each other's best interests in mind. I believe it may have been a while before I actually felt this kind of sincerity in a friend, but really good friends aren't easy to come by, and when you find one, you hold on to them.

Okay. So Dorothy goes through hell before she gets back to Kansas. But the bottom line was, she made it. And what I remember feeling when she clicked those heels was that you have to have faith and be a believer, for real, or nothing will ever materialize. Simple as that. And not only in life but even in your dreams there's always going to be adversity, obstacles, knots, or some kind of bullshit you're going to have to deal with in order to get on with your life. Dorothy had a good heart and it was in the right place, which is why I supposed she won out over the evil witch. I've learned that one, too. That good *always* overcomes evil; maybe not immediately, but in the long run, it does. So I think I vowed when I was little to try to be a good person. An honest person. To care about others and not just myself. Not to be a selfish person, because my heart would be of no service if I used it only for myself. And I had to have the courage to see other people and myself as not being perfect (yes, I had a heart and a brain, but some other things would turn up missing, later), and I would have to learn to untie every knot that I encountered—some self-imposed, some not—in my life, and to believe that if I did the right things, I would never stray too far from my Yellow Brick Road.

■

I'm almost certain that I saw *Oz* annually for at least five or six years, but I don't remember how old I was when I stopped watching it. I do know that by the time my parents were divorced (I was thirteen), I couldn't sit through it again. I was a mature teen-ager and had finally reached the point where Dorothy got on my nerves. Singing, dancing, and skipping damn near everywhere was so corny and utterly sentimental that even the Yellow Brick Road became sickening. I already knew what she was in for, and sometimes I rewrote the story in my head. I kept asking myself, what if she had just run away and kept going, maybe she would've ended up in Los Angeles with a promising singing career. What if it had turned out that she hadn't been dreaming, and the Wizard had given her an offer she couldn't refuse—say, for instance, he had asked her to stay on in the Emerald City, that she could visit the farm whenever she wanted to, but, get a clue, Dorothy, the Emerald City is what's happening; she could make new city friends and get a hobby and a boyfriend and free rent and never have to do chores . . .

I had to watch *The Wizard of Oz* again in order to write this, and my six-and-a-half-year-old son, Solomon, joined me. At first he kept asking me if something was wrong with the TV because it wasn't in color, but as he watched, he became mesmerized by the story. He usually squirms or slides to the floor and under a table or just leaves the room if something on TV bores him, which it usually does, except if he's watching Nickelodeon, a high-quality cable kiddie channel. His favorite shows, which he watches with real consistency, and, I think, actually goes through withdrawal if he can't see them for whatever reason, are "Inspector Gadget," "Looney Tunes," and "Mr. Ed." "Make the Grade," which is sort of a junior-high version of "Jeopardy," gives him some kind of thrill, even though he rarely knows any of the answers. And "Garfield" is a must on Saturday morning. There is hardly anything on TV that he watches that has any real, or at least plausible, drama to it, but you can't miss what you've never had.

The Wicked Witch intimidated the boy no end, and he was afraid of her. The Wizard was also a problem. So I explained—no, I just told him pointblank—"Don't worry, she'll get it in the end, Solomon, because she's bad. And the Wizard's a fake, and he's trying to sound like a tough guy, but he's a wus." That offered him some consolation, and even when the Witch melted he kind of looked at me with those *Home Alone* eyes and asked, "But where did she go, Mommy?" "She's history," I said. "Melted. Gone. Into the ground. Remember, this is pretend. It's not real. Real people don't melt. This is only TV," I said. And then he got that look in his eyes as if he'd remembered something.

Of course he had a nightmare that night and of course there was a witch in it, because I had actually left the sofa a few times during this last viewing to smoke a few cigarettes (the memory bank is a powerful place—I still remembered many details), put the dishes in the dishwasher, make a few phone calls, water the plants. Solomon sang "We're off to see the Wizard" for the next

few days because he said that was his favorite part, next to the **265**
Munchkins (who also showed up in his nightmare).

So, to tell the truth, I really didn't watch the whole movie
again. I just couldn't. Probably because about thirty or so years
ago little Dorothy had made a lasting impression on me, and this
viewing felt like overkill. You only have to tell me, show me, once
in order for me to get it. But even still, the movie itself taught me
a few things that I still find challenging. That it's okay to be an
idealist, that you have to imagine something better and go for it.
That you have to believe in *something*, and it's best to start with
yourself and take it from there. At least give it a try. As corny as
it may sound, sometimes I am afraid of what's around the corner,
or what's not around the corner. But I look anyway. I believe that
writing is one of my "corners"—an intersection, really; and when
I'm confused or reluctant to look back, deeper, or ahead, I create
my own Emerald Cities and force myself to take longer looks,
because it is one sure way that I'm able to see.

Of course, I've fallen, tumbled, and been thrown over all kinds
of bumps on my road, but it still looks yellow, although every once
in a while there's still a loose brick. For the most part, though, it
seems paved. Perhaps because that's the way I want to see it.

◣

ADULT

Cinema is sexual showing, a pagan flaunting.
—Camille Paglia

THE STAG FILM
A TALE OF NOT ENOUGH VICS
GORDON LISH

Q: We understand that you have been experiencing some difficulties in meeting the deadline you have with us.

A: Yeah, jeez, my God—I've been going *nuts* over it, yeah.

Q: But this is absurd—whatever for? All you need do is tell us about the movie that changed your life.

A: Sure, sure, I know, I know.

Q: Then what on earth is the difficulty? There was a movie that changed your life, wasn't there?

A: Oh, yeah, sure—my God, there was one that did *that*, all right. Jeez, wow, did that movie change my *life*.

Q: Splendid.

A: Yeah, I *know*.

Q: Then merely tell us all about it.

A: Yeah, but like *what*, for instance?

Q: Well, perhaps you could begin by telling us its title.

A: Oh, yeah, sure, its *title*.

Q: So?

A: Well, to tell you the truth, I don't think I ever heard anybody actually *mention* its title.

Q: Yes, yes, of course—but when the credits and so on played on the screen, the name of the movie must surely have been indicated.

A: Well, see, that's the *thing* of it—we never got to that *part* of it, seeing it on the *screen* or anything.

Q: Are you saying that you did not see this movie?

A: Yeah, well, jeez, you guys said you wanted me to tell you the *truth* and everything.

Q: Do we understand you to be making the claim that the movie that changed your life is a movie you never saw?

A: Hey, come on—jeez, I was doing everything I *could*. I mean, face it, with the situation the way it *was*, what more did you want me to do insofar as doing my best to give the right *impression* goes? But the thing of it was, it just wasn't in the *cards* for me, you know?

Q: And yet this unseen movie of yours made such a difference in your life.

A: Oh God, *yeah*. I mean, just for one thing, I couldn't even *think* about looking my mother or my sister in the eye after that. Even certain *aunts* I had—hey, skip it, forget it—it was *rough*.

Q: The movie was off-color, shall we say? This is your point, that the movie was off-color?

A: Really *dirty*, I think. Probably pretty *filthy*, I think. But, hey, like this is just an educated *guess*, you understand. But what happened was that Eddie and Donnie, neither one of them could get the *projector* going.

Q: Friends of yours.

A: Yeah, these two *guys*, okay?

Q: Eddie and Donnie.

A: Right. In other words, my best *friends*, you might say.

Q: One takes it, then, that the plan was for the three of you to witness this film together.

A: The plan, that was *it*, that was absolutely *it*—yeah, right, right, check, witness it *together*. Over at *Eddie's*, you understand— insofar as Eddie was the one whose folks were supposed to be away for the day. In Jersey, actually. Like I think Eddie said at a *wedding* or something.

Q: It was Eddie's projector.

A: Hey, that was just the thing—I mean, the fact that it wasn't *Eddie's*—because like if it was *Eddie's*, then probably the chances would have been that he would have known how to *work* the thing. But, hey, it was his uncle Vic's and he *didn't*.

Q: Eddie didn't.

A: Right, *Eddie*. I mean, the spools and things—the sprockets and so on—Eddie couldn't get them to go right so that when you had it all set up to go, it *did*. I mean, the motor went on and the light went on, but as far as the movie itself, hey, it *didn't*.

Q: But mightn't your friend Donnie have tried?

A: Yeah, yeah—you're right, that was the thing, Donnie kept screaming that Eddie should quit it and let *him* try—but you know what? Eddie *wouldn't*.

Q: Wouldn't let the other boy, the boy Donnie, have a try at getting the film threaded properly.

A: Jeez, that's right, that's right—Eddie *wouldn't*. Said it was his uncle Vic's *property* and that he, Eddie, had his *orders* that nobody was to lay a finger on it except somebody who was related to his uncle Vic the way Eddie himself was. As *family*, if you see what I am saying.

Q: So you were at an impasse.

A: That's *it*, that's *right*—I kept screaming to these guys that this thing we were at was an *impasse*. I kept screaming that somebody had to hurry up and do something about this *impasse.* Get us *out* of it and so on and so forth. But I have to grant you this, I think it was hard for anybody to *think,* you know what I'm saying? First of all, it was *dark.* I mean, I don't know if you know this, but we were down in Eddie's basement and it was really *dark* down there and I think that sometimes you just can't *think* straight when it's there in the *dark* and all, especially if it's three people *screaming.*

Q: Donnie was screaming for Eddie to let him have a crack at trying to operate the projector?

A: Hey, funny you should mention it—but what it actually was was *this*—getting *dirt* on it, Donnie was getting real *upset* over the question of us getting *dirt* on it, given the fact that Eddie finally got it *going* enough where what was *happening* was that the movie was running off on his mother's card table and then off on the *floor.* Hey, you got to bear in *mind* the fact that this was Eddie's *basement* we were in and like it *wasn't* what someone would call a *finished* basement. I mean, like we had this bedsheet hanging down from one of Eddie's mother's *clotheslines,* if you get the actual picture of it—and the thing was that it was one of Eddie's mother's *bedsheets*—but this didn't mean that the *floor* wasn't plenty dirty just because we had a nice clean *bedsheet.*

Q: You're suggesting to us that the circumstances were makeshift.

A: That's what I kept *saying* to these guys—that we were really dealing with some pretty makeshift *circumstances.*

Q: And your friend Donnie was fretful that the film would be harmed in some fashion.

A: Fretful—boy, that's the word, *fretful,* seeing as how it was his uncle *Vic* from who he, Donnie, had got his hands on the movie in the first place and then had to go ahead and get it back to before anybody was any the wiser, not to mention just his uncle *Vic* for starters.

Q: Then Donnie had an uncle Vic as well?

A: Yeah, there were *two* uncle Vics, *Donnie's* and *Eddie's.*

Q: And you fellows had, as it were, borrowed the projector from one of these uncles and the film from the other.

A: Hey, that's just what I have been sitting here trying to *tell* you. But like what was the *deal*? I mean, we weren't *getting* anywhere. All we had were these *boners*—but like what was the *deal*?

Q: It was very frustrating, you're saying.

A: God, man, it was just the *idea* of it, you know? But so like, okay, time is running out on us and what are we going to *do*? Whereupon what *happens* is that Eddie says, okay, let's just go ahead and look at it by like each guy just takes a turn holding it up to the *light* bulb and looking, okay?

Q: A reasonable proposal, it seems.

A: You know, like just *one* picture at a time and so forth.

Q: Yes, yes, I understand completely.

A: But then, jeez, Donnie starts screaming we'll get our *hands* all over it.

Q: Fingerprints.

A: And like his uncle Vic will look and *know*.

Q: I see the point, of course. And was there a counterproposal of some kind?

A: Me, I made a counterproposal—*I* was the one.

Q: Very good. And you said?

A: Yeah, well, I said, "Look, you guys, what do you say to the counterproposal that Eddie takes the projector back to *his* uncle Vic and that Donnie takes the movie back to *his* uncle Vic and that we all just go home and call it *quits*?"

Q: I'm impressed.

A: Yeah, well, thanks—I mean, *face* it—I think it was probably pretty clear to everybody at this stage of the game that what you were really ready to do was to get off by *yourself* somewhere and really, you know, loop the *mule*, as the fella says.

Q: I see, I see. Yes, of course—I expect this makes perfect sense.

A: Hey, come on, let's face it—the facts are the *facts*.

Q: So you adjourned at this juncture, is this correct?

A: I would have to say that I ran all the way *home.*

Q: To hasten to attend to your affairs, as we might say.

A: Hey, you hit the *nail,* as the saying goes, on the head.

Q: Ah, it all comes clear to me now—for it must have thereafter turned out that you were discovered in your nasty errand and that this trauma, then, your being surprised in the act, shall we say, is how it happens that the movie you never saw proved to exert such a power in your life. Hence, the shame you insist you felt when confronted by your mother. But of course—one sees the punchline coming—you are going to tell us that you were caught out by your mother.

A: Hey, are you *crazy?*

Q: By your sister, then? An aunt perhaps?

A: Hey, come on, be *nice.* You think I am the kind of an individual who would *sit* here and tell you anybody like that caught me *whacking off?*

Q: Your tale baffles me, then.

A: How *baffles?* I mean, I do not *get* it, *baffles.* Didn't you guys say to me you had to have the *truth?* Hey, I am not trying to pull some kind of a *fast* one on you—what I am sitting here doing is trying to tell you guys the *truth.*

Q: Which is?

A: All that stuff with the spools and *sprockets* and stuff—I knew how to *work* it.

Q: But you kept silent, did not offer assistance—allowed the project to succumb to failure.

A: Yeah, *succumb,* right—I just went ahead and *let* it.

Q: Threatened by the prospect before you—were afraid of it.

A: *Seeing* them, yeah, I was really *scared* of it.

Q: Naked women.

A: No, no—*guys* naked. You know, their *things.*

Q: Were suffocating in the embrace of an intimation that your private part would not measure up against these organs favorably.

A: Jeez, you are like some kind of like a *mind*-reader, you know?

Q: As if you would be shown up to be weak before . . .

A: Right, right, right—the *babes*—as if they, all of the *babes*, were right in there with them in the movie with them—like kind of already wise to the whole *deal*. Like even like they would be *looking* at me from it, would be *watching* me from it—hey, from right *inside* of—guess where—the *movie*.

Q: But that's incredible. Transumptively speaking, it's such a twisted piece of transference.

A: Hey, it really *hurt* me, man—almost, I think, for my *whole* life, I bet you could say—like almost really *permanently*, I bet somebody could say—me a guy with no uncle *Vic*, if you know what I mean. Not even one single lousy uncle Vic anywhere to my *name*.

Q: But what an abstruse metaphor—heavens, what in the world does it really mean?

A: Hey, it's a mystery to *me*, pal. But, you *know*, I can be sitting there watching *anything*—like let's say just any particular moving picture which it suits somebody to *name*, okay?—but even to this day and *age*, I still always *can't* get away from the funny feeling that it's a *test* which some *women* got together and set up and that *me*, they went ahead and picked *me* out *not* to be the one to *pass*.

Q: Then the movies are some sort of hyperreality for you, a context in which your defenses slip from place.

A: Hey, you think like it was maybe the *same* deal with *Donnie* and *Eddie*? I mean, like *back then*, you think that like *Eddie*, say— you think Eddie probably could have *really* got the projector to *go* right too, but didn't really *want* it to? And so forth and so on as also regards *Donnie*? Because maybe it's really too *much* for a person to really *handle*, like the vexatiousness of having really to *see.* So like maybe you *don't,* even when you *are,* hey, obviously so far as everybody *else* is concerned, even *yourself* maybe, actually *looking.* I mean, do you think it could be like *nobody* can *really* stand it to see anybody *else*—even if they're not *even* in a *movie?* Because it's like *forget* it, what kind of *crummy* payout did the big fella figure He was *pulling* on me here!

Q: Yes, yes, but didn't you make these persons up—Donnie and Eddie?

A: Hey, come on—Donnie *Wolf* and Eddie *Weisberg?* I mean, let's face it, you got to be kidding, make up *Donnie* Wolf and *Eddie* Weisberg when it's only *you* and like *myself* I did!

Q: But this is ridiculous—to close us off with such an erosive abridgement of the rules of discourse.

A: Well, it's what I was *telling* you, a put-upon character like me—Vicless *in,* Vicless *out.*

Q: Please—may I speak openly?

A: Sure, go ahead and speak openly—it's suddenly a *federal* case to speak *openly?*

Q: Quite frankly, these vagrant opinions of yours, they leave me utterly in the dark.

A: Hey, you *see?* Like I was telling you—*in the dark.*

Q: Very well, then. One further inquiry, please?

A: Shoot.

Q: This format of yours, interrogator versus respondent—you must be aware, are you not, of how preposterous it is.

A: Hey, yeah, I *know.* No kidding, I really *know.* I mean, what you said, you know, this is the same thing that I would have to say *too.* But like they came and said to me you had to have a certain number of *pages* before you went ahead and handed this thing *in.*

Q: In other words, one might put the argument that you accepted this assignment under false pretenses.

A: That's it, *false* ones, right! That's exactly the caliber of pretenses you could say I was going *along* with things, ones which were *false* ones, right! Hey, now that you mention it, it was the same deal in Eddie's *basement*—so let's *face* it, I guess you got a point.

Q: Then is it not necessary for you to take into account the contest between your fraudulence in the light and your fraudulence in the dark?

A: Nope, not if it's a photo *finish*, I don't.

◪

THE MOVIE
ON THE WHOREHOUSE WALL/
THE DEVIL IN MISS JONES

AN ESSAY ON INNOCENCE

LESLIE EPSTEIN

I

third of a century ago three young men, clinging still to their teens, pulled off the Pacific Coast Highway and prepared for a dip in the sea. The sky was hazy, the beach at La Jolla near deserted. Down below, the broken waves sizzled and hissed. The Pumpkin and the Duck settled down on the sand, while the Penguin—a dour fellow, worried and formal—waddled stiffly by the surf.

Duck: "Why the delay? What's the point? No one's going swimming today."

Pumpkin: "Who said anything about swimming? The delay *is* the point."

"What's that supposed to mean? The whole idea is to have fun in Tijuana."

"Fun?" echoed the Pumpkin. "Not fun: sex!"

"So?"

"So: what's sex but tension and release? That's the only known source of human pleasure. Think about it. Give me some other examples."

"What about beauty?" said the idealistic Duck.

"Come on. Get serious."

"I *am* serious. What about the pleasure you feel when you see something beautiful? Or hear a symphony, say?"

"Which wins—the most beautiful thing you ever saw: a Rembrandt, a flower, a sunset? Or a good shit? Give your opinion and not what they tell you to say at Yale."

A brief pause. "The shit wins hands down."

"Of course it does. That's because of the pressure on the colon and the sphincter. The greater the tension, the greater the release."

"According to you, we should go around constipated."

"Spare your wit, Duck. Most people most of the time settle for a little pleasure because they can take only a little pain. But we're in a once-in-a-lifetime situation here. Don't worry about the delay. Believe me, the frustration will pay off in all-time thrills. A few drinks, okay? Maybe a flick starring a girl and a burro. And then, Long Bar! We have to do what the Cow said and sit right next to the runway. This Mexican dropped her panties on his head! Talk about tension! And she made him smell the juice on her hand!"

"Do you believe that?"

The Pumpkin rolled over and scooped up a dank tangle of seaweed. "Believe it?" he cried, burying his face in the moss. "Oh, baby! Ambrosia! I can smell it now!"

The Pumpkin and I had known each other for years, both on and off the tennis courts at La Cienega; and my friendship with the Penguin went back even further, to the day camps for six- and seven-year-olds, Matson's Club and Tocaloma, where he claims to have tied a mackerel to my limp line, and where I distinctly recall catching a high fly ball off his bat: *third out, side retired!* The Pumpkin would go on to play Davis Cup and reach the quarter-finals at Wimbledon, while the Penguin, dressed like a lawyer anyway, would do important work for the Warren Commission and practice international diplomacy at The Hague. Meanwhile, the three of us, as was inevitable after the first year at different colleges, were drifting apart. I think it was because we sensed that the endless sets of tennis, the cruising on Hollywood Boulevard, the rubber rafts at Malibu or Will Rogers State Beach were coming to an end that we decided upon what was, in Southern California, a traditional rite of passage: the trip to T.J., the defloration of the freshman.

The Penguin came up the strand. "The golden years," he said, staring glumly at his foam-flecked shoes. "Yeah. Right. The best years of our lives."

◢

The weather turned at the border. The high haze gave way to thick brown clouds that shouldered their way over what were, in 1957, grass-covered hills. Now and then the setting sun would radiate upward, like spikes on a crown, or break through eerily, in patches, to make this acre or that acre a deeper green, a richer brown. Four or five fat raindrops struck the Century's windshield, and silent lightning raced horizontally in the clouds. *Don't touch metal*, I thought, part cowed by the ominousness of the landscape, in which Tijuana nestled like the recently studied Toledo of El Greco, and part amused by the corniness of the spectacle, this heavenly display before the Fatal Step: three virgins move south over the border; and who would cross north? *Los tres vagabondos!*

This was not, truth to tell, my first visit to lower California.

The Epsteins used to vacation at the Hotel del Coronado, the same sprawling resort that Tony Curtis and Jack Lemmon have the run of in *Some Like It Hot*. What are the middle-aged memories of this wonderful firetrap? Vichyssoise! The green circlets of chives floating on top, the creamy white residue on the spoon. And, still in the dining room, the string orchestra playing *Slaughter on Tenth Avenue*. From this beachhead we'd set out for Tijuana *en famille*. I remember myself, or a photograph of myself, sitting atop a donkey, cardboard cacti to either side, clutching the matted mane; short wiry men, hurling themselves halfway up walls, playing jai alai, of which Tijuana is something like the Cooperstown; and a large brass ring, skull-shaped, rubies in the sockets of the eyes, which left a green band on my finger that would not fade. I am less certain, however, whether the jumping beans—alive! with worms inside!—on my bureau, or the sugarcane dripping from my chin was purchased from the stalls of Tijuana or Olvero Street, downtown L.A., on one of the excursions of my fifth-grade class.

We parked at the edge of town and began to stroll along the arcade. Plan Pumpkin called for caution: first drinks, then flicks, followed by the runway at Long Bar. And after that? Not a word: it was as if, before the prospect of actual sexual intercourse, our minds had gone entirely blank. There was, on the main drag, no lack of *señoritas*—one, it seemed, for each of the negative spaces created by the arches that humped down the long promenade. At each encounter we veered aside, struck by a sudden thirst for beer. Our cruising career had been no different. One night, amidst the traffic of Hollywood Boulevard, the Penguin leaned out the back of the convertible and asked three chicks in a Ford where they were going. The plump-armed driver spoke for her companions:

"Anywhere that Buick is."

The Pumpkin grabbed my shoulder. "Did you hear that? Oh, boy! Get to the right. Fast! We're going to score!"

282   The red Ford tooted its horn and surged provocatively forward in the next lane.

From the back seat: "Get right, Duck! To the right!"

Pumpkin: "They're waiting for us. Jesus! They're holding up traffic!"

"Merge right! What are you waiting for? They're looking for our car!"

Said the Duck: "But fellas. It says left lane must turn left."

"Are you crazy? Did you see that babe? This is our shot!"

"Pull out for Christ's sake! You'll miss the damn light!"

Cars were honking. Someone shouted. The line of traffic in the right lane started forward. Up ahead the Ford's taillights, winking, gleaming, slowly shrank to the size of the ruby eyes, the bloody pupils, on my lost souvenir. Here were, after all, *Los Tres Hebreos*: we followed the arrows left.

◢

Up ahead, at the end of the gallery, the Penguin was arguing with the driver of a cab. "Three-fifty," cried he, with a flap of his arms. "For a stupid flick?"

"*Sí*. You wan' gorls, you pay ten dollar more."

"No girls, no girls," interjected the Pumpkin. "We're not interested. It'll ruin the plan."

The cautious Penguin: "How much for the ride out there? An arm and a leg?"

"One dollar fifty cents," said the driver.

"Each?" queried the Duck.

The Mexican grinned and threw open the back door of his Dodge, white with a blue top and a blue stripe down the side—in West Los Angeles folklore, one of the famed, fabled Blues. "*Sí!* Five dollar all together each."

"Okay," said the Pumpkin, stepping inside. "But no nooky!"

The Duck, last in, slid next to the Penguin, who hissed in his ear. "Get it out now. Don't let them see your wallet."

We three strained back to get at our hip pockets while the cab shot forward, hung a screeching U, and then swerved onto an unlit, unpaved road.

"Jesus," groaned the Penguin. "What are we doing?"

The driver began to sing: "Boom-bah, boom-boom-bah," striking the top of the dash with one hand, the wheel with the other.

"I don't like this."

"Relax, Duck. You act like you've never been to the movies be—" The words died on my friend's lips. Without slowing, without warning, the taxi left the road and careened up a rocky incline. Our heads hit the ceiling, our rumps slammed onto the springless cushion. Suddenly the cab was at the top of the embankment; it hung there motionless, its headlights casting crazed, cross-eyed beams into the black of the sky: then we slammed down and began burrowing across a rutted field. Ahead, dim, dark, was a cluster of what looked like tarpaper shacks.

"Boom-bah-bah!" crooned the driver, and hit the horn. Instantly the little settlement was ablaze. Strings of bare light bulbs winked on and off, and a score of figures, finery flapping, ran out to welcome the barnyard of innocents.

"It's a trick!" shouted the Penguin.

Pumpkin: "Girls!"

And so they were, with more waiting inside the largest of the shacks, into which, as if into the gaping maw of hell, we waded. Everywhere we looked—on chairs, on sofas, on the tabletops—the dark-haired women sat, legs crossed, sandals dangling from their painted toes.

"Look at him! That one for me!" cried a pretty *señorita*, meaning, all too plainly, neither my dour nor my cucurbitaceous companion.

"Calm down, Duck," the Penguin muttered from the side of his mouth. "She's not looking at you."

"She's wild about *you*, is that it? Lost her heart to the gentleman in the tux, I suppose?"

"Quack! Quack! Quack!"

At those sounds a ripple, a start of curiosity, passed through the ladies of the night.

Quickly the cabbie ushered us through the parlor to a small windowless room that contained nothing but a couple of chairs and, on a small table, an 8-mm projector. The single unshaded bulb went off. Simultaneously, a woman—she might have been forty, with coal-dark hair and surprisingly light skin—appeared on the wall in black and white. We watched as she paced to and fro, stomping her high heels and gazing longingly at her bedroom door, which finally opened.

"Here comes the burro!" said the Penguin, out of the dark.

But it was only a man, thin and middle-aged. He stood expressionless as the actress unzipped his fly and took his half-hearted member into her mouth. The film snapped. When the cab driver restored it, the actress was in bed, biting her shoulder and attempting to raise her breast to her mouth. This time, as if from shyness, the film halted and started to burn. When it resumed, the actor was also in bed, with the actress astride his belly, facing south; his penis, now feeling the part, stretched upward and backward, ending halfway inside what was for each of us our first glimpse of a mature vagina. The camera, from an angle between the man's legs, began to move forward, past his feet, still stockinged, and past his knees. Then it began to slide and bounce, as if it, like the straddling female, were caught up in the pleasure of intercourse: in fact, the film had slipped off the gears and was pooling onto the table. The cabbie bent over the projector, his plump face chalk white, scowling, while on the plasterboard the image of flesh violently shivered.

"Where's the damn donkey?" demanded the Penguin. "The Cow is full of crap."

"What about Long Bar? Was he bullshitting about that? About the panties?"

The perforations caught on the sprockets. A party was now in full swing. Three or four couples were tangled on the bed. One woman peeled a banana, pushed it between her thighs, and then took a bite. It was in this manner that the next moments flew by. Except for the fleeting scenes I have described—and even these may have been distorted by images that have crept in from shows on Forty-second Street—the film on the whorehouse wall has proved impossible to recall. Oddly enough, its very forgetability—rather, its elusiveness—is what has made it so memorable. That is to say, the tattered strip of celluloid, caught in wavering light, with its action halting, even derailed, and its blurred and trembling images, mere shadows, motes, remains for me the perfect symbol of the repressed unconscious as it wends its way through myriad defenses toward full exposure.

There is a second reason this muleless movie became, in addition to a milestone in my life, a remarkable aesthetic experience: for, well before the last frame had been wound onto the take-up reel, the work of art and reality, wish and fulfillment, had joined indissolubly together. In plain words, the door to the parlor opened and three living ladies darted into our half-lit room. One went straight for the dumbstruck Pumpkin and began to squirm on his lap. A redhead threw her arms about the Penguin's neck and, between fits of coughing, blew into his ear. The last girl, a woman really, about the same age as the actress on the makeshift screen, also with dark hair and pale skin, sat on my knees and unbuttoned my suede jacket. "What kind of job you want?" she asked. "I do any job on you."

For a brief span everything, save for the soft cough of the redhead and the whirr and whine of the old machine, was still.

286   Suddenly one of us was on his feet, his arms around his paramour. The Pumpkin!

"Have you lost your mind?" I cried. "What about the plan? The tension? What about the dancer at Long Bar?" But he only stood there, the chipped tooth in his smile making him look like a demented jack-o'-lantern. Then he took a step forward and tottered from the room.

"I guess this is it," said the Penguin.

"I guess so," I replied, and off we went, each to his cubicle: a mattress, a condom, a piece of toilet paper, a whore. It cost an extra five dollars to have her naked, more than my budget would allow; but barefoot, her dress thrown over her hips, she looked like a flower and the flower's stem, with, at the arrangement's center, the petals, the heavy dew. When I tried to touch her there, she cried, "Loco, you loco, you," and she continued this chant to the rhythm of our bodies, drowning, nearly, the thumping that came from the partition on my left, and, over the partition to the right, a hacking cough: *you loco you loco you.*

Fade-out, as they say in the movies, and then, in the familiar surrounds of the parlor, fade-in:

"Duck! Duck! I'm itching! It's the crabs!"

"What about me?" interrupted the Penguin. "I've got T.B.!"

No such ailments for me. The pleasure I had felt in the little cell had not ceased. Instead, a general platonic glow now illuminated not only me and the two other *señoritas*, but all those lolling about the parlor; it took in the handful of pimps, who came up to joke and tease; and, of course, it fell on our cabbie, the singing Charon who had ferried us over the Styx in his *Blue*, and to whom I now gave my jacket, brown suede, in an impulsive gesture of gratitude.

"Duck! Don't dawdle! We're getting out of here!"

"I've got to get home and wash my dick!"

Think of this: the happiness, the well-being, enfolded even

these two old friends, whom all too soon, with a continent between 287 us, and then an ocean, I would no longer see.

◤

Absurd, of course, to speak here of high art. Yet to the degree that the artist strives for immortality, what Shakespeare calls an eternal summer, the maker of this film succeeded:

> *Nor shall Death brag thou wander'st in his shade,*
> *When in eternal lines to time thou growest,*
> *So long as men can breathe, or eyes can see,*
> *So long lives this, and this give life to thee.*

The hookers of Tijuana are not, granted, the darling buds of May. Moreover, our experience was, if anything, an exile from the perpetual sun of summer, an initiation, a step from childhood not merely toward adulthood but into that shadow always associated with sexual union: desuetude, obsolescence, decay. At the same time, however, my friends and I had undergone a regression, a journey back to that Eden where there is no gap between wish and fulfillment, where repression and history and culture vanish, and where the sight of what is desired—white skin on a white wall, dark hair, high heels—is followed, as in any nursery rhyme or fairy tale, by the wish coming true.

> *Nativity, once in the main of light,*
> *Crawls to maturity, wherewith being crown'd,*
> *Crooked eclipses 'gainst his glory fight,*
> *And time that gave, doth now his gift confound.*

For Shakespeare, "crooked eclipses" stand for entropy, for exhaustion, and for wearing down, wearing out. But in relation to Tijuana, the phrase is as good a name as any for the flickering, filtered light, the hot incandescent bulb, silver nitrate and stained emulsion, that brought us back to the garden of instincts where art and life, illusion and reality, were as delicately joined as my mistress's finger and my own lips, which she had touched in order to reveal the two shining braces on my bottom teeth:

"Ooooh! Pretty!"

II

One needn't go south, of course, to make the connection between sex and the movies, since movies themselves, and the conditions in which we see them, represent the Baja of the psyche. Something about the darkened room; the kiddie food; the unseen presence of others, their breath about us; the shadow play—all that and my own preferred posture, feet up on the seat before me, head slowly going numb against the back of my own, put us, if not into a uterine environment, then one in which we are bathed by the free flow of infantile fantasy. And it almost goes without saying that it was in movie theaters that the majority of my generation first felt a breast or squeezed a thigh or took instruction, from that extra layer of cortex spread before us in the shape of a screen, on how to kiss.

My undergraduate years, 1956–60, when Kurosawa, Bergman, Fellini, Ray, and Truffault came into their own, were arguably the richest in the history of film. Yet for an entire academic year, the Lincoln in New Haven, erstwhile home of *Seven Samurai* and *The Seventh Seal*, played nothing but *And God Created Woman*. Standing room only, as the witty Elis had it. These many years later I can still see—is it a scene from the movie or the ubiquitous poster?—Brigitte Bardot sunning herself on her belly, dark glasses well down her nose, her half-tanned rump cleaving the air.

Once back in L.A., I spent modest amounts of time in a theater near Melrose and Santa Monica, which specialized in such features as *Blow the Man Down* and *The Spy Who Came*. From those years I remember best one film, in which three comical cops search for a psychopathic killer in, heaven help me, a woman's gym. Amid the usual shots of rowing machines and towel fights there was one extraordinary sequence that begins when the killer—we see only his hat brim and gloved hand—throws the bolt on the steam-bath door and turns up the pressure from the outside valve. Inside, obscurely seen through the mists, a brunette gasps from the heat and rattles the steam-covered door. What, precisely, makes this scene more memorable than all the others? I do not believe— perhaps I should say I do not wish to believe—that the appeal lay in the conjunction of eroticism and violence, the sadistic thrill of watching a desperate woman, her breasts and buttocks dissolving in a mantle of vapor, turn in circles, much like the crazed pirouettes of Lillian Gish in *Broken Blossoms*, while the needle of the pressure gauge trembles at DANGER. No: the pleasure was in the wisps, the fog, the shroud of droplets that make the victim little more than a blur, a patchwork, until the dark-haired phantom hurls herself against the opaque door and the audience gasps at the flattened red tips of her breasts, and the damp hair at the center, and the beauty of a puzzle solved, a mystery made clear.

Even then it had begun to dawn on me that there was no real need for skin in skin flicks at all. *Au contraire!* Perhaps the most erotic scene in all the sixties occurs in *Persona*, when, during a rainstorm, Bibi Andersson tells the half-catatonic Liv Ullmann about the time she and a friend had been lying on a beach and seduced two boys who wandered by. Nothing moves but the one actress's lips and the other's eyes. The rain beats down; the smoke from a cigarette rises. But what in the mind's eye we see is the

290 hot sand, a boy with his shorts about his ankles, and the sunbather reaching to fondle him as her friend looks on. *Show, don't tell*— that's the doctrine in every creative-writing course in America. The Greeks knew better, since Oedipus's discovery of his hanged mother, and the gouging out of his eyes, occurs only in words. And the death of Ophelia? Borne up, singing, mermaidlike, on her own spread gown? And that of Falstaff? Fumbling with the sheets, playing with flowers, babbling of green fields? That creeping coldness! From his feet to his knees and upward, "all was as cold as any stone."

But as the sixties passed into the seventies, words disappeared, every barrier fell, and the X-rated venture became too easy, too assessable, too complete. For a while after graduate school, living now in New York, I'd drop in at the Tivoli. It was at that theater, whose name, appropriately enough, spelled I-lov-it backward, that I heard the following snatch of dialogue: *"Sorry?* You pissed on my date and you're *sorry?"* It was there, too, that I walked out on my last pornographic film: imagine a blank screen, the roll of the credits, over which a solemn voice intones, "The United States Supreme Court has declared that nudity is not an obscenity!"— upon which an orchestra strikes up, the screen bursts into full color, and sixteen guys and gals, *tout ensemble* as they say in France, begin a game of volleyball. You may flee, but you may not hide. Nowadays one has only to flick on the TV, as I did recently in a hotel room on the Upper East Side. The remote control locked upon a show that was demonstrating the act of self-fellation. The star was a long, lean, flexible lad, and the witty title was *Head Over Heels.*

If film fails, what of the flesh? Once, well before college, the wise old Cow led his flock—Pumpkin, Penguin, and Duck—to a burlesque house near Pershing Square. From that excursion I retain the memory of one brief skit: the bosomy landlady tells the new tenant in the porkpie hat, "If any little thing should come up in the night, just call me."

The tenant (indignantly): "*Little* thing? You must have seen **291** me at the swimming hole last December!"

Many years later, in Amsterdam, I found myself third-row center at what was called a sex show. When the lights went down a Dutch woman and an Indonesian man—about twenty, I'd say, with dusky skin and matted hair—came out onto the stage. Without preliminaries, without plot, the youth dropped his pants and climbed aboard. How they had at it, all in the missionary position, though in this instance the colonial was on the bottom and the native on top. Why this jaunty tone? In plain fact, the scene before me, or perhaps it was the strobe lights in which it was bathed, filled me with heartsickness and nausea. I stood. I edged toward the aisle. As I reached the exit a scuffle broke out at the back of the hall. A score of Japanese men were pushing each other, squirming and jabbing, in a desperate attempt to claim my empty seat.

◪

The worst thing that can happen to an artist is to be burned at the stake by the Inquisition or shot dead by Stalin. The second worst is to be told that anything goes. On the evidence of the literature, what is needed is something like the oversight of Prince Dolgorukov, governor general of Moscow and confidant of the tsar. Make no mistake: I do not advocate censorship, least of all the sort that asks grant recipients to respect the diversity of their fellow citizens' beliefs. But if there are no taboos in society, there will be few in the psyche: so much, then, for the disguises, the tricks and sleight of hand, that the public, which shares the magician's repressions, calls art.

Something about modern films—their technical polish, the accuracy of the color, the fidelity of the sound; their ability, in short, to replicate life—seems foreign to that notion of quickness, pace, *hurry* (Charlie bends to tie his shoe and the seltzer strikes the face of the matron behind him, the whole speeded up by the gears of contemporary projectors) built into the very word "movie." Memory, like dreaming, is always in black and white; and, like old footage, it is fragmented, flickering, silent, dim. Was it in search of my own past, then, that even after I had abandoned the quasi-respectable Tivoli, I'd still drop in on the coin devices that dotted Times Square? The peep machine and kinetoscope and, behind them, the revolving drums through whose slats one could make out a horse jumping a hurdle or a man stifling a sneeze—in other words, the very origins of the cinema—are not far removed from those grim mechanisms, whose scenes were invariably small, cracked, nervous, fogged with the breath and thumb prints of thousands, an endless fifty-foot loop, a buried image, a forbidden scene (lesbians at play; a feeble phallus; will this be the burro?) on its eternal return.

III

In the basement of our building, sealed in tins, are a number of antique films, with such names as *Dangerous Dan*, *Willie and Tillie*, and *The Loves of Vivian*. A student of mine gave them to me twenty years ago. This was Spencer, my brilliant hippie, narrow-faced, thin-lipped, with a large Adam's apple and bulging blue eyes. He was as natural a writer as any teacher could hope for, incisive, sardonic, wildly funny. My agent, Sluggo, placed a story of his in, where else?, *Evergreen Review*; then she almost fainted when I sent over his full manuscript: "*Fuck*, a novel by Spencer Rotenberg." Spencer was, and surely still is, subject to fits of generosity: the best pot (Parents! Fear not! Students aren't seduced by their professors: vice versa); a complete set of City Lights books, including an early edition of *Howl*; and, of course, Willie, who looks to be in his sixties, and Tillie, with enormous thighs and breasts to her waistline, her hair unkempt, uncombed. This reel is so old, and undoubtedly rare, that it had to be shot outdoors, in natural light. Bald Will flounders atop Till next to the garden shrubs. They are like two moose, or elk, spied through a stand of firs. Vivian, if I remember correctly, is an English art dealer who shows a client a copy of Michelangelo's *Adam* receiving, from God Himself, the touch of life. Iris-out. The next thing we know, Vivian has assumed the pose, while his client, Savile Row trousers below his knees, begins to breathe life into the human dust. Dan proves not so dangerous, since all his mistress's ministrations fail to persuade his shrinking violet to bloom. Striking it is how bashful the men—or, at any rate how reluctant their male organs—in these early films. It is as if there were some correlation between the condition of the prints, brittle and scratched, mottled with bulb burns, and the inhibition of performing before an invention that primitive peoples still fear will capture their souls.

◧

Spencer's films remain locked in canisters, deep in the vault of our cellar, like forbidden thoughts, scenes from the distant past— *What kind of job you want? I do any job on you*—that cannot be brought often, or with ease, to light. The Videosmith, on the other hand, is just around the corner. The adult films are on the top shelf, stretching all the way around the store. That's just the trouble: not only are the tapes in full color, with soundtracks and no perforations to jam, nothing to thread, but one can browse freely through them, plucking down the fruits that hang no more than arm's length for all but a ten-year-old. The liberation of the repressed, that unattainable goal of Spencer's generation—think of R. D. Laing, or the polymorphous perverse in Norman O. Brown— is now available as a kind of push-button unconscious, two dollars and fifty cents, plus tax, over the counter.

The Duck: "You won't believe this, but I'm doing research for an essay."

The Blonde: "Yeah, I'll bet."

The Time: The present—or, at any rate, two weeks ago.

The Place: Interior of the Videosmith, off busy Coolidge Corner.

Action: The middle-aged mallard steps up to the counter. Under his arm, two tapes in plain boxes. The salesgirl, bright-eyed, bright-toothed, with an upturned nose like Bardot's, holds out her hand.

Close-up on customer's face: In spite of graying hair, lined cheeks, and slipping glasses, we cannot fail to note the startled look of an adolescent.

Flashback: The duckling in a drugstore. He has just asked another salesgirl—played by the same actress, in a fifties skirt and sweater—a confidential question. The girl, a novice, leans back and cups her hand at her mouth. She might have been—such is the power of her lungs, the blondness of her tresses, the redness of her alpine cheeks—a yodeler: "Hey, Frank!" she trills. "Where do we keep the condominiums?"

Slow dissolve: The Duck fleeing through the jing-jangling door.

"You got a videocard, Professor?"

We're back in the present, and I hold my ground. After all, this isn't so bad. I had looked forward to the task with some eagerness. Not only would I have an excuse to sample this expanded version of the Harvard five-foot shelf, but I would be paid for it as well. Why, I could even write off the cost of renting the tapes on my income tax, an ironic thrust to the vitals of Jesse Helms. My plan was to view perhaps a dozen films, starting with the classics of the seventies and working my way up to whatever Brigitte might whisper—in my ear?—was hottest in 1990. I've discovered that the most reliable guides, veritable Virgils, on such matters are the poets from my own department. That's why I might be seen handing over, along with my videocard, *The Devil in Miss Jones* and *Debbie Does Dallas*.

"I've been assured these are representative of the genre," I say, with a little chuckle.

The blonde fixes me with a piercing stare: "Yeah," she an- **295**
swers. "Sure. Right."

Back at home I draw the blinds and dim the lights. It's 10:15
in the morning. Wife at work, sons at school. I've got, with a break
for lunch, a good four hours. Into the VCR goes *The Devil in Miss
Jones*. At once I am confronted by a vestigial gasp from the world
of superego and repression: *Warning!* I see. And *FBI!* Then, before
I can register the twinge of guilt, we shift to a close-up of a middle
finger moving in and out of an open vagina. The camera pulls back
to reveal a dark-haired woman, her dress hiked well up her thighs,
eagerly masturbating. A man looks on, or, more accurately, looks
past, without interest. As best I recall, the woman says, "Get me
off! Get me off! I can't do it myself!" But the man answers in a
non sequitur, and the scene, so senseless and unexciting, fades out,
and a new one begins. The same woman is undressing in her
bathroom. She runs a tubful of water and climbs in. The camera
does the obligatory lingering on pockets of fat and flesh, and then
Miss Jones—for who else is this sad-faced woman?—takes out a
razor blade and slashes her wrists. The clear water turns red—or
so I suppose, since at this familiar conjunction of eroticism and
pain, I have shut my eyes.

Scene Three: The dead Miss Jones has her no-less-familiar
interview with the Devil, during which it is decided that before
descending to Hell proper, she will be allowed to experience all the
sensual gratification she had missed in her pinched and lonely life.
While she will be spared, at least for a time, the tortures of the
damned, it is already apparent that there will be no such relief for
the audience, which must endure another hour and a half of general
incompetence: amateur acting, marked by the characteristic combination of exaggerated gesture and uninflected speech; cheap sets
and harsh lighting; and, above all, the radical abdication of imagination that accounts for the great archetype of a pact with the
Devil becoming a cover for a series of unrelated and amoral sexual
adventures. Thus does the spinster step through the door to pur-

296   gatory transformed into a siren. Awaiting her is a guru in Jockey shorts. The film hasn't the wit or will to mimic the rhythms of foreplay. In a twinkling the quite nasty fellow has screwed some sort of plastic widget into the heroine's anus and has lain back to let her start vacuuming his penis with her lips. The telephone rings: not in the movie, but in the kitchen. After a moment's frantic fumbling in the dark with the pause button, I make it to the receiver. Here is a true torment, the twisted laughter of Hades: my daughter is calling from New Haven to ask about her paper on Henry James.

Flashback Number Two: Boston, the John Hancock auditorium, where an acquaintance has dragged me along to an *est* meeting. From the packed masses, out of the gloom, a single, quavering voice: "Why, Professor Epstein! What are you doing here?"

"Hi, Daddy," says the voice in the present, so bright, light, chaste, and chipper. "What do you know about *Daisy Miller?*"

In my state of utter mental paralysis I cannot even remember whether I've read the book or not. "Er, ah, isn't that about the, em, corruption of innocence?"

Through the half-open door the heroine is perpetually waiting, a smile of ecstasy and pale cum frozen on her features.

I leave the phone off the hook and hit the play button. In less than a moment the dilator that had been in Miss Jones's rectum has been transferred to her mouth. I watch in growing horror— horror not at the Boschian scenes unfolding before me, but at my own inner conviction, steadily growing, that, my God, *Jesse is right!* This isn't a matter of there being no socially redeeming qualities in the film. One doesn't ask for the vision—or the humor, or the formal artistic design—of a Bosch. Needless to say, as the heroine moves from one climax to another, there isn't the semblance of a plot, only the tatters of a theme: insatiability. Everything imaginable—bananas, of course, but a snake as well, a hose, fingers, phalli—disappears up both ends of the alimentary canal. What is lacking here is even the pretense of a point of view. One rough cut leads to another, and the camera is seduced by the scenes that it had implicitly promised—in a bow to the religiosity of the framing device, not to mention the obscenity statutes—to hold up for our pity and edification and scorn.

No: it is not because Miss Jones is ravaged vaginally and anally at one and the same time, and not because one does not forget for a moment that this is a real woman, perhaps with children of her own, that one wishes one were rocking on the senator's North Carolina porch, staring blissfully at a portrait of praying hands. It is because of what this film—and presumably all the others of its ilk (for Debbie shall have to do Dallas on someone else's screen) —does to oneself. I fast-forwarded. I watched through the interlaced fingers of my hands. I stopped to read the sports pages of that morning's *Globe*. And all the while I knew I was losing, or damaging, some critical aspect of my psyche. To say that the film was not arousing isn't the half of it. As image followed image I moved from dismay into what must be called despair. Old age? Perhaps. But I prefer to think that *The Devil in Miss Jones* does achieve, all unintentionally, and at cross-purposes, a vision of the underground. It is that Slough of Despond, the Valley of Humiliation, that Bunyan's Christian enters when he realizes he has fallen from the grace of God, that Hell which stares Raskolnikov in the face when he grasps that he is unable to love. It is not just savages who do well to flee the instrument that will steal their souls.

And what was stolen from me? At the end of *The Devil in Miss Jones* the frame is re-established. We are back at the scene with which we were first confronted, and realize that the heroine, her time up, has entered Hell itself. Once again she masturbates, more and more desperately, as the man, clearly insane now, talks about the buzzing of a fly. This scene, granted, has some power, though it does not derive from the little morality play into which it creeps to hide. The fact is, *we* are the ones who have been cast into the pit, denied that catharsis—the purging of pity and terror,

298   yes, and lustfulness—which is the artistic equivalent of the release
this actress busily seeks. In Tijuana the shadows played on one
side of the wall, the substance beckoned on the other. At that
collapse of the barrier between fantasy and fact, image and object,
one re-entered a kind of Eden of the instincts. Only great works
of art that deal with the full weight of reality, the wide arc of
significant and ordered experience, climax and resolution, can hope
to restore, however fitfully, the purity of soul all of us once knew.
The Devil in Miss Jones is the sword that expels us from the garden.
It is our youth, the seeds of our experience, that it severs us from,
leaving us alone and sullied on the flat plains and crowded cities
of this earth.

◪

ABOUT THE AUTHORS

RUSSELL BANKS

was born in New Hampshire in 1940. Currently teaching at Princeton University, he is the author of eleven books of fiction, most recently *Affliction* (1989) and *The Sweet Hereafter* (1991). Mr. Banks received the Literature Award from the American Academy and Institute of Arts and Letters. He is working on a novel about John Brown.

CLARK BLAISE

was born in Quebec, Canada, in 1940. His novels include *Lunar Attractions* (1979) and *Resident Alien* (1986), and he has also written *A North American Education* (1973), as well as two additional works of nonfiction in collaboration with Bharati Mukherjee, *Days and Nights in Calcutta* (1977), shortly to be made into a movie, and *The Sorrow and the Terror* (1988). Mr. Blaise teaches in the Creative Writing Program of the University of Iowa and is currently writing a memoir of his father.

HAROLD BLOOM

was born in New York City in 1930. A MacArthur Prize Fellow, he teaches at Yale University and at New York University. Among his many books are *The Anxiety of Influence*, *A Map of Mis-*

reading, and *Kabbalah and Criticism.* Mr. Bloom is the coauthor of both *The Book of J* (1990) and the forthcoming *The Book of Kabbalah.* He has recently completed *The American Religion.*

DAVID BRADLEY

was born in Bedford, Pennsylvania, in 1950. His first novel, *South Street* (1975), was followed by *The Chaneysville Incident* (1981). Mr. Bradley won the 1981 PEN/Faulkner Award. He has written numerous essays and is completing a nonfiction book, *The Bondage Hypothesis.* He divides his time between La Jolla, California, and the east coast, where he has taught most recently at Temple University.

E. M. BRONER

was born in Detroit in 1932. She lives in New York City and is the author of five books, including *A Weave of Women* and *Her Mothers,* both novels. Recent essays have appeared in *Testimony: Contemporary Writers Make the Holocaust Personal* (1989) and *The New York Times* (1991), and stories have recently appeared in *Ms.* (1991) and *North American Review* (1991). Her new novel is *The Repair Shop.*

LESLIE EPSTEIN

was born in Los Angeles in 1938. His six volumes include *King of the Jews,* a novel, and his most recent books, *Pinto and Son,* a novel (1990), and *Goldkorn Tales,* stories. Mr. Epstein is the director of the graduate creative writing program at Boston University.

LOUISE ERDRICH

was born in Wahpeton, North Dakota, in 1954. She lives in Maine with her husband and co-author of *The Crown of Columbus* (1991), Michael Dorris. Ms. Erdrich is also the author of *Love Medicine, The Beet Queen,* and *Tracks.*

DONALD HALL

was born in New Haven, Connecticut, in 1928. Among his many books of poems, *The One Day* (1988) won the National Book Critics Circle Award. *Old and New Poems* (1990) and *Here at Eagle Pond*, essays (1990), are recent works. Mr. Hall has published numerous books of essays, stories, and nonfiction, and makes his home in New Hampshire.

GEOFFREY HARTMAN

was born in Germany and emigrated in 1939. His works include *Wordsworth's Poetry* (1964), which won the Christian Gauss Prize, and *Criticism in the Wilderness* (1980). Recent books are *Easy Pieces* and *Bitburg in Moral and Political Perspective*. Mr. Hartman has taught at Yale University since 1955 and is a member of the American Academy of Arts and Sciences.

AMY HEMPEL

was born in Chicago in 1951. Her recent collections of stories are *Reasons to Live* (1985) and *At the Gates of the Animal Kingdom* (1990). Ms. Hempel lives in New York City.

GORDON LISH

was born in Hewlett, New York, in 1934. Among his novels are *Dear Mr. Capote*, *Peru*, and *Extravaganza*, and his story collections include *What I Know So Far* and *Mourner at the Door*. His most recent novel is *My Romance* (1991).

PHILLIP LOPATE

was born in New York City in 1943. He currently teaches at Bennington College and at Columbia University, and is the author of books of poetry and nonfiction. His most recent novel is *The Rug Merchant* (1988), and his current book of essays is *Against*

Joie de Vivre (1990). On the selection board of the New York Film Festival since 1987, Mr. Lopate has also written film criticism for *Esquire* and *Vogue* magazines. He is currently writing a screenplay for the Australian director Jane Campion.

TERRY MCMILLAN

was born in Port Huron, Michigan, in 1957. Her novels include *Mama* (1987) and *Disappearing Acts* (1989). Ms. McMillan is the editor of *Breaking Ice*, an anthology of contemporary African-American fiction, and is completing *Waiting to Exhale*, a novel. She lives in Tucson and is currently on a sabbatical year from the University of Arizona.

LEONARD MICHAELS

was born in New York City in 1933. In addition to *The Men's Club*, a novel (1981), he is the author of *Going Places* and *I Would Have Saved Them If I Could*, collections of stories, and, most recently, *Shuffle*, an autobiographical fiction (1990). Mr. Michaels is the coeditor, with Christopher Ricks, of two volumes called *The State of the Language*; and he coedited *West of the West* with David Reid and Raquel Scherr. He has taught at the University of California, Berkeley, since 1969.

BHARATI MUKHERJEE

was born in Calcutta, India. *The Middle Man and Other Stories* won the National Book Critics Circle Award in 1988. *Darkness* (1985) and *Jasmine* (1989) are her most recent novels. She is coauthor, with Clark Blaise, of *Days and Nights in Calcutta* (1977), *The Sorrow and the Terror* (1988), works of nonfiction, and a screenplay, *Orbiting*. Ms. Mukherjee is Distinguished Professor at the University of California, Berkeley.

JOYCE CAROL OATES   **303**

was born in Lockport, New York, in 1938. She is the Roger S. Berlind Distinguished Professor in the Humanities, Princeton University, and the author of numerous works of fiction and nonfiction. Her most recent books are *The Rise of Life on Earth*, a novella (1991), and *Heat*, a book of stories (1991). Ms. Oates won the 1990 Rea Award in the Short Story and the 1990 Bobst Award for Lifetime Achievement.

JAYNE ANNE PHILLIPS

was born in West Virginia in 1952. She is the author of *Black Tickets* (1979), stories, and *Machine Dreams* (1984), a novel, and several works published in limited editions, including *Counting* (1978) and *Fast Lanes* (1987). Ms. Phillips recently completed the text for *The Last Day of Summer* (photos by Jacques Sturges). She lives in Newton, Massachusetts.

FRANCINE PROSE

was born in New York in 1947. Her seven published novels include *Household Saints* (1981) and *Bigfoot Dreams* (1986); a story collection, *Women and Children First*, appeared in 1988. Ms. Prose was a Guggenheim Fellow in 1991 and recently completed a new novel, *Primitive People*.

DAVID ROSENBERG

was born in Detroit in 1943. He is the author of several volumes of poetry, as well as *A Poet's Bible* (1991) and *The Book of J* (coauthor, 1990). Mr. Rosenberg is also the coauthor of the forthcoming *The Book of Kabbalah* and is currently finishing *The Song That Was Solomon's*. He has edited *Congregation* and *Testimony*, and is currently editing *Personal Gods*—all collections of original essays.

304

JUDITH ROSSNER

was born in New York in 1935. Among her novels are *Looking for Mr. Goodbar* (1975) and *August* (1983). Her most recent book, *His Little Women*, a novel, appeared in 1990.

VALERIE SAYERS

was born in Beaufort, South Carolina. Her first novel, *Due East* (1987), was followed by *How I Got Him Back* (1989) and, most recently, *Who Do You Love* (1991). Ms. Sayers lives in Brooklyn, New York.

GRACE SCHULMAN

was born in New York City. She is professor of English at Baruch College of the City University of New York, and is poetry editor of *The Nation* magazine. Her books of poetry include *Burn Down the Icons* (1976) and *Hemispheres* (1984), and her nonfiction includes *Marianne Moore: The Poetry of Engagement* (1986). New poems have appeared in *The New Republic* and *Boulevard* magazine, among others.

MEG WOLITZER

was born in Brooklyn, New York, in 1959. Her recent novel *This Is Your Life* has been adapted for the screen by Nora Ephron. Earlier novels include *Sleepwalking* and *Hidden Pictures*, and Ms. Wolitzer is coauthor of *Nutcrackers*, a book of puzzles (1991).